Southern Treasures

Our Famous Yellow Cookbook

Due to overwhelming demand,
we are proud to present in this edition
Valdosta Recipes and *Taster's Luncheon*
reprinted in their entirety.

Valdosta Junior Service League
Valdosta, Georgia
www.vjsl.org

The purpose of the Valdosta Junior Service League is to improve cultural, welfare, recreational, civic and educational conditions in the community, to promote volunteerism, and to cooperate with other organizations performing similar services.

Copies of Southern Treasures may be obtained by contacting the Valdosta Junior Service League at valdostajsl@yahoo.com, by using the order forms provided in the back of this edition, or at the address provided below.

Valdosta Junior Service League
P.O. Box 2043
Valdosta, GA 31603-2043

Other cookbooks published by the Valdosta Junior Service League include *Who's Cooking in Valdosta, Valdosta Recipes, the hors d'oeuvre tray, Taster's Luncheon, The Holiday Hostess,* and *Timeless Treasures.*

ISBN: 0-9635249-1-7

WIMMER
COOKBOOKS
ConsolidatedGraphics
1-800-548-2537

About Valdosta Recipes
and Taster's Luncheon

Southern Treasures is a compilation of two extremely popular Valdosta Junior Service League Cookbooks, *Valdosta Recipes* and *Taster's Luncheon*. *Valdosta Recipes,* or as it is known locally, "the yellow cookbook" was compiled over several years by Associate Members of the Valdosta Junior Service League. This local treasure was first printed in 1968 and was reprinted in 1970. *Taster's Luncheon* was the centerpiece of the 1980 Valdosta Junior Service League Provisional Class fundraising project. Only two hundred and fifty copies were printed. Both books have remained sought after, yet unavailable, for more than two decades.

To the many women who contributed to these timeless classics, we thank you. It was an honor to have the opportunity to update and reprint these traditional southern recipes loved by so many generations.

The laurel wreath is found at the top of each page throughout *Southern Treasures* is traditionally a symbol of distinction, honor, and achievement. Intricate woodcarvings of the laurel wreath are seen throughout the interior and exterior of the historic Converse-Dalton-Ferrell House, home of the Valdosta Junior Service League.

 In this edition, a lovely leaf design signifies recipes from *Taster's Luncheon*.

About the Artists

Cover Artist

We are honored to feature on the cover of *Southern Treasures,* a beautiful watercolor by talented Georgia native Edward Norris. This elegant rendering was created exclusively for *Southern Treasures.*

Eddie Norris took his first art class at the age of six and has been painting ever since. His official career was in banking. At the time of his retirement from the business world, he was the President and CEO of First State Bank and Trust in Valdosta, an affiliate of Synovus Financial Corporation. Mr. Norris's wife Ann was an Affiliate Member of our organization. He has also found time to become a highly accomplished artist. Watercolor is and has been his dominant medium for the last 30 years. Studies each year under nationally know artists at the Grand Strand Watercolor Workshop in Myrtle Beach, South Carolina have enhanced his ability to capture the essence of his favorite subjects. His love of the outdoors is easily seen in the rich colors of his palette.

Mr. Norris has won countless awards and has been juried into many exhibitions. By invitation, he has had one-man shows throughout Georgia. On February 18, 1999, the Georgia Citizens for the Arts named him artist of the year for the state of Georgia. His painting, "Fall Feathers in South Georgia", hangs in the permanent collection at the Georgia State Capitol. As an artist, one of Eddie's concerns has been to use his "God Given" talent to promote the enjoyment appreciation of art in all its dimensions. Every year Mr. Norris donates many of his paintings to charities and civic causes. He truly feels that art challenges the individual to find the best within himself and others. Mr. Norris currently resides in Columbus, Georgia with his wife Ann.

Section Divider Artist

Throughout *Southern Treasures* we proudly feature the breathtaking photography of local artist, John Vickers Neugent.

Vick Neugent was born in Brunswick, Georgia. His parents were Johnie Neugent and Bessie Vickers. He attended Berry College in Rome, Georgia, and Emory University in Atlanta, Georgia, until 1946. That same year, he entered the United States Army as a Technical Sergeant in the Judge Advocate General's Office Headquarters Korea Based Command, Inchon, Korea, until he was honorably discharged in 1948. He then returned to Emory University, graduating in 1949 with a B.A. Degree and following in 1950 with a L.L.B. from Emory Law School. Mr. Neugent began a private practice as an attorney in Pearson, Georgia, and was elected Solicitor General in 1960. He began serving for the Alapaha Judicial Circuit in 1961. He held this position until his retirement in, 1982. Mr. Neugent was appointed District Attorney Emeritus by the Governor. He has served as President of the District Attorney's Association of Georgia, Judge of the Atkinson County Court, and is presently a member of the Georgia Bar Association, Alapaha Bar Association, Lakeland Masonic Lodge #434, and the First Baptist Church of Lakeland, Georgia. Mr. Neugent is married to Martha Bruce, Clerk of Superior Court, Lanier County, Georgia. He has four daughters, two stepchildren and ten grandchildren.

Mr. Neugent has always maintained a strong interest in photography because he feels that it "allows one to preserve for self and others so much of nature's beauty". He refers to these objects of beauty as being captured "by the side of the road" in his photography. Mr. Neugent feels that his ability to preserve and share this beauty with his fellowman is most rewarding.

Favorite Recipes

From My Cookbook

Recipe Name	Page Number

Acknowledgements

Thank you to Dawn Rodgers, a valued member of our organization, for her suggestion of the title *Southern Treasures*. This title perfectly represents the recipes included in this edition and the women who contributed them. *Southern Treasures* was chosen to grace this cover by majority vote of the Valdosta Junior Service League General Membership.

Special thanks to league members Meg Douglass, Julie Godbee, Beth Howell, Rebecca Mutert, and Leslie Sherwood; also to Britt Peeples, special friend of our League, all of whom graciously volunteered their time to this project.

2001-2002 Cookbook Committee

Wendy Bahnsen

Karen Campbell

Danita Cooper

Bridget Corbett

Tanya Davis

Laura Elliott

Amanda Holmes

Amy King

Beth Odom

Laura Singletary

Renee Smith

I would also like to personally thank the members of the 2001-2002 Cookbook Committee for all of their hard work and dedication. Whether typing, proofing, editing, or consulting, each of these women made important contributions to this amazing collaboration that has spanned more than thirty years. For me, it has been an incredible honor to work on this project and truly an experience I will never forget.

Stephanie Hughes
2001-2002 Cookbook Chairman

About the Valdosta Junior Service League

The Valdosta Junior Service League was founded in 1936 by a group of young Valdosta women in order to work for the betterment of their community. Some of the current projects of the League include:

The Converse-Dalton-Ferrell House

Educational Scholarships

Habitat for Humanity

Kid's Café

Koats for Kids

Learning Enhancement Grants

The Lowndes-Valdosta Arts Commission

School Hearing and Vision Screening

Our civic-minded members are dedicated to identifying and meeting our community's current and future needs. Your purchase of Southern Treasures will allow us to continue to serve our community and it's surrounding areas. We appreciate your support of our organization.

Valdosta Junior Service League

Active Members	Carol Crews	Stephanie Hughes
Jennifer Allen	Nita Cross	Catherine Hutchinson
Laura Allison	Donna Culbreth	Cheryl Johnson
Cadden Anderson	Tanya Davis	Kristy Johnson
Wendy Bahnsen	Meg Douglass	Meredith Jordan
Cheryl Beall	Cathy Durland	Elaine Keener
Jeana Beeland	Laura Elliott	Amy King
Melissa Boatenreiter	Stacy Evans	Sherri Kirbo
Jan Brice	Gaye George	Evelyn Langdale
Stephanie Broome	Julie Godbee	Kimberly Langdale
Kelly Call	Susan Haynes	Lori Lovell
Karen Campbell	Anne Henry	Julie McLeod
Amy Carter	Jennifer Hight	Cindy McTier
Kathi Clifton	Casey Hogan	Brandi Mackey
Danita Cooper	Amanda Holmes	Heidi Moody
Bridget Corbett	Debbie Holt	Rebecca Mutert
Katharine Courson	Angie Hornsby	Beth Odom
Lalee Cregger	Beth Howell	Leslie Parker

Deidre Parramore
Jane Peeples
Donna Perry
Debra Peterman
Pam Pitts
Stephanie Powell
Sala Prain
Tania Reames
Julie Sanderbeck
Lane Sayre
Deann Scruggs
Leslie Sherwood
Missy Sherwood
Laura Singletary
Amy Smith
Renee Smith
Karen Steinberg
Rhonda Steinberg
Laura Talley
Rhonda Thagard
Beth Veal
Laura Washnock
Nicole Watts
Molly Webb
Kelly Wilson
Lynne Wilson
Susan Wilson
Robyn Woodruff

Non-Resident Members

Sandy Chambless
Tiffany Cox
Kameron Girardin
Meg Procopio
Julie Lovein
Tenia Workman

Associate Members

Donna Adams
Cathy Alday
Susan Allison
Jan Anderson
Cheryl Arnold
Janice Baker
Barbara Bankston

Jamie Bird
Karen Bishop
Janet Blalock
Jan Blanton
Vallye Blanton
Becky Bowling
Rosemary Brannen
Elaine Bridges
Joey Broadwater
Brenda Brown
Julie Budd
Jane Burgsteiner
Elizabeth Butler
Shirlee Carroll
Melissa Carter
Dorothy Chandler
Pam Chapman
Pat Chitty
Donna Clary
Ellen Clary
Sue Clary
Robin Coleman
Kay Coleman
Mary Corbett
Jeanne Cowart
Carol Cowart
Sue Cox
Susan Crago
Dale Crane
Jane Crick
Becky Crosby
Patty Dalponte
Debbie Davis
Pam Davis
Lyn Dickey
Pam Edwards
Sharon Everson
Jan Fackler
Marcia Felts
Sally Gaskins
Libby George
Carol Giles
Mary Gray
Barbara Hacker

Laura Hansen
JaBra Harden
Caroline Harris
Lisa Henry
Debbie Hobdy
Marie Holland
Clod Holt
Judith Joseph
Marilyn Kemper
Honey Kendrick
Christy Kirbo
Merry Jo Kurrie
Sally Kurrie
Renee Land
Margaret Langdale
Sybil Langdale
Suzanne Lastinger
Russell Lawrence
Allison Leonard
Lee Limbocker
Kathy Lincoln
Floye Luke
Pam Mackey
Mary Young Manning
Zan Martin
Kay McBride
Debbi McNeal
Marcia McRae
Kellie McTier
June Mercer
Mary Beth Meyers
Claire Miller
Donna Miller
Jessie Miller
Linda Miller
Teresa Minchew
Lynn Minor
Stephanie Mize
Jan Moseley
Carole Newbern
Janet Nichols
Debbie Parker
Sarah Parrish
Sue Ellen Patterson

Terry Peacock
Mary Perry
Jadan Pitcock
Jamie Pitts
Mary Powell
Brenda Pridgen
Jane Rainey
Anita Reames
Denise Retterbush
Chris Roan
Martha Rock
Dawn Rodgers
Denise Rountree
Stacy Sasser
Stuart Lynn Simpson
Monique Sineath
Debbie Smith
Janice Smith
Kaye Smith
Tonya Smith
Sharon Stalvey
Susan Steel
Teresa Steinberg
Diane Stewart
Julie Street
Kim Strickland
Leslie Strickland
Beth Sullivan
Amy Swindle
Sharon Swindle
Cheri Tillman
Marcia Tillman
Kathy Turner
Kelly Turner
Barbara Turrentine
Jan Warren
Vickie Wilkinson
Carol Woodall
Pam Woodward
Sally Woods
Janice Worn
Patti Wright

Lifetime Members
Sue Addington
Sandra Allen
Emily Anderson
Gloria Anderson
Sandra Anderson
Jane Anthony
Carol Barker
Joann Bassford
Virginia Beckman
Sue Bentley
Myra Jane Bird
Dee Broadfoot
Patsy Brogdon
Dean Brooks
Ann Burnette
Ingrid Carroll
Jan Carter
LaVerne Coleman
Sharon Coleman
Marion Anise Cross
Ann Dasher
Judy DeMott
Sue Dennard
Nancy Dewar
Mary Dickey
Martha Dover
Phyllis Drury
Peggy Durden
Carolyn Eager
Karen Eager
Beverly Edwards
Cindy Fann
Billie Ruth Fender
Jean Fowler
Peggy Gayle
Ann Godbee
Frances Golivesky
Barbara Griffen
Margaret Ann Griffin
Jeneane Grimsley
Jeannie Grow
Lilla Kate Hart
Mary Ann Heard

Marilyn Henderson
Barbara Hornbuckle
Lamar Jackson
Susie Kaiser
Dottie Keller
Susan Klanicki
Lamb Lastinger
Barbara Lester
Laurie McCall
Jane McLane
Susan Mackey
Shirley Miller
Sharon Mink
Sally Moritz
Beverly Moye
Emma Murrah
Shelia Myddleton
Joyce Paine
Barbara Parks
Nancy Parris
Ginger Paulk
Jean Pipkin
Ann Plageman
Jerry Powers
June Purvis
Marsha Rudolph
Sue Nell Scruggs
Careen Shapiro
Sadie Shelton
Jane Sherwood
Harriett Smith
Janet Smith
Leigh Smith
Morris Smith
Jane Stanaland
Suzanne Sullivan
Polly Talley
Cissy Taylor
Betty Dow Templeton
Georgia Thomson
Tootsie Tillman
Mala Vollotton
Rose Ware
Joanne Youles

Table of Contents

Beverages & Appetizers 13

Salads, Salad Dressings & Sauces 41

Sandwiches & Soups 79

Entrées 91

    Beef 94

    Corned Beef, Veal & Lamb 109

    Pork 112

    Game 119

    Seafood 121

    Poultry 135

    Egg Dishes 157

Sides 163

    Vegetables 165

    Grits 196

    Pasta 197

    Potatoes 198

    Rice 202

Breads 205

Sweet Treasures 225

    Cakes 229

    Frostings, Icings, Fillings & Sauces 265

    Pies 269

    Brownies, Cookies, & Candy 285

    Desserts 311

    Frozen Desserts 330

Jellies, Jams & Preserves 337

Pickles & Relishes 345

Equivalents Tables 357

Index 359

Beverages
& Appetizers

Beverages

Brunch Bloody Mary Mix 15
Hot Chocolate Mix 15
Mrs. Clelland's Cubes 15
Glug 16
Hot Buttered Rum Cider 16
Party Punch 17
Punch 17

Tingle Bells Punch 17
Ramos Fizz 18
Wassail Bowl 18
Tea Syrup 18
Russian Tea 19
Iced Tea 19
Wine 19

Appetizers

Hot Bacon-Cheese Roll Ups 20
Bacon Crisps 20
Cauliflower Dip 20
Beef and Mushrooms 21
Cereal Nibbles 21
Flaming Cabbage 22
Marinated Cauliflower 22
Hot Cheese Dip 22
Hot Broccoli Dip 23
"Brahma" Cheese Dip 23
Cheese Ball 24
Cheese Roll 24
Ham and Cheese Balls 24
Hot Cheese Puffs 25
"Crispen Island" Cheese Straws 25
Chee Wees 25
Foolproof Cheese Straws 26
Cheese Straws #1 26
Cheese Straws #2 26
Salt-Rising Bread Cheese Straws 27
Cheese Wheels 27
Cream Cheese and Caviar 27
Cream Cheese Pickapeppa 28
Cream Cheese Log 28
Hot Cheese Spread 28
Pineapple Cheese Ball 29
Roquefort Mound 29
Chicken Liver Wrap-Ups 30

Chili Meat Turnovers 30
Swiss Fondue 31
Honey Chicken Wings 31
Chafing Dish Crab 31
Hot Clam Dip #1 32
Hot Clam Dip #2 32
Crab Newburg Dip 32
Hot Crab Spread 33
Guacamole 33
Barbecued Meatballs 34
Cocktail Meatballs 34
Brandied Mushrooms 35
Marinated Mushrooms 35
Mushroom Appetizers 35
Olive Surprises 36
Glorified Onions 36
Sesame Bread Sticks 36
James' Marinated Oysters 37
Picadillo Dip
    (from San Antonio Country Club) 37
Shrimp and Artichoke Dip 38
Shrimp Dip 38
Dip For Shrimp 38
Marinated Shrimp 39
Shrimp Pâté 39
Shrimp and Crab Mousse 40
Swamp Salad 40
Dip for Vegetables 40

Brunch Bloody Mary Mix

1	quart tomato juice	3	teaspoons salt
3	tablespoons sugar	3	ribs celery, minced
3	tablespoons vinegar	½	medium onion, grated
3	tablespoons Worcestershire sauce		Dash of Tabasco sauce, optional

Mix all ingredients. Prepare in advance so flavors will blend.

Rose Ware

Hot Chocolate Mix

1	(2-pound) box Nestlé Quick	1	(11-ounce) jar Coffeemate
1	(1-pound) box powdered sugar	1	(8-quart) box powdered milk

Mix together and sift. Store in jars. When ready for a cup of hot chocolate, fill cup half full of mix and finish filling cup with hot water.

Marsha Rudolph

Mrs. Clelland's Cubes

1	pint milk	½	cup lemon juice
	Dash of salt		Orange, pineapple or
¾	cup sugar		cranberry juice

Mix and freeze in ice cube tray. Serve in juice.

Mrs. James Allen

15

Glug

Spice Bag

1	cup almond slivers	10	whole cardamoms
1	cup raisins	5	whole cloves
1	stick cinnamon	1	piece gingerroot

In a gauze bag mix above spices.

Wine Mixture

⅕	Port	⅕	Cognac
⅕	Bordeaux	1	cup sugar

Mix wines. Add sugar to the mixture of wines. Place spice bag in liquid and bring mixture to the simmering point. Do not boil. Keep mixture hot and serve in preheated mugs with 1 raisin and 1 almond in mug.

Mrs. Tom Smith

Hot Buttered Rum Cider

1	teaspoon maple syrup	⅙	lemon
1	teaspoon brown sugar	2-3	whole cloves
	Pinch of nutmeg	1	thin slice orange
2	teaspoons butter	¾	cup hot apple cider
	(not margarine)	1	stick cinnamon stick
3	tablespoons dark rum		

In a mug, mix maple syrup, brown sugar, nutmeg, butter and rum. Squeeze juice from lemon into mug, and then add the lemon. Stud cloves into orange slice and add to mug. Fill mug with hot apple cider. Stir with cinnamon stick. Leave stick in mug while serving.

Serves 1

Susan Hogan

Party Punch

1	cup sugar	1	can pineapple chunks
1	cup water	10	bottles lemon lime soda
	Juice of 12 oranges	1	pint grape juice
	Juice of 12 lemons		

Boil sugar and water 8 minutes, then chill. Add remaining ingredients. Pour over ice in punch bowl.

Serves 25

Mrs. James Allen

Punch

2	packages lime cool-aid	1	cup sugar
2	cans frozen orange juice	3	quarts water
2	cans frozen lemonade	2	large bottles of ginger ale
2	(18-ounce) cans pineapple juice		

Combine ingredients in punch bowl and stir until well blended.

Serves 40

Mrs. Grady Durden

Tingle Bells Punch

2	quarts cranberry juice	½	cup maraschino cherry juice
1	can frozen lemonade concentrate (thawed)	6	(10-ounce) bottles lemon-lime soda, chilled

Combine all ingredients. Serve over ice in punch bowl. Garnish with lemon slices, orange wedges and cherry alternated on cocktail picks.

Makes 40 (4-ounce) servings

Mrs. Fred Dodson

Ramos Fizz

¼	cup gin	2	teaspoons lemon juice
2	egg whites	½	teaspoons vanilla
½	cup whipping cream	1	cup crushed ice
2	teaspoons sugar		

Cover and blend 10 seconds on high.

Serves 4 to 6

Rose Ware

Wassail Bowl

2	quarts apple cider or apple juice		Whole cloves
3	oranges	½	cup lemon juice
			Cinnamon sticks

Preheat oven to 350 degrees. Press cloves about ¼-inch apart into oranges. Put in shallow pan and bake 30 minutes. Heat cider or juice until small bubbles show around edge. Remove from heat. Stir in lemon juice. Pour into heatproof punch bowl. With ice pick, pierce oranges in several places, and then add to cider. Serve in mugs, with fragrant cinnamon sticks.

Serves 10 to 12

Mrs. Fred Dodson

Tea Syrup

12	cups water	1	(5-pound) bag of sugar less 2 cups
¼	pound loose tea		

In large pot, bring water to a boil. Add loose tea and cover, set off eye for 10 minutes. Pour sugar in another large pot. Pour hot tea through strainer into sugar. Pour half of tea, then stir. Then remaining tea. Pour into gallon jug. If it does not make a gallon, add hot water to tea leaves and strain into jug. This keeps 4 to 6 weeks in refrigerator.

To serve, mix 1 cup tea syrup plus 4 cups water.

Jeneane Grimsley

Russian Tea

½ cup sugar	¼ cup orange juice
½ cup water	2 tablespoons lemon juice
1 (2-inch) cinnamon stick	¼ cup pineapple juice
1 teaspoon grated lemon rind	3 cups boiling water
1½ teaspoons grated orange rind	3 tablespoons tea

Combine sugar, water, cinnamon stick, lemon rind and orange rind in saucepan. Boil 5 minutes. Then remove the cinnamon stick. Add orange, lemon and pineapple juice; keep hot. Pour boiling water over tea leaves; steep 5 minutes. Combine tea and fruit mixtures. Serve hot in tea or punch cups.

Serves 6 to 8

Tea is much better kept in the refrigerator and reheated the next day.

Mrs. C. E. Davis

 # Iced Tea

2 cups water	2 quarts cold water
2¼ cups sugar	2 cups orange juice
4 tablespoons loose tea or 8 tea bags	1 cup lemon juice

Combine water and sugar, boil for 5 minutes. Steep tea in 1 quart of boiling water for 5 minutes. Put into 2 quarts cold water. Add remaining ingredients.

Serves 12 to 24

Polly Talley

Wine

8 quarts grapes	3 pounds sugar
2 quarts boiling water	

Mash grapes. Pour boiling water over grapes. Let stand 36 hours. Strain and add sugar. Bottle and let stand uncorked until all fermentation is over, keeping bottles full. Then cork.

Mrs. Conner Thomson

Hot Bacon-Cheese Roll Ups

Thinly sliced bread   **1   pound bacon**
1   jar cheese spread

Remove crusts from bread. Cut each slice in half. Spread lightly with cheese spread. Roll up, wrap with half slice of bacon, and secure with wooden toothpick. Bake on rack at 400 degrees until bacon is crisp. These may be cooked halfway, cooled, and frozen until needed. When ready to use, put frozen roll ups on cookie sheet and bake.

Mrs. Henry Brice

Bacon Crisps

1   box Waverly crackers   **Paprika**
1-2 pounds thin sliced bacon

Break crackers along perforation. Wrap ½ piece bacon around cracker (may need to secured with a toothpick). Sprinkle heavily with paprika. Bake slowly in a 200 degree oven until bacon is done, about 45 minutes or 1 hour. Let set a few minutes until bacon is crisp. Serve warm.

Mrs. Jack Sullivan

 Cauliflower Dip

1   cup mayonnaise   **1   tablespoon minced onion**
1   cup sour cream   **1   tablespoon parsley**
1   tablespoon dill weed

Mix together and refrigerate.

LaVerne Coleman

Beef and Mushrooms

1	(5-pound) beef tenderloin	2	tablespoons catsup
1	stick butter, melted	3	large jars mushroom caps
	Juice of 1 lemon		Salt and pepper to taste
1	small bottle A-1 steak sauce		

Strip membrane from tenderloin. Place in roasting pan and bake, uncovered, for 20 minutes at 400 degrees. Baste with melted butter and lemon juice. Remove meat to platter to cool, saving drippings. Add steak sauce, catsup, salt and pepper to taste to drippings. Heat to boiling. Cut beef into 1-inch cubes. Add beef and mushrooms to sauce. Let cool. Refrigerate for 24 hours. Heat to boiling and serve in chafing dish with toothpicks.

Serves 20

Mrs. Walton Carter

Cereal Nibbles

Mix

1	box O shaped oat cereal	1	small box pretzels
1	box bite-sized rice cereal squares	2-4	cups pecans
		1	jar pumpkin seeds

Sauce

1	pound butter	¼	teaspoon red pepper
1	bud garlic, crushed	3	tablespoons Worcestershire sauce
2	teaspoons savory		

Place all ingredients except pumpkin seeds in large roasting pan and mix well with the sauce, which has been heated. Cook in 200 degree oven 1 hour. Stir carefully every 15 minutes. Add pumpkin seeds, stir and cook 1 more hour. Let cool in pan.

Mrs. Grady Durden

Flaming Cabbage

1	large cabbage	1	package cocktail sausages
1	large jar stuffed olives	1	Sterno

Wash a large cabbage, preferable a purple one. Curl outer leaves out from top. Hollow out center, about 6 inches deep. Place a small Sterno in cavity. Place a stuffed olive and a cocktail sausage on each wooden toothpick and stick into sides of cabbage. Light Sterno and let guests roast their own sausages.

Note: A sharp mustard or barbecue sauce is nice to dip these in.

Mrs. Henry Brice

Marinated Cauliflower

1	medium cauliflower	½	teaspoon red pepper
1½	cups vegetable oil	½	teaspoon black pepper
½	cup white vinegar	1	teaspoon sugar
1	teaspoon prepared mustard	1	minced clove garlic
2	teaspoons salt		Dash Tabasco sauce
½	teaspoon Worcestershire sauce		

Wash and break cauliflower into florets. Put in a covered dish or large jar. Mix remaining ingredients and shake well. Pour over cauliflower florets. Let marinate several hours.

Mrs. Marshall Parks

Hot Cheese Dip

1	cup sharp grated cheese	1	medium onion, grated
1	cup Hellmann's mayonnaise	1	teaspoon dry mustard

Mix ingredients together and bake at 350 degrees for 30 minutes or until brown. Serve hot on crackers.

Catherine Parramore

Hot Broccoli Dip

½ cup chopped onion
½ cup chopped celery
½ cup chopped mushrooms
3 tablespoons butter, melted
1 (10-ounce) package frozen chopped broccoli, cooked and well drained
1 (10¾-ounce) can cream of mushroom soup undiluted
1 (6-ounce) package diced garlic cheese

Sauté onion, celery, and mushrooms in butter until tender. Combine cooked broccoli, soup, and cheese; cook over low heat until cheese melts, stirring occasionally. Add sautéed vegetables to broccoli mixture, stirring well. Serve hot.

Makes 1 quart

Betty Dow Templeton

"Brahma" Cheese Dip

1 pound sharp Cheddar cheese
1 pound whipped cheese spread (two 8-ounce containers)
3 tablespoons dry mustard
1 tablespoon garlic powder
½ teaspoon Tabasco sauce
3 tablespoons Worcestershire sauce
1 tube anchovy paste
½ bottle warm beer

Whip all ingredients, excluding beer, together at medium speed in mixer for 6 minutes. Add beer, whip for 3 minutes more. Refrigerate to store. Serve at room temperature with any assortment of crackers.

Mrs. B. J. Wetherington

Cheese Ball

1	jar Vera Sharp Cheese (a Spanish goat cheese)	1	cup chopped pecans, divided
4	ounces blue cheese	1	teaspoon red pepper
12	ounces cream cheese	¼	teaspoon salt
1	tablespoon Worcestershire sauce	1	teaspoon garlic powder
		½	cup chopped parsley

Mix cheeses at room temperature. Add ½ cup of the nuts and all seasonings. Spread other half of nuts and parsley on large sheet of waxed paper. Shape cheese in ball in center of that and roll on the paper until covered with nuts and parsley. Chill overnight. Can be kept indefinitely in freezer.

Mrs. Bill Keller

Cheese Roll

1	pound sharp Cheddar cheese	2	cloves garlic
1	(3-ounce) package cream cheese	1	cup pecans

Grind all together in food processor. Roll into 2 long rolls, about 1½ inches in diameter. Roll in paprika or chili powder. Will freeze well.

Mrs. B. J. Wetherington

Ham and Cheese Balls

¼	pound cooked ham, ground very fine	1	tablespoon catsup
4	ounces cream cheese	½	teaspoon pepper
2	teaspoons Worcestershire sauce	1	teaspoon lemon juice
			Salt to taste
			Chopped chives

Blend all ingredients except chives. Form into balls. Roll in chopped chives.

Makes 30 balls

Mrs. Ferrell Singleton

Hot Cheese Puffs

2	jars cheese spread	1¼	sticks margarine
1	egg	1	loaf sandwich bread
	Red pepper		

All ingredients should be room temperature. Whip all, except bread, until well blended. Remove bread crusts. For every 2 slices of bread, make 4 small sandwiches with a thin layer of the mixture in the middle. Then spread a thin layer of cheese mixture on the sides and tops of each small sandwich. Freeze on cookie sheet. Bake while frozen at 350 degrees for 10 to 12 minutes.

Jane McLane

"Crispen Island" Cheese Straws

1½	sticks butter	1	teaspoon dry mustard
2	cups softened sharp Cheddar cheese (grated and packed)	1	tablespoon water
		1	teaspoon Worcestershire sauce
2	cups flour		
1	teaspoon salt	2	teaspoons baking powder
½	teaspoon Tabasco sauce		

Combine butter and cheese in food processor. Gradually add flour, then remaining ingredients. Use cookie press (either star or flat design) to squirt on ungreased cookie tin. Bake at 375 degrees for 15 minutes.

Mrs. Jack Sullivan

Chee Wees

1	jar cheese and bacon spread	¾	cup plain flour
½	stick butter		

Blend; shape as desired and bake in moderate oven.

Mrs. Stanley Bishop

25

Foolproof Cheese Straws

1	cup sifted all-purpose flour	½	cup butter or margarine
½	teaspoon baking powder	3	tablespoons cold water
1	cup grated Cheddar cheese		

Sift flour and baking powder into a bowl. Cut in cheese and butter with a pastry blender. Add water and mix well. Fill cookie press. Form straws on ungreased cookie sheet using star plate. Bake 8 to 10 minutes at 375 degrees. Cut into desired length immediately and remove from sheet.

Makes 3 dozen

Mrs. Bill Keller

Cheese Straws #1

1	pound grated cheese	½	teaspoon salt
½	pound butter	¼	teaspoon red pepper
3	cups bread flour		

Blend and cook at 450 degrees. Good with chopped nuts added.

Mrs. Stanley Bishop

Cheese Straws #2

1	cup grated sharp cheese	Dash of Tabasco sauce
½	cup butter	Dash of salt
1½	cups flour	Dash of cayenne pepper
3	teaspoons water	

Cream cheese and butter, then add flour and seasonings. Roll very thin and cut in desired shapes or use decorators' tube. Bake at 350 degrees about 5 minutes. Sprinkle with salt while hot.

Mrs. Charles D. Richards

Salt-Rising Bread Cheese Straws

Salt-rising bread **Red pepper**
Butter, melted **Parmesan cheese**

Cut bread slices into sticks. Dip each stick into butter, sprinkle with red pepper, and cover sides with Parmesan cheese. Put on cookie sheet and refrigerate until time to use. Cook in 300 degrees oven until toasted. Serve hot.

Mrs. Joyce Mixson

Cheese Wheels

Bread **Parmesan cheese, melted**
Butter, melted

Cut rounds of bread. With a smaller cutter, take circles from the center of each round; toast on one side; spread the other side with melted butter. Cover the buttered side thickly with grated Parmesan cheese. Toast. Watch closely so that cheese does not burn. Serve cold. Can be made a day ahead. Store in a tin. Good with soups and salads.

Mrs. Maxwell Oliver

Cream Cheese and Caviar

1 **large package cream cheese** 1 **small jar black or red**
3 **teaspoons grated onion** **caviar**

Place block of cream cheese on serving tray. Sprinkle onion over cheese. Pour caviar over cheese. Serve with crackers.

Mrs. Richard Beckmann

Cream Cheese Pickapeppa

1 large block of cream cheese   **1 jar Pickapeppa sauce**

Cover 1 block of cream cheese with Pickapeppa sauce. Serve with crackers.

Mrs. Michael Drumheller

Cream Cheese Log

**3 (3-ounce) packages cream
cheese**
¼ cup finely chopped celery
½ teaspoon grated fresh onion

**Dash of Worcestershire
sauce**
1 cup chopped pecans

Beat cream cheese until fluffy. Blend in celery, onion, and Worcestershire sauce. Shape into log; roll in pecans. Wrap in waxed paper. Chill.

Mrs. Bill Keller

Hot Cheese Spread

¾ cup mayonnaise
⅓ cup Parmesan cheese
1 tablespoon chives

Onion salt to taste
3 drops Worcestershire sauce

Spread on party rye bread and broil until lightly browned and bubbly, about 1 minute. Serve hot.

Mrs. Joe Taylor

Pineapple Cheese Ball

2	(8-ounce) packages cream cheese	¼	cup chopped bell pepper
2	(4-ounce) cans crushed pineapple, drained	2	tablespoons chopped onion
		1	cup chopped nuts
		1	teaspoon salt

Soften cream cheese and mix with pineapple. Mix in peppers, onion, nuts and salt. Shape into balls. Refrigerate overnight. Roll in 1 cup chopped nuts or sprinkle over the top.

Ann Dasher

Roquefort Mound

½	pound Roquefort cheese	1	small grated onion
¼	pound sharp Cheddar cheese	1	teaspoon Tabasco sauce
1	(8-ounce) package cream cheese		Pinch of salt
			Red pepper to taste
			Dash of lemon juice

Soften cheese and mix well. Add other ingredients; then roll ½ cup of pecans between waxed paper until crushed. Cover molded cheese. Place in refrigerator to chill. Better prepared day before serving.

Mrs. Bill Keller

Chicken Liver Wrap-Ups

½   **pound chicken livers, cut into thirds**
¼   **cup soy sauce**
1   **clove garlic, minced**

1   **(5-ounce) can water chestnuts, cut into thirds**
15   **slices thin sliced breakfast bacon, cult into halves**

Marinate livers in soy sauce and garlic 3 hours at room temperature or overnight in refrigerator. Wrap livers and water chestnuts in bacon and secure with toothpick. Place on wire rack over shallow pan and bake at 425 degrees for 25 minutes. Cook until bacon is crisp, turning occasionally. Keep some water in shallow pan to keep drippings from burning. May also be charcoaled.

Mrs. Fred Dodson

Chili Meat Turnovers

1   **tablespoon oil**
1   **onion, minced**
¾   **pound ground beef**
½   **teaspoon salt**
¼   **teaspoon pepper**
½   **teaspoon chili powder**
⅛   **teaspoon cayenne**

2   **tablespoons flour**
½   **cup diced sautéed mushrooms**
6   **stuffed olives, minced**
6   **black olives, minced**
⅓   **recipe quick puff pastry**

Heat oil in skillet. Sauté onion. Add beef and stir constantly. Add seasonings. When beef has browned and moisture evaporated, mix in flour and stir well over flame. Mix in mushrooms and olives. Adjust seasonings. Cool thoroughly. Roll out dough in 2 pieces, 6x18 inches. Cut into 3 parts each, 2x18 inches. Cut 2-inch squares. Place a teaspoonful of meat on each square and bring corner over to make a triangle. These may be frozen at this point or refrigerated until ready to use. Brush each pastry with a mixture of 1 egg yolk and 1 tablespoon water. Bake at 400 degrees for 15 minutes.

Makes 54 turnovers

Mrs. Tenney S. Griffin

Swiss Fondue

For each person use:

⅓ **pound Swiss cheese, sliced in thin slices**

1 **wine glass of dry Sauterne**
1 **clove of garlic**

Place sliced cheese in chafing dish or top of double boiler that has been rubbed well with garlic clove. Melt cheese slowly, adding one glass of wine at a time, stirring very slowly. Keep warm. Cut one day old French bread into 1-inch squares and dip into cheese dish. Serve as appetizer, or with green salad for supper.

Mrs. Jim Tunison

Honey Chicken Wings

3 **pounds chicken wings, tips cut off and cut into 2 pieces**
   Salt
   Pepper
1 **cup honey**

½ **cup soy sauce**
2 **tablespoons vegetable oil**
2 **tablespoons catsup**
½ **cup chopped garlic clove**

Cook 6 to 8 hours on low in crock-pot.

Sue Nelle Scruggs

Chafing Dish Crab

4 **(8-ounce) packages cream cheese**
1 **cup mayonnaise**
4 **teaspoons sugar**
1 **clove garlic, minced**

4 **teaspoons prepared mustard**
2 **pound claw crabmeat**
12 **tablespoons dry white wine**

Melt cheese, stirring constantly. Add mayonnaise, sugar, garlic and mustard. Heat thoroughly. Add crabmeat and wine and heat thoroughly again.

Mrs. James Dowling, Jr.

Hot Clam Dip #1

3	tablespoons butter	4	tablespoons catsup
1	small onion, finely chopped	1	tablespoon Worcestershire
½	green pepper, finely chopped		sauce
1	(10½-ounce) can clams,	1	tablespoon sherry
	drained	¼	teaspoon cayenne pepper
½	pound or more processed		
	cheese loaf		

In top of a double boiler, melt 3 tablespoons butter. Sauté onion and green pepper over direct heat for 3 minutes. Add remaining ingredients. Cook in double boiler until cheese has melted, stirring often. Transfer to chafing dish. Serve with toast rounds.

Mrs. Henry Brice

Hot Clam Dip #2

2	cans minced clams	½	onion, chopped finely
3	(8-ounce) package cream	1½	tablespoons Worcestershire
	cheese		sauce
	Clam juice to thin		Salt and cayenne pepper to
3	tablespoons lemon juice		taste

Mix, heat and serve in chafing dish with toast rounds.

Mrs. Marshal Parks

Crab Newburg Dip

1	(6-ounce) package frozen	1	can shrimp soup
	crabmeat	¼	cup sherry

Combine, heat and serve with toasted bread sticks.

Mrs. John McTier

Hot Crab Spread

1	(8-ounce) package cream cheese	½	teaspoon cream style horseradish
1	tablespoon milk	¼	teaspoon salt
1	(6½-ounce) can crabmeat, flaked		Dash of pepper or Tabasco sauce
2	tablespoons finely chopped onion	⅓	cup toasted sliced almonds Paprika to taste

Combine cream cheese and milk. Add crabmeat, onion horseradish, salt, and Tabasco. Blend well and spoon into a glass pie plate. Sprinkle with almonds and paprika. Bake at 375 degrees for 15 minutes. Serve with crackers.

Mrs. Henry Brice

Guacamole

2	ripe avocados	¼	teaspoon cayenne pepper
1½	tablespoons lemon juice	1	teaspoon finely grated onion
1	tablespoon Worcestershire sauce	1	scant teaspoon salt
1	medium clove garlic, mashed with press		

Mash avocados and lemon juice together. Stir in other ingredients. If not smooth, press through coarse sieve. When ready to serve, sprinkle with paprika and serve with crackers or corn chips.

Mrs. Henry Brice

Barbecued Meatballs

Meatballs
1   **pound hamburger**   **Onion salt**
1   **slice white bread, crumbled**   **Garlic salt**
    Salt   ⅛ **cup catsup**
    Pepper

Mix all above and roll into very small balls. Place in large glass baking dish or aluminum pan with sides and cook ½ hour in oven at 250 degrees. Drain off grease.

Sauce
½ **bottle barbecue sauce**   2   **teaspoons flour**
1   **small can tomato sauce**   ½ **cup water**

Mix barbecue sauce, tomato sauce, flour and water to make sauce. Pour over meatballs. Cook 20 to 30 minutes at 250 degrees. Garnish with stuffed olives.

Sue Bentley

Cocktail Meatballs

1   **pound ground beef**   **Small cubes sharp Cheddar**
1   **jar Smithfield ham spread**   **or blue cheese**
    Salt   **Red wine**
    Pepper

Mix beef and ham spread together. Season with salt and pepper. Mold meat mixture around cubes of cheese, making small balls. Place in a bowl and pour red wine over. Let stand in refrigerator about 2 or 3 hours. Put small amount of margarine in frying pan. Add a little of the wine, and pan fry the meatballs. Serve from chaffing dish.

Makes 20 meatballs

Mrs. Henry Brice

Brandied Mushrooms

1	pound sliced mushrooms	Salt
2	tablespoons butter	Pepper
¼	cup brandy	Chopped parsley

Sauté mushrooms in butter over high heat. When the mushrooms are browned pour on brandy. Set a match to it for flaming. Shake the skillet as the flame catches and gradually dies away. Season with remaining ingredients.

Mrs. Tenney S. Griffin

Marinated Mushrooms

½	pound fresh mushrooms, thinly sliced	½	teaspoon cracked pepper
		¼	teaspoon basil
½	cup salad oil	¼	teaspoon marjoram
½	cup lemon juice	¼	teaspoon oregano
2	teaspoons seasoned salt	¼	teaspoon salt
½	teaspoon sugar	¼	teaspoon garlic powder

Wash mushrooms. Combine all other ingredients and shake well in a jar. Pour over mushrooms. Cover and allow to absorb flavors.

Mrs. Jack Sullivan

Mushroom Appetizers

1	(8-ounce) package cream cheese, softened	1	clove minced garlic
2	tablespoons butter, softened	2	small can drained and chopped mushrooms

Mix together all ingredients. Heap onto party bread slices and broil.

Serves 48

Russell Lawrence

Olive Surprises

½ cup soft butter or margarine
1 cup grated sharp Cheddar cheese
¼ teaspoon salt
¼ teaspoon pepper
½ cup sifted flour
36 stuffed olives, drained

Cream butter and cheese until blended. Add remaining ingredients, except olives, and mix well. Chill 15 to 20 minutes. Shape a small portion of dough around each olive. Bake at 400 degrees for about 15 minutes. If desired, these may be frozen on cookie sheet, put in plastic bags, and stored in freezer until needed. Best when served hot.

Mrs. William Oliver

Glorified Onions

5-6 medium purple onions
½ cup vinegar
1 cup sugar
2 cups water
½ cup mayonnaise
1 teaspoon celery salt

Slice onions and soak 2 to 4 hours in refrigerator in vinegar, sugar and water. Drain well and toss with mayonnaise and celery salt.

Mrs. George Shelton

Sesame Bread Sticks

White bread
Parmesan cheese
Sesame seeds

Butter white bread on both sides. Sprinkle both sides of bread with Parmesan cheese and sesame seeds. Cut into finger strips. Bake 1 hour at 250 degrees.

Mrs. Jack Sullivan

🌿 *James' Marinated Oysters*

2	pints fresh or frozen oysters	½	cup salad or olive oil
1	pint cherry tomatoes	½	cup water
½	pound fresh mushrooms	2	cloves minced garlic
6	green onions cut into 2-inch lengths	1	teaspoon sugar
		1	teaspoon salt
¼	cup chopped pimento	½	teaspoon oregano leaves
1	cup cider vinegar	¼	teaspoon pepper

Drain oysters and remove any shell particles. Wash vegetables and pat dry. Cut large mushrooms in half. In a 2- to 3-quart bowl, combine oysters, tomatoes, mushrooms, green onions and pimento. In a 1-quart bowl combine vinegar, salad oil, water, garlic, sugar, salt, oregano, and pepper; mix thoroughly until sugar is dissolved. Pour marinade over oysters and vegetables. Cover loosely and marinade in the refrigerator at least 12 hours. Serve with toothpicks and crackers.

Teresa Steinberg

Picadillo Dip
(from San Antonio Country Club)

½	pound ground beef	¾	cup toasted almonds, slivered
½	pound ground pork	2½	cloves garlic, cut up
1-1½	teaspoons salt	1	(6-ounce) can tomato paste
¼	teaspoon pepper (or to taste)	2	canned jalapeño peppers, chopped
4	tomatoes, peeled and diced, or 1 can	¾	cup seedless raisins
3	green onions, finely chopped	¼	teaspoon oregano
3	medium potatoes, diced		

Barely cover ground beef and pork with water and simmer half hour with salt and pepper. It must be well seasoned. Add remaining ingredients. Cook until potatoes are done, about 1 hour. Drain if too much juice. Serve from chafing dish with corn chips.

Mrs. Joyce Mixson

Shrimp and Artichoke Dip

2 cans small deveined shrimp or equal amount of fresh cooked shrimp	1 jar Catalina salad dressing
1 can chopped mushrooms	2 dashes Worcestershire sauce
2 jars artichoke hearts	Salt
1 small jar pimento	Pepper

Drain everything. Chop artichokes. Mix all ingredients together. Serve with tortilla chips. Can prepare two days ahead.

Betty Jean Daugharty

Shrimp Dip

1 (16-ounce) package cottage cheese	Dash of Tabasco sauce
1 cup chili sauce	Dash of lemon juice
1 tablespoon white pepper	Dash of Worcestershire sauce
2 tablespoons horseradish	

Combine above in blender. Add at least 1 pound of shrimp and serve with corn chips.

Mrs. Michael Drumheller

Dip For Shrimp

1 can tomato soup	3 teaspoons salt
2 garlic cloves, cut	3 teaspoons Worcestershire sauce
2 teaspoons dry mustard	1 cup oil
½ cup sugar	½ cup vinegar
4 teaspoons grated onion	

Combine ingredients, adding vinegar and oil last. Use cold peeled shrimp for dipping.

Mrs. Richard Beckmann

Marinated Shrimp

2	pounds shrimp, boiled and peeled	¼	teaspoon dry mustard
2	large onions, sliced into rings	4	medium bay leaves
		1	small gingerroot
2	lemons, thinly sliced	1	blade mace
1½	cups salad oil	1	teaspoon sugar
1	pint apple cider vinegar	½	teaspoon black peppercorns
1	teaspoon salt	⅓	cup mixed pickling spices

Combine first 4 ingredients. Bring remaining ingredients to a boil. Cool and strain and pour over shrimp mixture. Marinate overnight.

This will keep for days in the refrigerator.

Mrs. Fred Dodson

Shrimp Pâté

3-4	tablespoons Pernod (or 3 tablespoons sherry and ½ teaspoon tarragon)	1	teaspoon Dijon mustard
		¼	pound butter, softened
	Juice of ½ lemon		Salt and pepper to taste
½	teaspoon mace	1	pound cooked, peeled shrimp
	Dash of Tabasco sauce		

Put all except shrimp in blender. Cover and blend well. Flipping switch, add 3 or 4 shrimp at the time until coarsely chopped. Chill and serve.

Mrs. Marshall Parks

🌺 *Shrimp and Crab Mousse*

1	can tomato soup	1	small can crabmeat
1	package plain gelatin	1	small can shrimp
¼	soup can cold water	½	cup finely chopped onion
1	(8-ounce) package cream	½	cup finely chopped celery
	cheese	½	cup finely chopped green
1	cup mayonnaise		pepper

Heat tomato soup to a boil. Dissolve gelatin in water and add to soup. Add cream cheese and mayonnaise. Add cream cheese and mayonnaise and blend in blender. Add remaining ingredients and pour into mold.

Lyn Dickey

Swamp Salad

Tomatoes
Onions
Cucumbers

Ice cubes
Vinegar

Slice desired amount of tomatoes, onions and cucumbers into large bowl. Cover with ice cubes and vinegar. To be eaten on saltine crackers.

Dip for Vegetables

1	package blue cheese salad	½	pint sour cream
	dressing mix	½	cup mayonnaise

Mix and refrigerate several hours. Serve with carrots, cauliflower, and celery cut into bite-size pieces.

Mrs. Jack Sullivan

Salads, Salad Dressings & Sauces

Salads

Jellied Ambrosia 44
Apricot Aspic 44
Apricot Salad 45
Artichoke Hearts Salad 45
Asheville Salad 45
Molded Asparagus Salad 46
Mother's Avocado Salad 46
Bean Salad 47
Three Bean Salad 47
Bing Cherry Salad 47
Bing Cherry Congealed Salad 48
Blue Cheese Ring Mold 48
Buttermilk Salad 49
Blueberry Jello Salad 49
Cold Broccoli Mold 49
Broccoli Salad 50
Chicken Salad 50
Consommé Salad 51
Corned Beef Salad 51
Cranberry-Raspberry Salad 52
Congealed Salad #1 52
Congealed Salad #2 52
Corn Salad 53
Hot Crab Rice Salad 53
Cranberry Ring Mold 53
Cranberry Mold 54
Raw Cranberry Salad 54
Frozen Cranberry Salad #1 55
Frozen Cranberry Salad #2 55
Cucumber Marinade 55
Cucumber Salad 56
Faucon Salad 56
Five Cup Salad 56
Egg and Cheese Salad 57
Frozen Fruit Salad 57

Fruit Salad 58
Grapefruit Salad 58
Grapefruit-Avocado Mold 58
Green Bean Congealed Salad
    with Cucumber Dressing 59
Guacamole-Tomato Salad 59
Green Bean Salad 60
Onion Salad 60
Mincemeat Gelatin Salad 61
Frosted Orange Salad 61
Macaroni Salad 61
Orange Fluff 62
Pink Frozen Salad 62
Pineapple-Marshmallow Salad 62
Potato Salad 63
Oriental Salad 63
Potato Salad with Blue Cheese-
    Sour Cream Dressing 64
Salad Surprise for Jean 64
Sea Dream Salad 65
Strawberry Jello Salad 65
Jan Carter's Slaw 65
Marinated Shrimp Salad 66
Tea Garden Salad 66
Tart Salad 67
Tomato Chicken Mold 67
Perfect Tomato Aspic 68
Herbed Tomato Platter
    & Dutch Cucumbers 68
Tomato Soup Salad 69
Tomato Aspic
    with Crab Mayonnaise 69
Tossed Club Salad 70
Tuna Garden Salad 70
White Salad 71
Wilted Lettuce Salad 71

Salad Dressings

Avocado Salad Dressing 72
Blue Cheese Dressing 72
Celery Seed Dressing 73
French Dressing 73
Fruit Salad Dressing 73
Dressing for Grapefruit Salad 74
Green Goddess Dressing 74

Roquefort Dressing 74
Kum Bak Dressing 75
Thousand Island Dressing 75
Lemon-Caper Mayonnaise 75
Tomato Salad Dressing 76
Homemade Mayonnaise #1 76
Homemade Mayonnaise #2 76

Sauces

Tangy Sauce for
    Cabbage, Broccoli, Etc. 77
Barbecue Sauce 77
Barbeque Sauce for Chicken 77

Barbecue Sauce for Steaks 78
Ridgewood Bar-B-Q Sauce 78
Hollandaise Sauce 78

Jellied Ambrosia

1	envelope unflavored gelatin	1½	cups fresh orange segments
¼	cup sugar	¼	cup coconut
½	cup boiling water	½	cup maraschino cherries,
1¼	cups orange juice		halved
1	tablespoon lemon juice	1½	cups banana slices

Soften gelatin in ¼ cup cold water. Add boiling water and sugar and stir until dissolved. Add remaining juices and chill until partially set. Fold in fruits and pour in 1-quart mold. Chill until set.

Serves 6

Gloria Anderson

Apricot Aspic

2	(1-pound) cans peeled apricots	1	(7-ounce) bottle of lemon-lime carbonated beverage
2	(3-ounce) packages orange gelatin		Lettuce
	Dash of salt		Mayonnaise
1	(6-ounce) can orange juice concentrate		Whipped topping

Drain apricots, reserving 1½ cups syrup. Puree apricots in blender or sieve. You will need 2 cups apricot puree. Combine reserve syrup and orange gelatin. Add dash of salt and heat to boiling, stirring to dissolve gelatin. Remove from heat; add apricot puree and orange juice concentrate (undiluted). Slowly pour lemon-lime carbonated beverage down side of the pan. To keep bubbles, mix gently with up and down motion. Pour into a 6½-cup ring mold. Chill until firm. Unmold on bed of lettuce and fill center with a dressing made by folding together equal parts of mayonnaise and whipped topping.

Nancy Paris

✤ *Apricot Salad*

1 large package apricot or lemon jello	2 cans apricot nectar
1 package plain jello	1 large package cream cheese
1 medium can crushed pineapple	1 cup chopped nuts

Dissolve jello and cream cheese in juices. Add other ingredients. Chill until gelled.

Ann Stone

✤ *Artichoke Hearts Salad*

1 package chicken flavored Rice-A-Roni, cooked and cooled	⅓ teaspoon curry
	⅓ tablespoon mayonnaise
2 green onions	½ green pepper
8 green olives	2 jars marinated artichoke hearts

Slice onions, pepper, olives and artichoke hearts. Save artichoke juice. Mix artichoke juice with curry powder and mayonnaise. Mix onions, pepper, olives and artichoke hearts with Rice-A-Roni. Pour artichoke juice, curry powder and mayonnaise mixture over other ingredients. Refrigerate for a few hours.

Serves 10

Teresa Minchew

Asheville Salad

2 packages cream cheese	½ cup nuts
2 cans tomato soup	1 cup celery, onion, and green pepper, cut fine and mixed
1 envelope gelatin dissolved in ⅓ cup cold water	1 cup mayonnaise

Heat cream cheese and soup together to dissolve. Add gelatin and mix well. Add nuts, vegetables, and then mayonnaise. Congeal.

Mrs. Nettie Keller

Molded Asparagus Salad

2 tablespoons butter	1 cup almonds, blanched and
2 tablespoons flour	chopped fine
1 large can green asparagus	Juice of 1 lemon
tips, reserve liquid	1 cup mayonnaise
4 egg yolks	½ pint cream, whipped
1 tablespoon gelatin	Salt and pepper to taste
¼ cold water	

Melt butter, stir in flour until well mixed. Add asparagus liquid making a cream sauce. Beat egg yolks well. Add a little of hot cream sauce gradually to beaten yolks, stirring well, then add all of egg yolk mixture to cream sauce. Cook until thick. Dissolve gelatin in water and add to hot mixture. When slightly cool, add almonds, lemon juice, asparagus, mayonnaise, whipped cream, salt and pepper. Pour in individual molds or one large mold. Serve on lettuce leaves with a teaspoon of mayonnaise on top.

Mrs. Joyce Mixson

Mother's Avocado Salad

1 small package lime jello	1 cucumber; grated, drained
1 cup hot water	and strained
1 cup mayonnaise	1 avocado, scraped and diced
1 cup sour cream	1 small onion, grated

Combine all ingredients and stir until blended. Pour into mold or 1½-quart casserole dish and chill until firm.

Sharon Coleman

Bean Salad

1	can green beans	½	cup yellow onion, chopped
1	can yellow beans	½	cup salad oil
1	can red kidney beans	½	cup cider vinegar
1	can chick peas	¾	cup sugar
½	cup chopped green pepper		Salt and pepper

Drain beans. Combine in bowl with green pepper and onion. Mix oil, vinegar, sugar, salt and pepper and pour over beans. Toss mixture and refrigerate overnight.

George Hart

Three Bean Salad

1	cup sugar	1	can cut green beans, drained
¾	cup oil		
1½	teaspoons salt	1	can wax beans, drained
1	cup vinegar	1	can kidney beans, drained
1	teaspoon garlic powder	1	medium onion, thinly sliced
1	teaspoon celery seed		

Mix sugar, oil, salt, vinegar, garlic powder, and celery seed and heat. Pour over beans. Add onion. Refrigerate. Will keep for several weeks.

Sara Holt

Bing Cherry Salad

1	package cherry gelatin		Chopped pecans
1	can drained pitted Bing cherries	1¾	cups liquid (juice plus water)
1	large can drained crushed pineapple	¼	cup cooking sherry

Dissolve gelatin in hot liquid. Add other ingredients. Refrigerate.

Mrs. Stanley Bishop

47

Bing Cherry Congealed Salad

1   small package lemon jello
1   small package cherry jello
3½ cups water
1   can Bing cherries, drained
    and pitted

1   can crushed pineapple,
    drained
½   cup celery (diced)
1   (8 ounce) package cream
    cheese
½   cup chopped nuts

Combine jello and add 1 cup boiling water. Stir until jello is completely dissolved and add remaining 2½ cups cold water. Set in refrigerator to congeal. When jello begins to hold shape, add Bing cherries, pineapple, and celery. Make cream cheese and nuts into balls, about the size of the end of your thumb. Add fruit and cream cheese balls evenly to jello. Place in mold and continue chilling until firm.

Mrs. Fred Dodson

Blue Cheese Ring Mold

1   envelope plain gelatin
½   cup water
2   cups cottage cheese
½   cup sour cream
½   cup crumbled blue cheese
½   cup mayonnaise

Season to taste with the following: vinegar, Tabasco sauce, onion salt, Worcestershire sauce, and garlic salt

Soften gelatin in water, then heat over low heat until gelatin dissolves. Cool. Combine remainder of ingredients and pour dissolved gelatin over. Put in ring mold and place in refrigerator to congeal. Unmold on large platter of lettuce and garnish with tomato wedges, avocado slices, cold asparagus, etc.

Mrs. Oris Blackburn

🍃 *Blueberry Jello Salad*

1   large package black cherry jello
1   (20-ounce) can crushed pineapple
1   (20-ounce) can blueberries

1   carton sour cream
1   (8-ounce) package cream cheese
½   cup sugar

Drain fruits and add enough water to juice to make 2 cups. Boil and stir into jello. Chill and stir in fruit. Congeal. Combine sour cream, cream cheese and sugar. Spread onto jello mixture. Sprinkle with flaked coconut.

Betty Dow Templeton

🍃 *Buttermilk Salad*

2   (3-ounce) packages strawberry jello
1   large can crushed pineapple

2   cups buttermilk
1   (9-ounce) container whipped topping

Drain pineapple. Heat juice, adding enough water to make 1 cup. Use to dissolve jello. Add pineapple and let cool. Then add buttermilk. Stir well and refrigerate until mixture thickens. Fold in whipped topping and let congeal. This is also good using orange jello and Mandarin oranges with pineapple.

Patty Castleberry & Mrs. Earl Mayo

🍃 *Cold Broccoli Mold*

3   packages chopped broccoli, cooked and drained
1   package gelatin
½   small jar pimentos
⅔   cup mayonnaise
1   teaspoon salt

1   tablespoon Worcestershire sauce
1   can beef consommé
3-4   chopped boiled eggs
4   teaspoons lemon juice

Heat ¼ can consommé to dissolve gelatin. After dissolved, mix all the ingredients together and pour into mold. Chill until firm. Unmold on bed of lettuce. Garnish with whole pimento.

Serves 8 to 10

Frances Golivesky

Broccoli Salad

2	packages frozen chopped broccoli	1	tablespoon Worcestershire sauce
1	envelope plain gelatin		Salt and red pepper to taste
1	can beef consommé	6	hard-boiled eggs, sliced
	Juice of 2 lemons	¾	cup mayonnaise
2	shakes of Tabasco sauce		

Cook and drain broccoli. Soften gelatin in ¼ cup cold consommé. Heat remainder of consommé and dissolve the softened gelatin in heated consommé. Let cool. Add seasonings. Place half of sliced hard-boiled eggs in bottom of mold. Just before gelatin mixture begins to gel, fold in mayonnaise and broccoli. Pour half over sliced eggs, and add another layer of hard-boiled eggs, then remainder of gelatin, broccoli, and mayonnaise mixture. Place in refrigerator to congeal.

Mrs. Jack Sullivan

Chicken Salad

1	hen	Salt and cayenne pepper to
1	bunch celery, diced	taste
3-4	hard-boiled eggs	Mayonnaise
	Lemon juice to taste	

Boil the hen until very tender. Remove from the water and chill. Pull the meat from the bones, discarding all skin, gristle, and veins. Cut with scissors into small cubes. Mix chicken with celery, hard-boiled eggs and lemon juice with mayonnaise. Season to taste and serve on a bed of lettuce.

Shrimp Salad. Replace chicken with 2 pounds of shrimp. Boil shrimp in salt water until they turn pink and are tender. Rinse in cold water, peel and de-vein. Break shrimp into small pieces. Shrimp should boil approximately 10 minutes. Follow remaining directions.

Mrs. John B. Lastinger

Consommé Salad

1 envelope unflavored gelatin	1 cup artichoke hearts, cut in
2 cans undiluted beef	half
consommé	Lemon juice, salt, pepper,
⅔ cup chopped celery	grated onion and Tabasco
⅓ cup grated carrots	to taste

Dissolve gelatin in ½ cup water. Add 2 cans heated consommé. Add seasonings. Refrigerate until partially congealed. Add remaining ingredients. Pour into greased mold. Chill for several hours until congealed. The vegetables may be varied. Use peas, tomatoes, shrimp or any combination you prefer. Just artichokes are good. Serve with shrimp mayonnaise.

Shrimp Mayonnaise

2 cups cooked chopped shrimp	Grated peel of ½ lemon
1 small onion, chopped	

Marinate the above in:

½ cup vegetable oil	Juice of ½ lemon
½ cup vinegar	

Marinate several hours. Drain. Add to 1½ cups mayonnaise.

Serves 4 to 6

Mr. John B. Lastinger

Corned Beef Salad

2 small packages lemon jello	1 tablespoon minced bell
1 can corned beef, shredded	pepper
⅔ cup water	1 cup mayonnaise
2 teaspoons minced onion	3 hard-boiled eggs
2 cups chopped celery	

Mix jello with hot water. Add corned beef. Add celery, onion and pepper. Fold in mayonnaise and chopped eggs. Chill several hours and cut in squares. Serve on lettuce, top with pepper ring and grated cheese.

Jeneane Grimsley

🌿 Cranberry-Raspberry Salad

1 (3-ounce) package raspberry gelatin	1 (10-ounce) package frozen raspberries
1 (3-ounce) package lemon gelatin	1 (16-ounce) can jellied cranberry sauce
1½ cups boiling water	1 (7-ounce) bottle lemon-lime soda

Dissolve gelatins in boiling water. Stir in frozen berries, breaking up large pieces. Break up cranberry sauce with a fork, stir into gelatin mixture. Chill until partially set. Carefully pour in lemon-lime soda, stirring gently. Turn into 6-cup mold and chill 5 to 6 hours. Unmold on crisp greens.

Laurie McCall

Congealed Salad #1

1 package lime jello	1 small can crushed pineapple, with juice
1 can pears, cut up with juice	
1 cup water	Handful tiny marshmallows
Nuts (optional)	

Dissolve jello in cup of hot water. Add all ingredients except marshmallows. Refrigerate. Fold in marshmallows when partially congealed.

Mrs. John Howell

🌿 Congealed Salad #2

1 large head lettuce, chopped	1 tablespoon sugar
2 large cans English peas, drained	1 pint mayonnaise
6-8 stalks celery, chopped	1 medium can Parmesan cheese
6 green onions mixed with water chestnuts	

Place in large casserole layered as listed. Cover tightly with plastic wrap and chill at least 6 hours.

Dee Broadfoot

Corn Salad

1	jar pimento	½	cup oil
1	green pepper, chopped	1	cup sugar
2	small cans shoe peg corn	1	cup vinegar
1	large can French green beans	1	tablespoon salt
5	stalks celery, chopped	1	onion chopped

Drain corn and beans and mix ingredients. Let set overnight.

Sue Bentley

Hot Crab Rice Salad

1	cup cooked rice	½	teaspoon red pepper
1½	cups mayonnaise	⅛	teaspoon black pepper
1	cup cooked or Alaskan canned flaked crabmeat	1	cup cream
			Individual sized pasty shells
6	hard-boiled eggs, chopped		Butter
1	tablespoon parsley, chopped	½	cup Cheddar cheese, grated
1	teaspoon salt		

Combine all ingredients except cheese, mix well. Place in buttered individual pastry shells, sprinkle with grated cheese. Bake 350 degrees for 20 minutes. Serve hot.

Kitty Fricks

Cranberry Ring Mold

2	packages cherry jello	1	can whole cranberry sauce
2	cups hot water or fruit juice	1	cup nuts
1	tall can crushed pineapple	1	cup diced apples

Dissolve jello with hot liquid. Add pineapple and cranberry sauce. When partially congealed, add nuts and diced apples. Pour into ring mold and chill until firm.

Mrs. Rudolph Howell

Cranberry Mold

1	(8-ounce) can crushed pineapple	2	tablespoons salad dressing or mayonnaise
1	(1-pound) can of whole cranberry sauce	1	cup heavy cream or 1 (8-ounce) package whipped cream
2	(3-ounce) packages raspberry jello	½	cup chopped pecans (more if desired)
1	package cream cheese		

Drain fruit. Reserve liquid and add water to make 2 cups. Bring to boil. Dissolve jello in hot liquid. Chill until partially set. Beat softened cream cheese and salad dressing together until fluffy. Gradually beat in jello mixture. Fold this mixture into whipped cream. Set aside 1½ cups of this mixture. Add fruit and nuts and pour into 12x7x2-inch glass dish and refrigerate until surface sets, about 20 minutes. Frost with reserve topping. Refrigerate several hours. Salad may be frozen if desired. Remove from freezer to refrigerator 1 hour before serving.

Serves 20

Mrs. Jack Rudolph

Raw Cranberry Salad

1	cup sugar	1	package plain gelatin
1	ground whole orange with juice	½	cup boiling water
2	cups ground raw cranberries	1	small can crushed pineapple
1	package lemon flavored gelatin		Nuts
			Celery, if desired

Mix sugar, orange and cranberries together. Dissolve gelatin in water. Add other ingredients and congeal.

Mrs. Nettie Keller

Frozen Cranberry Salad #1

1	carton whipping cream, whipped	1	small can crushed pineapple, drained
1	(8-ounce) package cream cheese, softened	¼	cup chopped celery
¾	cup mayonnaise	½	cup chopped ripe olives
		1	can cranberry sauce, diced

Blend whipping cream, cream cheese and mayonnaise in mixer. Fold in pineapple, celery, olives and cranberry sauce. Reserve a few slices of the cranberry sauce for garnishing top of salad. Freeze salad in ice trays overnight. Serve on lettuce leaf and garnish top with cranberry sauce.

Mrs. Fred Dodson

Frozen Cranberry Salad #2

1	(16-ounce) can jellied cranberry sauce	¼	cup mayonnaise
3	tablespoons lemon juice	¼	cup confectioners' sugar
1	cup heavy cream, whipped	1	cup chopped pecans

Crush cranberry sauce with fork. Add lemon juice. Pour into individual molds. Combine rest of ingredients and spread over cranberry mixture. Freeze until firm. Unmold on crisp lettuce.

Serves 6 to 8

Mrs. Richard Beckmann

Cucumber Marinade

1	small onion, thinly sliced	⅓	cup vinegar
2	teaspoons salt	2	small cucumbers, peeled and thinly sliced
2	tablespoons sugar		

Soak cucumbers for 30 minutes in ice water. Drain; reserve ⅔ cup ice water. Mix vinegar, ⅔ cup ice water, sugar, salt and onion. Pour over cucumbers and stir slightly. Let stand in refrigerator at least 1 hour. Serve drained.

Mala Vallotton

Cucumber Salad

1	package lime jello	4	tablespoons lemon juice
1	cup cottage cheese	1	large cucumber, grated
1	cup mayonnaise	1	large onion, grated
1	pinch of salt		

Dissolve jello in ½ cup boiling water. Add all other ingredients and chill.

Mrs. John W. Lastinger and
Mrs. Tillman Lane of Brunswick, Georgia

Faucon Salad

1	head of lettuce	½	teaspoon salt
4	hard-boiled eggs, sliced	¼	pound Roquefort cheese
1	teaspoon dry mustard (less if desired)	3	tablespoons oil
1	teaspoon cayenne (less if desired)	1	tablespoon vinegar Crisp bacon

Rub bowl with garlic, cut up lettuce, put sliced eggs over it. Mix other ingredients and pour over lettuce and eggs. Top with crisp bacon.

Raw spinach may be used instead of or with the lettuce.

Serves 4

Mrs. Maxwell Oliver

Five Cup Salad

1	cup sour cream	1	cup Mandarin oranges
1	cup coconut	1	cup miniature marshmallows
1	cup diced pineapple		

Combine and serve chilled.

Mrs. Jack Gayle

🌿 *Egg and Cheese Salad*

7-8	hard-boiled eggs, sliced	½	pound American cheese, grated

Dressing

1	egg, beaten in pan	1	cup sugar
3	tablespoons flour	1	teaspoon salt
	Dash red pepper	2½	teaspoons mustard
½	cup water	½	cup vinegar
½	cup sweet milk		

Add a small amount of one of the liquids to dry ingredients and egg (of dressing) and mix well. Then add other liquids and cook until thickened, stirring constantly. Cool. Place a layer of the sliced egg, one of the cheese and one of the dressing in a bowl. Then repeat 2 layers. Sprinkle cracker crumbs on top if desired.

Carolyn Eager

Frozen Fruit Salad

1	(20-ounce) can fruit salad (may add cherries)	¼	teaspoon salt
1	can apricots, cut in several pieces	⅓	cup orange juice
1	(3-ounce) package cream cheese	1	teaspoon grated orange rind
3	tablespoons lemon juice	1	cup whipping cream
¼	cup sugar	1	tablespoon finely chopped preserved ginger

Drain fruit thoroughly. Soften cream cheese and blend in lemon juice, sugar, salt, orange juice and orange rind. Whip cream until barely stiff. Fold in cheese mixture. Fold in drained fruit and ginger. Freeze in aluminum loaf pan or refrigerator trays.

Mrs. Maxwell Oliver

Fruit Salad

1	package lime jello	1	cup mayonnaise
1	cup boiling water	½	cup nuts
1	can evaporated milk	1	large can fruit cocktail
1	cup cottage cheese		

Dissolve jello in boiling water and cool. Add other ingredients and freeze.

Mrs. Grady Durden

Grapefruit Salad

1	celery stalk	1	teaspoon salt
2	grapefruits, sectioned	¼	teaspoon oregano
3	tablespoons oil		Pepper
½	teaspoon sugar	1	tablespoon vinegar

Cut a stalk of celery into medium size cubes. Mix with grapefruits. Mix oil, sugar, salt, oregano and pepper together. Add vinegar. Pour on grapefruit and let set in refrigerator for 1 hour. Serve on lettuce.

Mrs. Diane Smith

Grapefruit-Avocado Mold

3½	cups boiling water	2	teaspoons grated onion
2	packages lime jello	2	avocados, peeled and diced
4	tablespoons lemon juice	2	grapefruit, peeled and
2	tablespoons horseradish		sectioned

Dissolve jello in boiling water. Add lemon juice, horseradish, and onion. Refrigerate. When mixture begins to set, beat with rotary beater and fold in grapefruit and avocado. Place in molds and refrigerate.

Serves 10

Mrs. Henry T. Brice, Jr.

Green Bean Congealed Salad with Cucumber Dressing

1   can French style green beans
1   package lemon flavored gelatin
1   envelope plain gelatin
½   cup pecans, diced
¼   cup chopped onion
½   cup celery, diced

Drain green beans and save liquid. Add enough water to liquid to make 2 cups. Heat to boiling. Dissolve gelatins in a little cold water. Mix pecans, onion, and celery with gelatin mixture. Add green beans and place in greased mold. Refrigerate until firm.

Cucumber Dressing
½   cup mayonnaise
1   teaspoon vinegar
1   tablespoon chopped bell pepper
¼   cup chopped cucumber
   Salt and pepper to taste

Mix all ingredients together and serve over Green Bean Congealed Salad. Always double Cucumber Dressing recipe.

Mrs. Howard Dasher, Jr.

Guacamole-Tomato Salad

6   medium tomatoes, peeled
2   teaspoons salt, separated
1   medium onion, chopped
1-2 canned chili peppers, finely chopped
2   teaspoons lemon juice
2   ripe avocados, mashed
6   lettuce leaves
3   slices bacon, crisply cooked and crumbled

Core tomatoes and scrape out centers, reserving shells. Finely chop tomato centers. Sprinkle inside of tomato cups with ½ teaspoonful salt, then turn upside down on paper towels to drain. Chill. Combine chopped tomato, onion, green chilies, lemon juice and remaining salt. Chill. Just before serving, mash avocados. Blend into tomato mixture. Arrange tomato cups on lettuce leaves, fill with guacamole. Top with crumbled bacon.

Mrs. J. K. Bland, Jr.

Green Bean Salad

1	large clove garlic	¾	cup salad oil
¼	teaspoon dried dill weed	1	small jar chopped pimento, drained
2	teaspoons salt (seasoned or plain)	1	can mushrooms, drained
½	teaspoon black pepper	2	cans green beans, drained well
1	teaspoon grated lemon rind		
¼	cup lemon juice		

Crush the garlic to a smooth paste and put into a large jar, which will eventually hold all of the ingredients. Add remaining ingredients. Close jar and gently shake. Refrigerate several hours and periodically shake during the chilling time. It is good to make first thing in the morning if you plan to use it for the evening meal. To make it a main dish luncheon salad, add cooked shrimp. This recipe can easily be doubled or tripled.

Mrs. John Bosch

Onion Salad

2	cups thinly sliced onions	½	teaspoon celery seed
½	cup water	¼	teaspoon salt
	Vinegar	2-3	tomatoes, peeled and sliced
1	tablespoon sugar		Lettuce
¼	cup mayonnaise		

Place onion in shallow dish. Pour the water over onion and add enough vinegar to cover. Sprinkle with sugar. Cover and chill for 3 or 4 hours. Just before serving, drain and mix onions with mayonnaise, celery seed and salt. Serve with sliced tomatoes on a bed of lettuce.

Mrs. Joe Stubbs

Macaroni Salad

1	medium box elbow macaroni	½	pound grated sharp cheese
1	green pepper, chopped	1	bunch celery, chopped
1	can pimento, chopped		Grated onion to taste

Mix all ingredients together with mayonnaise. The longer it sets, the better it is.

Mrs. Cleve Hunt

Mincemeat Gelatin Salad

2	packages black cherry jello	½-1	cup pecans, chopped
1	package dry mincemeat		

Cook mincemeat with 1 cup water until thick. Cool. Add to jello that has been blended with scant 3 cups hot water. Add nuts. Mold.

Mrs. Richard Beckmann

Frosted Orange Salad

1	small package orange jello	1	(3-ounce) package cream cheese
1	small grated carrot	1	cup chopped nuts
1	small can crushed pineapple	½	pint whipped cream

Drain pineapple, reserving juice. Heat juice with enough water to make 1 cup of liquid. Dissolve jello in liquid. When cool add whipped cream and other ingredients and congeal.

Martha Dover & Jane McLane

Orange Fluff

2	packages orange jello	4	temple oranges, peeled and
3	cups water		sliced with sugar to taste
½	cup sugar	½	pint whipping cream,
			whipped

Dissolve jello in water, add sugar and congeal until thick. Fold in sliced oranges and whipped cream. Mold until firm.

Mrs. Ed Garvin

Pink Frozen Salad

1	can condensed milk	1	(20-ounce) can crushed
1	quart whipped topping		pineapple
1	(20-ounce) can cherry pie filling		

Mix and freeze in pan approximately 8x12-inch. Cut in squares and serve.

Kay Coleman

Pineapple-Marshmallow Salad

2	small packages lime gelatin	1	small can crushed pineapple
2½	cups boiling water	1	cup ground pecans
12	marshmallows, chopped	1	cup heavy cream, whipped

Dissolve gelatin in boiling water. Add marshmallows to melt, cool. Add pineapple and pecans. Fold in whipped cream. Place in mold. Serve with cream cheese dressing, below.

Cream Cheese Dressing

1	(3-ounce) package cream cheese	1	tablespoon mayonnaise
		¼	teaspoon green food coloring

Mix together the above ingredients.

Kay McBride

Oriental Salad

2 (10-ounce) packages cooked frozen peas with onions	1 (7-ounce) package frozen shrimp, cooked
1 cup celery, chopped	1 (7½-ounce) can or box frozen crabmeat
1 can bean sprouts, drained	1 tablespoon lemon juice

Combine cooked peas, celery, bean sprouts, shrimp, crabmeat and sprinkle with lemon juice.

Blend

½ cup mayonnaise	1 teaspoon salt
¼ teaspoon curry powder	¼ teaspoon pepper
1 teaspoon soy sauce	

Pour over salad and toss well. Chill overnight or for several hours before serving.

Serves 6

Beverly Moye

Potato Salad

7 medium potatoes, cooked and cubed	½ medium head lettuce, cut in small wedges
4 hard-boiled eggs, sliced	1 cup mayonnaise
1 cup thinly diced celery	¼ cup lemon juice
½ cup sliced green onions and tops	¼ cup grated Parmesan cheese
⅓ cup diced stuffed green olives	2 tablespoons chopped chives
¼ cup sliced sweet pickles	

Combine potatoes, eggs, celery, onions, olives, pickles and lettuce. Blend mayonnaise with lemon juice, cheese and chives. Mix well. Add mayonnaise to potato mixture and mix gently. Season to taste with salt and pepper and chill.

Serves 8

Mrs. James S. Oliver

🎋 *Potato Salad with Blue Cheese-Sour Cream Dressing*

4	cups cooked, sliced potatoes	½	pint sour cream
1	cup sliced celery	¼	cup vinegar
¼	cup sliced green onions	1	tablespoon blue cheese
¼	cup sliced radishes		salad dressing
1	tablespoon celery seed		Salt and pepper to taste

Combine all ingredients and chill.

Serves 6

Mrs. Maxwell Oliver

Salad Surprise for Jean

Rémoulade Sauce

2	tablespoons Dijon mustard	Vinegar, salt, pepper, and
½	cup salad oil	tarragon to taste

Place mustard in small mixing bowl. With wire whip beat in oil, one drop at a time. Add vinegar and spices.

Salad

1	cup rice	Cherry tomatoes
2	cups water	Raw mushrooms, thinly
¾	pound small shrimp, boiled	sliced
1	can artichoke hearts	Gherkin pickles
	Lettuce	Ham, thinly sliced
	Black olives	

Cook rice in water. While hot, mix well with ¾ of the Rémoulade Sauce. Refrigerate. Marinate shrimp and artichoke hearts in remaining sauce. Refrigerate. To serve heap rice, shrimp and artichoke hearts in bowl lined with lettuce leaves. Garnish with olives, tomatoes, mushrooms, and gherkins that have been wrapped in ham.

Mrs. Dan Haight

Sea Dream Salad

1	package lime jello	¾	teaspoon grated onion
1	cup hot water	½	teaspoon salt
1	tablespoon vinegar		Dash of Tabasco sauce
1	cup grated cucumber		

Dissolve jello in hot water. Add remaining ingredients. Pour into mold and chill until firm.

Mrs. Stanley Bishop

Strawberry Jello Salad

1	large package strawberry jello	½-1 cup pecans	
2	cups water, separated	2	bananas, mashed
1	(20-ounce) can crushed pineapple	2	packages thawed frozen strawberries
		1	pint sour cream

Dissolve jello in ½ cup boiling water. Then add the remaining 1 and ½ cups water. Add the fruit and nuts. Put ½ of mixture in 8x10-inch dish. Let congeal. Spread sour cream over this. Put back in refrigerator for 20 minutes then add remaining mixture over layer of sour cream. Let congeal.

Mrs. Wade Pierce

Jan Carter's Slaw

1	head cabbage, shred fine but don't chop	1	cup vinegar
2	onions	1	teaspoon celery seed
⅔	cup sugar	1	teaspoon salt
1	teaspoon regular mustard	⅔	cup oil

Bring to a boil-sugar, vinegar, celery seed, regular mustard, and salt. Then add oil and bring to a boil again. Pour while hot over layered cabbage and onions. Prepare 24 hours ahead.

Susan Hogan

Marinated Shrimp Salad

1	can sliced broiled mushrooms	1	cup diced celery
1	pound cooked shrimp	½	cup raw cauliflower florets
¼	cup seasoned Italian dressing	¼	cup mayonnaise
		½	teaspoon salt
		⅛	teaspoon curry powder

Place mushrooms and shrimp in bowl. Add Italian dressing and mix. Cover and let stand in refrigerator for at least 2 hours. Add celery and cauliflower. Stir in mayonnaise, salt and curry powder. Serve on lettuce.

Serves 4

Mrs. Marshall Parks

Tea Garden Salad

1	cup hot tea	1	can Mandarin oranges, drained
1	package orange jello, softened in hot tea	1	cup drained juices added to tea and jello
1	cup crushed pineapple, drained	1	cup water chestnuts, sliced thin

Combine all ingredients and mold. The following salad dressing is delicious on this.

Salad Dressing

¼	pint cream, whipped stiff		Pinch of mace
½	cup mayonnaise folded into cream	½	orange rind, grated

Mix these ingredients together and serve on top of Tea Garden Salad.

Mrs. Joyce Mixson

Tart Salad

¾ cup sugar
½ teaspoon salt
½ cup vinegar
1½ cups water, separated
2 envelopes gelatin
1 cup chopped celery

½ cup broken pecans
1 small can cut up asparagus spears
1 small jar slivered pimento
½ onion, grated
Juice of ½ lemon

Boil the sugar, salt, vinegar and 1 cup water for 5 minutes. Dissolve gelatin in ½ cup cold water and add to hot mixture. When cool, add celery, pecans, asparagus spears, pimento, grated onion and lemon juice. Place in ring mold and congeal.

Mrs. Dave Wainer

Tomato Chicken Mold

2 envelopes unflavored gelatin
1 (10½-ounce) can condensed consommé
1 (17½-ounce) can tomato juice
½ teaspoon salt or to taste

2 tablespoons lemon juice
¼ teaspoon Tabasco sauce
2 (5-ounce) cans boned chicken or turkey, diced
1 cup chopped celery
½ cup chopped cucumber
¼ cup chopped stuffed olives

Sprinkle gelatin on 1 cup of the consommé to soften. Place over boiling water and stir until gelatin is thoroughly dissolved. Add remaining consommé, tomato juice, salt, lemon juice and Tabasco sauce. Chill until mixture is the consistency of unbeaten egg whites. Fold in diced chicken, celery, cucumber and olives. Turn into a 6 cup mold. Chill until firm. Unmold on salad greens.

Mrs. C.W. Warner

Perfect Tomato Aspic

¼   **cup cold water**
1   **envelope plain gelatin**
2   **cups tomato juice**
1   **beef bouillon cube**
    Juice of ½ lemon

1   **small bottle Spanish olives, sliced or chopped**
2-3   **stalks celery, cleaned and chopped fine**

Pour cold water in a bowl. Sprinkle gelatin on top to dissolve. Heat tomato juice to boiling, dissolve bouillon cube in it. Pour tomato juice over gelatin. Add 1 lemon juice, olives and celery. Mix well and congeal until firm. Serve on lettuce with a spoonful of mayonnaise on top.

Mrs. John T. McTier

Herbed Tomato Platter
& Dutch Cucumbers

6   **ripe tomatoes**
⅔   **cup salad oil**
¼   **cup vinegar**
¼   **cup chopped parsley**
¼   **cup slice spring onions**
1   **teaspoon salt**

¼   **teaspoon coarsely ground pepper**
½   **teaspoon dried basil**
½   **teaspoon dried thyme**
½   **teaspoon dried marjoram**
1   **clove garlic, minced**

Peel tomatoes. Place in a deep bowl. Make dressing and pour over tomatoes. Cover and chill, baste occasionally. Before serving baste well again. Served with Dutch Cucumbers.

Dutch Cucumbers
2   **cups thinly sliced cucumber**
1   **cup thinly sliced onions**
½   **cup vinegar**
½   **cup cold water**

¼   **cup sugar**
¾   **teaspoon salt**
    Generous sprinkling of coarsely ground pepper

Place cucumbers and onions in deep bowl. Combine vinegar and cold water, sugar, salt, and ground pepper. Pour over cucumbers. Chill and baste often. Serve drained.

Mrs. Maxwell Oliver

Tomato Soup Salad

2	(3-ounce) packages cream cheese
1	cup mayonnaise
2	envelopes plain gelatin
½	cup water

1	can tomato soup
1	tablespoon lemon juice
½	cup diced green peppers
¼	cup minced onions
½	cup diced celery

Have cream cheese at room temperature, blend with mayonnaise. Soften gelatin in water. Heat tomato soup, add gelatin, stirring until it dissolves. Remove from heat. Combine all ingredients and pour into a slightly greased 1½-quart mold. Chill 4 to 5 hours.

Serves 10

Mrs. Mack Anthony, Jr.

Tomato Aspic with Crab Mayonnaise

2	cups tomato juice
1	cup cold water
2	envelopes gelatin
1	medium onion, chopped
2	stalks celery, chopped
½	cup cold water for gelatin

	Juice of 1 lemon
1	tablespoon tarragon vinegar
¼	teaspoon sugar
	Salt and cayenne pepper to taste

Simmer tomato juice, 1 cup cold water, onion and celery 15 minutes. Strain. Dissolve gelatin in ½ cup cold water. Add to hot tomato juice and stir until completely dissolved. Add lemon juice, vinegar, sugar, salt and cayenne pepper. Pour into 6 large individual molds or a 1-quart mold that has been dipped in cold water. This is a basic recipe. Chopped olives, toasted almonds, cooked shrimp, or crabmeat may be added to mold.

Crabmeat Mayonnaise Dressing

1	cup mayonnaise
½	tablespoon lemon juice

1	(6-ounce) can crabmeat, shredded

June Purvis

Tossed Club Salad

½	pound bacon, cooked and crumbled	1⅓	cups seasoned croutons
3	cups cooked and diced chicken breasts	2	tomatoes, peeled and quartered
			Fresh spinach

Cut bacon in half and fry until crisp. Drain. When ready to serve, combine bacon, croutons, turkey or chicken, tomatoes and spinach. Serve dressing on the side.

Dressing

¾	cup mayonnaise	1	tablespoon chives
1	tablespoon Worcestershire sauce	1	teaspoon salt
1	tablespoon fresh parsley, minced	1	tablespoon capers
		1	teaspoon seasoned pepper

Blend.

Serves 6

Carolyn Eager

Tuna Garden Salad

1	package Italian dressing mix, prepared	1	cup diced cucumber
1	(16-ounce) box cooked seashell macaroni	2	cans tuna packed in water
½	cup chopped celery	½	cup mayonnaise (may need more)
			Cherry tomatoes (optional)

Pour dressing over noodles, and then mix in other ingredients. Chill at least 2 hours.

Dorothy Chandler

70

White Salad

4   **egg yolks, beaten and slightly sweetened**
1   **cup milk**
1   **tablespoon gelatin**
1   **pint cream, whipped**
1   **(30-ounce) can pineapple chunks**

1   **(30-ounce) can white cherries, seeded and halved**
¾   **pound marshmallows, cut**
     Juice of 1 lemon
½   **pound chopped, blanched almonds**

Mix beaten egg yolks with milk; scald in double boiler. Soak gelatin in water to moisten, and add to mixture. Fold in whipped cream and remaining ingredients. Let stand 24 hours in refrigerator. Garnish with lettuce.

Serves 20

Mrs. C. W. Warner

Wilted Lettuce Salad

   Small head lettuce
1   **tablespoon grated onion**
2   **hard-boiled eggs**
3   **pieces bacon, cooked**
3   **tablespoons vinegar**

1½   **tablespoons sugar**
1   **tablespoon water**
     Salt
     Pepper

Tear lettuce into bite size pieces, add grated onion and chop hard-boiled eggs in. Cook bacon. Remove from pan when done and add vinegar, sugar and water to bacon grease left in pan. Pour this hot mixture over lettuce, onion and eggs and watch the lettuce "wilt." Add salt and pepper to taste.

Mrs. Jack Sullivan

Avocado Salad Dressing

1	large avocado	¼	teaspoon garlic powder
1	small onion	½	teaspoon monosodium
2	teaspoons sugar		glutamate (optional)
1	tablespoon fresh lemon juice	2	drops green food coloring
1	teaspoon Worcestershire	⅔	cup sour cream
	sauce	½	cup real mayonnaise
1-2	dashes Tabasco sauce, or to		Salt and pepper to taste
	taste		

Finely grind avocado and onion in blender. Put in mixing bowl and add sugar, lemon juice and other seasonings. Mix well. Add green food coloring, mayonnaise and sour cream and blend until smooth. Taste and adjust seasonings to suit your taste. Add more onion if you like. Serve on crisp lettuce wedge or on your favorite green mixed salad. This dressing can be used as a sauce for seafood cocktail. This dressing is better if mixed a day ahead, or at least several hours before you plan to use.

Mrs. William H. Morris

Blue Cheese Dressing

1	small can milk	1	teaspoon white or black
4	tablespoons lemon juice		pepper
1-2	cloves garlic	¼-½	pound blue cheese,
1	teaspoon salt		crumbled

Chill and whip milk. Fold in 1 cup mayonnaise. Add remaining ingredients. Store in refrigerator. Stir before using.

Mrs. Courtney B. Foy

Celery Seed Dressing

1 teaspoon salt	1 teaspoon paprika
1 teaspoon celery seed	1 cup salad oil
1 teaspoon dry mustard	½ cup sugar
1 teaspoon grated onion	¼ cup tarragon vinegar

Mix dry ingredients. Add oil and vinegar alternately.

Mrs. Richard Beckmann

French Dressing

1½ cups salad oil	2 teaspoons sugar
½ cup vinegar	1 teaspoon paprika
Cloves of garlic, minced	½ teaspoon black pepper
1 can tomato soup	1 teaspoon Worcestershire
Juice of 1 lemon	sauce
3 teaspoons salt	1 small onion, grated

Mix all ingredients together. Shake well. Will keep indefinitely in refrigerator.

Mrs. Howard Dasher, Jr.

Fruit Salad Dressing

5 tablespoons vinegar	1 teaspoon paprika
⅓ cup honey	¼ teaspoon salt
1 teaspoon celery seed	1 tablespoon lemon juice
½ cup sugar (less if desired)	1 cup salad oil
1 teaspoon dry mustard	1 teaspoon grated onion

Mix first 8 ingredients in blender or on medium in an electric mixer. Gradually add salad oil and continue blending; then add grated onion. Blend and store in refrigerator.

Makes 2 cups

Mrs. Joyce Mixson

Dressing for Grapefruit Salad

1 cup oil	⅓ cup catsup
½ cup sugar	1 teaspoon salt
⅓ cup vinegar	1 teaspoon paprika
Juice of ½ a lemon	1 medium onion, chopped

Mix and shake well. Serve over fruit salad, grapefruit, avocados, etc.

Mrs. Walton Carter

Green Goddess Dressing

1 egg yolk	¼ cup cream
2 tablespoons tarragon vinegar	1 tablespoon lemon juice
1 tablespoon anchovy paste	1 teaspoon onion salt
½ teaspoon salt	Dash of garlic salt
1 cup salad oil	2 tablespoons chopped chives
	2 tablespoons chopped parsley

Mix egg yolk, vinegar, anchovy paste and salt well in bowl. Beat in salad oil, 2 tablespoons at a time. Stir in cream, lemon juice, onion salt, garlic salt, chives and parsley. Pour in jar and refrigerate. Keeps well.

Mrs. Maxwell Oliver

Roquefort Dressing

1 package imported Roquefort cheese	¾ cup mayonnaise
	Salt to taste
2 tablespoons olive oil	2 hard-boiled eggs
3 tablespoons vinegar	2 cloves of garlic

Mash cheese fine. Add oil and vinegar, slowly, beating well. Fold in mayonnaise and salt. Add chopped eggs. Place the garlic cloves, which have been stuck on toothpicks, in the dressing, to be removed before serving.

Mrs. Wynona C. Parramore

Kum Bak Dressing

2 cloves garlic, crushed	1 teaspoon black pepper
1 cup mayonnaise	Dash of Tabasco sauce
½ cup chili sauce catsup	Dash of paprika
1 tablespoon prepared mustard	1 medium onion
½ cup vegetable oil	2 tablespoons water
1 tablespoon Worcestershire sauce	½ teaspoon salt

Blend all ingredients well in electric mixer or blender. Will keep indefinitely in refrigerator and is excellent on combination or fruit salad.

Mrs. Joyce Mixson

Thousand Island Dressing

1 cup mayonnaise	½ cup sliced stuffed olives
1 teaspoon paprika	1 small onion, slivered
¼ cup ketchup or chili sauce	2 tablespoons minced parsley
2 tablespoons vinegar	3 hard-cooked eggs, coarsely diced
¼ cup chopped walnuts	
½ cup chopped celery, chopped in ½-inch pieces	

Mix and chill.

Serves 8

Mrs. M. M. Harris

Lemon-Caper Mayonnaise

½ cup mayonnaise	1 tablespoon drained capers
2 teaspoons lemon juice	

Stir all together and refrigerate until needed.

Mrs. E. G. Barham

Tomato Salad Dressing

½	cup vinegar	1	bud garlic
2	cups olive oil	1	tablespoon sugar
1	cup ketchup	1	teaspoon salt
1	onion, grated	½	teaspoon Tabasco sauce

Combine above ingredients and refrigerate before using. Shake well before serving.

Delicious over avocado.

Mrs. Franklin J. Eldridge

Homemade Mayonnaise #1

1	pint vegetable oil	1	teaspoon prepared mustard
2	egg yolks	1	teaspoon salt
	Juice of 1 lemon		Lots of red pepper
1	tablespoon vinegar		

Slowly add oil to egg yolks. Add lemon juice, vinegar, mustard, salt and red pepper while adding oil. Beat until firm.

Soak a garlic clove in the oil for several hours before mixing it with the egg yolks for a different flavor.

Mrs. Marshall Parks

Homemade Mayonnaise #2

½	large onion	½	teaspoon paprika
1	egg, unbeaten	¼	teaspoon pepper
1	teaspoon salt	1	tablespoon white vinegar
¾	teaspoon sugar	1½	cups salad oil
¼	teaspoon dry mustard	1	tablespoon lemon juice
½	teaspoon cayenne		

Combine first 9 ingredients in mixing bowl. Slowly add ½ cup of oil a tablespoon at a time as you mix at high speed with electric mixer. Alternating oil and lemon juice, add remaining oil, 1 to 2 tablespoons at a time, and lemon juice, a small amount at a time. Beat until thick for about 3 minutes at high speed.

Mrs. Frank Eldridge

Tangy Sauce for Cabbage, Broccoli, Etc.

⅓ **cup mayonnaise**   1 **teaspoon sugar**
¼ **cup milk**   ½ **teaspoon prepared mustard**
4 **teaspoons vinegar**

Put mayonnaise and milk in small saucepan and stir until smooth. Add vinegar, sugar and prepared mustard. Mix well and stir over low heat until hot. Pour over well drained cabbage or broccoli.

Mrs. E. G. Barham

Barbecue Sauce

½ **cup vinegar**   1 **teaspoon dry mustard**
½ **cup apple juice**   ½ **teaspoon Tabasco sauce**
1 **clove garlic, crushed**   1 **tablespoon sugar**
2 **tablespoons Worcestershire** ½ **cup catsup**
    sauce   1 **teaspoon salt**

Combine and simmer for 10 minutes.

Mrs. Virginia Beckmann

Barbeque Sauce for Chicken

1 **pint vinegar**   1 **tablespoon salt**
½ **pint corn oil**   1 **tablespoon black pepper**
½ **bottle Worcestershire sauce** ¼ **bottle chili powder**
    Juice of 2 lemons   ¼ **can paprika**
1 **lemon, sliced**   ¾ **teaspoon Tabasco sauce**
    (3 lemons in all)   **(more if desired)**

Bring to boil; cook slowly for 5 to 10 minutes. This will not turn meat dark and may be stored in refrigerator.

Barbecue Sauce for Steaks

1	stick butter	1	tablespoon chili powder
2	small onions, chopped	1	tablespoon peppercorns,
1	(5½-ounce) can tomato juice		cracked
¼	cup white vinegar	1½	cups catsup
¼	cup Worcestershire sauce	2	tablespoons brown sugar
1½	cups water	1	tablespoon salt

Mix in saucepan and simmer on stove for 45 minutes.

Makes 4 cups

Mrs. Sam L. Harvey, Jr.

Ridgewood Bar-B-Q Sauce

32	ounces ketchup	½	tablespoon onion salt
2⅔	ounces Worcestershire sauce	½	tablespoon monosodium glutamate
⅓	small bottle Tabasco sauce	2	ounces browning and
⅔	ounce mustard		seasoning sauce
2⅔	ounces vinegar		(or 4 teaspoons)
5⅓	ounces oil	½	teaspoon salt
3⅓	ounces sugar	½	teaspoon pepper
½	tablespoon garlic salt		

Mix well, simmer 1 hour.

Nancy Parris

Hollandaise Sauce

½	cup butter or 1 stick	½	teaspoon salt
½	cup cold water	3	teaspoons lemon juice
4	eggs yolks		Dash of red pepper

Cook in double boiler. Do not let water touch pan. Beat while cooking. Takes 5 or 6 minutes. Do not stir after cooked.

Martha Feely and Mrs. C. W. Warner

Sandwiches & Soups

Sandwiches

Asparagus Roll-Ups 81
Corned Beef for Sandwich Filling 81
Bacon Sandwich Spread 81

Shrimp Sandwich Filling 82
Ham and Chutney Spread 82
Tuna Sandwich Torte 82

Soups

Thick Beef Soup 83
Black Bean Soup 83
Clam Chowder 84
Crab-Shrimp Bisque 84
Crab Soup #1 85
Crab Soup #2 85
Old-Fashioned Split Pea Soup 85
French Onion Soup 86

Oyster Stew 86
Spinach and Mushroom Soup 87
Turkey Soup 87
Homemade Vegetable Soup 88
Vegetable Soup 88
Vichyssoise 89
Jodie's Avocado Vichyssoise 89
Quick Vichyssoise 89

Asparagus Roll-Ups

Fresh bread, thinly sliced
Butter, softened
Seasoned salt

Chives, finely chopped
Asparagus

Cut crust away from bread. Spread with butter. Season with seasoned salt and finely chopped chives. Place 1 asparagus spear on bread and roll up. Bake in medium oven until brown. Can be made the day before and refrigerated, but brush with melted butter before baking.

Mrs. Michael Drumheller

Corned Beef for Sandwich Filling

1   **can corned beef**
1   **bell pepper, chopped**
1   **onion, grated**
1   **jar pickle relish**

1   **pint mayonnaise**
Sugar, vinegar and celery
seed to taste

Take can of corned beef, break up with fork and add bell pepper, onion and relish. Mix mayonnaise to taste with sugar, vinegar and celery seed. Combine mayonnaise mixture with corned beef mixture until it is of spreading consistency.

Mrs. Courtland Smith

Bacon Sandwich Spread

Finely chopped almonds
Cream cheese
Crisp bacon

Green onion, chopped
Mayonnaise

Mix first 4 ingredients together. Add enough mayonnaise to moisten.

Mrs. Henry T. Brice

Tuna Sandwich Torte

2	jars cheese spread	2	hard-boiled eggs, grated
½	cup soft butter	½	cup ripe olives, chopped
2	eggs	⅔	cup mayonnaise
2	cans white tuna	1	loaf white bread

Mix cheese spread, butter and eggs together in mixer to make cheese mixture. Mix tuna, hard-boiled eggs, olives, and mayonnaise together to make filling. Cut bread into circles. You may use tuna can to cut. Use 3 circles for each serving. Spread with filling and over top and sides with cheese mixture. Can do this ahead and refrigerate until used. Bake at 450 degrees for 10 minutes.

Serves 8

Mrs. Jack Sullivan

Shrimp Sandwich Filling

1	(3-ounce) package cream cheese	¼	cup celery, finely chopped
2	tablespoons mayonnaise	1	teaspoon onion, finely chopped
1	tablespoon catsup	1	cup shrimp, chopped
1	teaspoon prepared mustard		Butter
	Dash of garlic powder	1	loaf bread

Blend above ingredients together. Lightly butter bread. Spread mixture onto bread and cut into 4 triangles.

Makes 20 small sandwiches

Mrs. Henry T. Brice

Ham and Chutney Spread

2	cups ground ham	½	cup mayonnaise
¾	cup chopped chutney	⅛	teaspoon curry powder

Blend together. Good on icebox rye.

Mrs. Henry T. Brice

Thick Beef Soup

1	pound ground beef
1	onion, sliced
	Salt to taste

2-3 cooked potatoes, diced
2-3 ears fresh corn, grated cream style.

In a large pot put beef and onion and at least half fill pot with water. Bring to a boil. Cover and reduce heat to simmer. Cook approximately 45 minutes. With a slotted spoon scoop out beef and onion and run through a grinder. Return to stock in pot. Salt to taste. Add potatoes and grated corn and simmer approximately 5 more minutes.

Mrs. John Bosch

Black Bean Soup

4   cups black beans
5   quarts cold water
3   stalks celery
3   large onions, finely chopped
½   cup butter
2½ tablespoons flour
½   cup chopped parsley
    Rind and bone of a cooked smoked ham
3   leeks, thinly sliced

4   bay leaves
1   tablespoon salt
½   teaspoon freshly ground black pepper
1   cup dry Madeira cooking wine
2   hard-boiled eggs, finely chopped
    Lemons, thinly sliced

Pick over and wash beans. Soak beans in enough cold water to cover. Soak overnight. Drain them the following morning. Add cold water and cook the beans over low heat for 1½ hours. In a soup kettle over low heat sauté celery and onions in butter for about 8 minutes, or until they are tender. Blend in flour and chopped parsley and cook the mixture, stirring, for 1 minute. Gradually stir in the beans and their liquid. Add the rind and bone of a cooked smoked ham, leeks, bay leaves, salt and pepper. Simmer the soup for 4 hours. Remove and discard the ham bone, rind and bay leaves and force the soup through a sieve. Combine the pureed beans and their broth and add Madeira. Heat the soup, remove it from the stove, and stir in chopped hard-cooked eggs. Float a thin slice of lemon on each serving.

Mrs. Richard Beckmann

Clam Chowder

3	strips bacon, finely chopped	1	(20-ounce) can tomatoes
1	onion, finely chopped	1	pint milk
1-2	cans minced clams and liquid	1	tablespoon Worcestershire sauce
1	pint of water	⅛	teaspoon black pepper
4	medium potatoes, grated		Salt to taste
1	green pepper, finely chopped		Lemons, thinly sliced

Brown bacon and onion slowly in kettle. Add clams and liquid, water, potatoes, pepper and tomatoes. Cook until potatoes are just done. Just before serving, add milk and Worcestershire sauce, black pepper, and salt. Do not let boil after milk has been added. Serve with a thin slice of lemon in each bowl.

Mrs. Walton Carter

Crab-Shrimp Bisque

4	tablespoons butter	1	small jar chopped pimento, drained
4	tablespoons plain flour		
2½	cups milk	1	teaspoon Worcestershire sauce
1	can frozen cream of shrimp soup, defrosted		
		1	flat can crabmeat, drained
		1	can minced clams and juice

In a large, heavy saucepan, melt butter. Stir in flour. Cover over low heat a minute or so, stirring constantly. Slowly add milk and cook over low heat stirring constantly until mixture begins to thicken. Add cream of shrimp soup, pimento, Worcestershire sauce, crabmeat, and clams and juice. Heat thoroughly, but watch carefully, so as not to scorch. If thicker than desired, add more milk or half-and-half.

Mrs. John Bosch

Crab Soup #1

1	cup chopped onion, peppers and celery		Salt to taste
1	stick butter		Pepper to taste
1	cup milk		Worcestershire sauce to taste
2	tablespoons cornstarch		Tabasco to taste
	Remainder of quart of milk	½	cup sherry
1	pound crabmeat		Nutmeg (if desired)

Sauté onion, peppers, and celery in butter. Add milk, thickened with cornstarch. Add remainder of quart of milk. When milk is warm, add crabmeat, salt, pepper, Worcestershire sauce, Tabasco and sherry. Do not allow to boil. Sprinkle nutmeg on top if desired.

Mrs. James Oliver

Crab Soup #2

1	cup white celery, cut fine		White pepper to taste
2	quarts of milk	¼	pound butter
2	pounds white crabmeat	½	cup sherry
	Salt to taste		Lemons, thinly sliced

Simmer celery in a little water until tender. Add milk and crabmeat. Heat. Add salt, pepper, butter and sherry. Serve with slices of lemon on top of each serving.

Mrs. Richard Beckmann

Old-Fashioned Split Pea Soup

	Ham bone		Pepper
3	quarts water	1	medium onion, sliced
2	cups spilt green peas	1½	cups slivered, cooked ham
2	teaspoons salt		

In kettle, place ham bone, water, peas, salt, pepper and onion. Simmer, covered over low heat 2½ to 3 hours. Remove bone from soup, cut off any bits of ham. Add to soup, along with slivered, cooked ham.

Serves 8

Mrs. Tenney S. Griffin

French Onion Soup

4	large onions, sliced	1	quart chicken broth
3	tablespoons bacon drippings	½	cup white wine
1	tablespoons flour	1	tablespoon cognac or other brandy
½	teaspoon salt	4-6	slices mozzarella cheese
½	teaspoon pepper	4-6	slices French bread, dried in oven
1	pinch sugar	4-6	tablespoons grated Parmesan cheese
1	crushed garlic clove		
1	sprig of parsley		
1	pinch of thyme		

Sauté onions in hot bacon drippings. Add flour, salt, pepper, sugar and garlic and cook until golden brown. Add parsley, thyme, stock, and wine. Bring to boil, reduce heat and simmer 45 minutes. Add cognac. In individual casseroles, place a slice of cheese and then a slice of bread. Pour hot soup over all. Cover thickly with grated Parmesan and a lump of butter and bake 10 to 15 minutes until bubbly hot and top begins to brown.

Sheila Myddelton

Oyster Stew

1	cut garlic clove	⅛	teaspoon pepper
4	tablespoons butter	2	dozen (or more) raw oysters
½	onion, chopped	4	cups milk
1	teaspoon Worcestershire sauce	1½	teaspoons salt
			Dash paprika

Rub inside of pan with garlic. Discard garlic. Melt butter over low heat; add onions and sauté slightly. Add Worcestershire and oysters. Heat 2 to 3 minutes or until edges of oysters begin to curl. Add remaining ingredients. Heat well, gently stirring. Do not bring to a boil or milk will curdle.

Carol Barker

Spinach and Mushroom Soup

2	tablespoons butter	2	cups chicken broth
1	small onion, minced	⅛	teaspoon curry powder
6	mushrooms, sliced	⅛	teaspoon allspice
2	cups fresh spinach, shredded with a knife	½	cup sweet cream
1	tablespoon flour	1	hard-boiled egg, minced

Melt butter in an 11-quart saucepot, add onion and mushrooms. Stir and cook about 2 minutes, until glazed. Add spinach and stir. Lower heat, add flour and mix well. Blend in chicken broth, a little at the time. Adjust seasoning with curry and allspice. Heat soup to a simmer and allow to cook for 5 minutes uncovered. Add cream the last few minutes. Garnish with slices of hard-boiled egg.

Serves 6

Mrs. Tenney S. Griffin

Turkey Soup

1	turkey carcass with some meat	1	tablespoon parsley flakes
6	pieces celery, diced		Salt and pepper to taste
1	large onion, chopped	½	cup raw rice
½	cup barley	1	cup raw spaghetti, broken
2	chicken bouillon cubes, dissolved in 1 cup boiling water		

Combine all ingredients in large kettle with water to cover. Simmer for 2 hours. Cool. Remove bones. Thirty minutes before serving, bring to boil and add rice and spaghetti.

Mrs. Walton Carter

Homemade Vegetable Soup

Leftover steak bones and any fat and meat left on bones
1½ quarts water
1 medium diced onion
3-4 diced carrots
2 cans okra and tomatoes
Salt and pepper to taste
1 can tomato sauce
1 small can white cream style corn
2 cups diced potatoes

Place leftover steak bones into 4½-quart sauce pan. Pour in water. Add onion, carrots, and okra and tomatoes. Add salt and pepper. Simmer about 2 hours, covered. Add tomato sauce, corn and potatoes. Simmer 1 hour longer. If soup needs thickening, cook while uncovered.

Mrs. Gus Elliott

Vegetable Soup

1 soup bone
2 carrots, chopped
2 onions, chopped
2 potatoes, chopped
2 ribs celery, chopped
1 large can tomatoes
Any leftover or frozen vegetables
Beef bouillon cubes, if desired
1 handful spaghetti, broken
Salt, pepper and Worcestershire sauce to taste

Boil soup bone, stew beef, brisket stew, roast beef bone (any or all) in a large Dutch oven type container, with enough water to cover well for 4 to 6 hours. Refrigerate overnight and skim congealed fat from surface next morning. Bring to boil and add carrots, onions, potatoes, celery, tomatoes, and any other vegetables. Cook 1 to 2 hours. You may need to add more water. Beef bouillon cubes can be added for more flavor. Break and add a few spaghetti noodles, and cook until these are done. Season with salt, pepper, and Worcestershire sauce.

Mrs. Jack Sullivan

Vichyssoise

4	tablespoon butter	2	sprigs parsley
4	green onions, finely chopped	2	small stalks celery
1	white onion, finely chopped	2	potatoes, sliced thin
4	cups chicken stock or canned broth		Salt, pepper, nutmeg or curry powder to taste
		1	cup cream

In glass baking dish, melt butter. Add onions and cook until tender. Add chicken stock and remaining ingredients. Cook until potatoes are tender. Blend in blender. Add enough stock to make 2 cups. Before serving, stir in cream. Make a day ahead.

Mrs. Marshall Parks

Jodie's Avocado Vichyssoise

1	quart vichyssoise	1	teaspoon Worcestershire sauce
1	pint coffee cream		
2	ripe avocados		Salt and pepper to taste
½	teaspoon Tabasco sauce	1	avocado, thinly sliced

Blend all ingredients in blender until well blended. Chill several hours or overnight. Float thin slices of avocado in each bowl. Chives may be added and green food coloring if desired.

Serves 8

Mrs. Marshall Parks

Quick Vichyssoise

1	package frozen, condensed cream of potato soup	Sour cream
2	chicken bouillon cubes	Chives, chopped

Mix up soup according to package directions. Add bouillon cubes. Serve hot or cold garnished with a spoonful of sour cream and lots of chopped chives.

Mrs. C.W. Warner

Notes

Entrées

Beef

Beef Burgundy 94
Beef Kabobs 94
Chinese Beef & Rice Casserole 95
Beef Pan Pie 95
Beef Ragoût 96
Chili 96
Hamburger Casserole
    with Leftover Vegetables 96
Company Casserole #1 97
Company Casserole #2 97
Ground Beef Casserole 98
Hamburger Pie 98
Easy Lasagna Casserole 99
Macaroni and Hamburger Casserole 99
Lasagna 100
Meat Pie 101

Meat Loaf 101
Peppercorn Steak 102
Savory Pepper Steak 102
Deep Dish Pizza 103
Pizza-Style Meat Pie 103
Rolled Round Steak in Wine 104
Roast in Foil 104
Sauerbraten 105
Sirloin Tip Roast or Steak 105
Beef Stroganoff 106
Skid Row Stroganoff 106
Spaghetti 107
Stay-Abed Stew 107
Swiss Steak 108
Taghiarena 108
Tamale Pie 109

Corned Beef, Veal & Lamb

Corned Beef.. 109
Corned Beef Hash 110
Veal Scaloppini 110

New England Boiled Dinner 111
Barbecue Leg of Lamb 111

Pork

Asparagus and Ham Casserole 112
Barbecued Spareribs 112
Barbecued Pork Chops 113
Overnight Broccoli and Ham Strata 113
Ham and Cheese Fondue 114
Plantation Casserole 114
Smithfield Ham 115
Grilled Pork Chops 115

Pork Chop Supreme 115
Neapolitan Pork Chops 116
Party Bake Pork Chops 116
Pork Chops and Dressing 117
Dot's Sausage-Wild Rice Casserole 117
St. Paul's Rice Casserole 117
Stuffed Pork Chops Calle 118
Sweet and Sour Pork 118

Game

Dove or Quail 119
Doves with Orange Sauce Glaze 119
White Oak Hunting Lodge Quail 119
Quail with Mushrooms 120

Venison Steak 120
Wild Duck 120
Venison Pot Roast 121

Seafood

Dearing Street Casserole 121
Savannah Seafood Casserole 122
Crab Casserole 122
Seafood Casserole Supreme 123

Crabmeat and Hollandaise 123
Crab Mornae 123
Deviled Crab 124
Poached Trout Marinier 124

Seafood continued

Crab Pie 125
Court Bouillon 125
Baked Shrimp 125
Baked Fish 126
Chinese Skewered Shrimp 126
Shrimp Creole 127
Shrimp and Cheese Casserole 127
Golden Shrimp 128
Shrimp Curry 128
Shrimp Casserole #1 129
Shrimp Casserole #2 129

Shrimp Delight 130
Shrimp Gumbo 130
Shrimp Valencia 131
Minced Oysters 131
Shrimp Fried Rice 132
Shrimp Pilau 132
Tuna Burgers 132
Lobster and Chicken Cantonese Dinner ... 133
Salmon Loaf 134
Foolproof Salmon Croquettes 134
Scalloped Oysters 134

Poultry

Brunswick Stew 135
Chicken Breast Supreme 135
Arroz Con Pollo 136
Chicken and Almond Casserole 136
Chicken with Almonds 137
Creamy Baked Chicken 137
Chicken Breast Sauté 138
Oriental Chicken Casserole 138
Chicken Casserole #1 139
Chicken Casserole #2 139
Chicken Casserole #3 140
Chicken Casserole #4 140
Chicken Casserole #5 141
Cordon Bleu Chicken Breasts 141
Chicken 'n Cream 142
Chicken and Dressing Casserole 142
Chicken Chow Mein #1 143
Chicken Chow Mein #2 143
Chicken Cashew Casserole 144
Chicken Country Captain 144
Chicken and Kraut 145
Aunt Willie's Chicken Dish 145
Chicken Divine 146

Chicken Loaf 146
June's Easy Chicken 147
Chicken Spaghetti 147
Chicken with Pecans 147
Chicken Devoni 148
Biscuit Crust for Chicken Pie 148
Chicken Pie 148
Party Chicken Bake 149
Two Layer Chicken Pie 149
Chicken and Stuffing Bake 150
Chicken Soufflé 150
Chicken and Pork Caribbean 151
Polynesian Chicken 151
Chicken Loaf and Sauce 152
Pressed Chicken 152
Paella 153
Chicken with Oysters 153
Lemon Barbeque Chicken 154
Chicken and Oyster Dressing 154
Chicken Royal 155
Turkey Gumbo 155
Chicken Tetrazzini #1 156
Chicken Tetrazzini #2 156

Egg Dishes

Creamed Eggs Chartres 157
Creamed Eggs 157
Breakfast Casserole 158
Blender Cheese Soufflé 158
Cheese Omelet 158
Cheese Strata 159
Creamed Stuffed Eggs 159
Curried Deviled Eggs 159

Curried Eggs 160
Eggs Continental 160
Eggs Benedict ~
    Quick Version of Old Classic 161
Mushroom Quiche 161
Impossible Quiche 162
Quiche Lorraine 162

Beef Burgundy

1   (2-pound) round steak, cut
    into 1x2-inch strips
    Clove of garlic
3   onions, chopped
½   cup butter
1   tablespoon flour

1   can beef bouillon
1   cup Burgundy wine
1   (3- to 4-ounce) can
    mushrooms, drained
½   teaspoon thyme
    Salt, pepper to taste

In a skillet or Dutch oven, brown first 3 ingredients in butter and add remaining ingredients. Cover and simmer slowly for about 3 hours. If need more liquid, add 2 parts wine to 1 part bouillon. Serve over rice.

Mrs. Jack Sullivan

Beef Kabobs

1   beef tenderloin, cut into
    large chunks
½   cup salad oil
½   cup wine vinegar
2   tablespoons soy sauce
4   tablespoons minced green
    onions
1   clove garlic, minced
½   teaspoon pepper
1   tablespoon sugar

Green pepper, cut in
chunks
Cherry tomatoes
Large mushrooms
Fresh potatoes, parboiled
and cut in chunks
Fresh onions, parboiled and
cut in chunks
Bacon, thickly sliced

Marinate meat all day in oil, wine vinegar, soy sauce onion garlic pepper and sugar. Remove meat from marinade and on skewers alternate beef, cut up green pepper, cherry tomatoes, mushrooms, onion, potatoes and bacon. Pieces should be placed on both sides of meat to give it a good flavor. You may use any or all above suggested vegetables. Cook over charcoal coals, turning often.

Serves 4

Mrs. Arthur McLane

Chinese Beef & Rice Casserole

1	(1-pound) stew beef, cut in small cubes	1	can cream of mushroom soup
1	cup celery, chopped	1	cup water
1	cup onion, chopped	1	can English peas, drained
1	cup green pepper, chopped	2	teaspoons soy sauce
½	cup rice	1	can Chow Mein noodles

Brown beef. Add celery, onions and green pepper. Cook until all are well browned. Add rice, soup, water, peas and soy sauce. Cook until bubbles. Place in casserole dish. Bake at 325 degrees for 1½ hours. Add noodles on top, then heat through.

Mrs. Alex Culbreth

Beef Pan Pie

2	pounds cubed beef chuck		Salt and pepper
2	tablespoons shortening	1	tablespoon bottled browning sauce
3	cups boiling water		Pie crust mix
1	teaspoon lemon juice		Water
1	can beef consommé	1	egg, beaten
1	tablespoon Worcestershire sauce		Melted butter
2	tablespoons soy sauce		

Brown meat in shortening. Add water, lemon juice, consommé, Worcestershire sauce, soy sauce and seasoning. Simmer until tender. Remove meat and thicken liquid. Add browning sauce for a rich brown color. Place meat in a 2-quart casserole dish and pour gravy over meat, should be about 3 cups. Make pastry using pie crust mix, water mixed with egg. Cut in rounds with biscuit cutter. Cover top beef with pastry rounds and brush top with melted butter. Bake at 375 degree for 45 minutes.

Serves 8

Mrs. Jack Sullivan

Beef Ragoût

½	cup butter	2	tablespoons flour
½	cup diced onion	½	teaspoon salt
½	pound mushrooms	1	teaspoon sugar
3	pounds beef, sliced in 1-inch pieces	1	can beef consommé
		1	cup dry red wine

Melt butter in a heavy skillet. Add onions and mushrooms and brown. Roll beef lightly in the flour and add to the onions and mushrooms. Add salt, sugar, consommé and wine. Simmer at low heat until done.

Mrs. H. W. Parramore

Chili

3	pounds onions, chopped	2	cans tomato soup
2	cloves garlic, minced	2	(8-ounce) cans tomatoes
¼	cup butter		Chili powder, salt, pepper
2	pounds ground beef		to taste
2	(8-ounce) cans kidney beans		

In a large skillet or Dutch oven, cook onions and garlic in butter until tender and slightly brown. Add ground beef and brown or brown in separate skillet. Add remaining ingredients and cook 3 to 4 hours.

Mrs. Jack Sullivan

Hamburger Casserole with Leftover Vegetables

1	pound ground beef	1	cup canned tomatoes
3	tablespoons chopped onion	2	teaspoons salt
1	tablespoon salad oil	1	teaspoon sugar
1	cup leftover snap beans (or leftover asparagus)	⅛	teaspoon black pepper
			Canned biscuits, rolled thin

Sauté meat and onions in oil. Add vegetables, salt, sugar and pepper. Put in casserole dish (if not juice enough, add a little water). Place biscuits on top. Bake at 450 degrees 10 to 20 minutes.

Mrs. Dave Wainer

Company Casserole #1

	Salt and pepper to taste	1	can cream of chicken soup
⅓	cup flour	1	package onion soup
1	(2-pound) round steak, cut into 1-inch cubes	1	tablespoon Worcestershire sauce
2	medium onions		Rice, pasta or potatoes
1	can sliced mushrooms	4	green pepper rings
1	bay leaf		

Salt, pepper and flour steak cubes. Place in casserole with onion slices, mushrooms and bay leaf. Combine soups and Worcestershire sauce. Pour over steak. Bake at 325 degrees for 2 hours. Remove bay leaf. Serve over rice, pasta or potatoes. Garnish with green pepper rings.

Mrs. Lane Renfroe

Company Casserole #2

1	(8-ounce) package pasta	1	(8-ounce) package cream cheese
3	tablespoons butter, separated	¼	cup sour cream
1	pound ground chuck	⅓	cup chopped green onions
2	(8-ounce) cans tomato sauce	1	tablespoon chopped green pepper
1	cup cottage cheese		Pepper

Preheat oven to 375 degrees. Cook pasta as directed on package; drain. Melt butter in skillet. Sauté ground chuck until brown. Stir in tomato sauce and remove from heat. Combine cottage cheese, cream cheese, sour cream, onions and green pepper. In 2-quart casserole dish, spread half of noodles; cover with cheese mixture, then with rest of pasta. Pour in 2 tablespoons of melted butter, then meat mixture. Bake uncovered at 375 degrees for 30 minutes.

Serves 6

Ann Godbee

Ground Beef Casserole

1 large onion, chopped	1 can whole grain corn
1 large green pepper, chopped	1 can ripe olives
	Salt and pepper to taste
4 tablespoons vegetable oil	2 cups uncooked noodles, broken in small pieces
1 pound ground beef	1 cup grated cheese
1 can tomato paste	
1-2 cups water	

Sauté onion, green pepper in oil until tender. Add ground beef and cook until slightly brown. Add tomato paste, water, corn, olives, salt, pepper and broken noodles. Pour entire mixture into glass casserole dish and place grated cheese on top. Bake in at 325 degrees for 45 minutes.

Mrs. R.B. Anderson Sr.

Hamburger Pie

1 pound ground beef	1 can tomatoes
⅓ cup onions, chopped	1 (8-ounce) can drained kidney beans
Salt and pepper	
2 teaspoons chili powder	½ (7-ounce) box of corn muffin mix, made as directed on box
1 tablespoon Worcestershire sauce	

Brown beef, onions seasoned with salt and pepper in skillet. Add chili powder, Worcestershire sauce, and tomatoes. Simmer 15 minutes, and then add kidney beans. Place in greased casserole dish. Top with muffin mix. Bake at 425 degrees for 20 minutes.

Mrs. Chandler Blanton

Easy Lasagna Casserole

1 pound ground beef
1 chopped onion
2 (6-ounce) cans tomato sauce
1 (3-ounce) package cream cheese

1 (8-ounce) carton sour cream
1 package wide egg noodles
   Grated Cheddar cheese

Brown hamburger and chopped onion. Add tomato sauce and cook several minutes. Mix cream cheese and sour cream. Cook egg noodles and drain. Layer in casserole in this order: noodles, cheese mixture, and meat sauce. Repeat if necessary. Top with grated cheese. Bake at 350 degrees for 30 minutes.

Jane Stanaland

Macaroni and Hamburger Casserole

1½ cups uncooked elbow macaroni
1 pound ground beef
1 can cream of mushroom soup
¾ cup shredded Cheddar cheese

1 (14½-ounce) can whole tomatoes, cut up
¼ cup chopped green pepper
¾ teaspoon seasoned salt
1 (3-ounce) can French fried onion rings

Prepare macaroni as directed on package, drain. Brown ground beef; drain. Combine all ingredients except onions. Pour ½ mixture into 2-quart casserole dish. Add ½ can onions. Pour remaining mixture over onions. Cover and bake at 350 degrees for 30 minutes. Top with remaining onions and bake uncovered for 5 minutes longer.

Linda Miller

Lasagna

Meat Sauce

1	large onion, chopped	2	tablespoons dried parsley
¼	cup salad oil	1	large can tomatoes
2	pounds ground beef	2	small cans tomato paste
2	cloves garlic, minced		Salt and pepper to taste

Sauté onion in oil. Add meat, stirring until meat is brown. Add remaining ingredients and cook covered for 2 hours.

Cheese Sauce

6	tablespoons butter	1	cup grated Parmesan
1	small onion, finely chopped		cheese
6	tablespoons flour	2	egg yolks
3	cups milk		Salt

Melt butter and sauté onion. Stir in flour. Add milk and cook until thickened, stirring constantly. Remove from fire and stir in cheese until well blended. Add hot mix to egg yolks. Salt to taste.

Lasagna Filling

1	box lasagna, cooked according to package directions	2	pepperoni sausages, skinned and cut into thin rounds
1	package mozzarella cheese, cut in thin strips		

Line buttered casserole with pasta, layer of meat sauce, layer of mozzarella cheese, layer of pepperoni, layer of cheese sauce. Repeat layers until all is used up. Top with mozzarella cheese. Bake at 375 degrees for 30 minutes or until bubbly.

Mrs. Richard Beckmann

Meat Pie

¾ pound ground beef or ground sausage
¾ cup milk
1½ teaspoons cornstarch
2 eggs
Salt
Pepper
½ teaspoon garlic salt
¾ cup mayonnaise
½ cup spring onions, chopped
1 teaspoon Worcestershire sauce
1½ cups sharp cheese
1 (9-inch) pie shell

Brown meat. Mix milk, cornstarch, beaten eggs. Stir in meat and remaining ingredients and bake in pie shell for 35 to 40 minutes at 350 degrees or until knife comes out clean.

Ellen Oliver

Meat Loaf

1 slice bread or 6 saltines
¼ cup milk
1 pound ground chuck or ground round
1 tablespoon Worcestershire sauce
1 egg, beaten
Salt and pepper
1 small onion, finely chopped
1 can beef consommé
Lemon pepper marinade

Pour milk over bread or crackers. Mix remaining ingredients together lightly, reserving some of the consommé to be added while cooking to baste with. Cook in loaf or brownie pan with foil to cover at 325 degrees for 45 minutes. Remove foil and cook 15 minutes longer.

Mrs. Jack Sullivan

Peppercorn Steak

1	(3-pound) chunky sirloin tip roast or steak, 3 inches thick
1	teaspoon seasoned meat tenderizer

Liquid smoke
Lemon Pepper marinade or coarsely crushed black pepper

Sprinkle steak generously with liquid smoke. Pierce with a fork or ice pick and rub the tenderizer into both sides of meat. Sprinkle both sides with the lemon-pepper marinade and press in with palm of the hand. Roast at 400 degrees for approximately 50 minutes, or until meat thermometer reads desired doneness.

Mrs. John Bosch

Savory Pepper Steak

¼ cup flour
½ teaspoon salt
⅛ teaspoon pepper
1 (1½-pound) round steak, ½-inch thick, cut in strips
¼ cup cooking oil
1 (8-ounce) can tomatoes
1¾ cups water
½ cup chopped onion

1 clove garlic, minced
1 tablespoon beef flavored gravy base
1½ teaspoons Worcestershire sauce
2 large green peppers, cut in strips
¼ cup sherry wine (optional)
Mushrooms (optional)

Combine flour, salt and pepper and dredge meat in this. Use large skillet and brown meat in hot oil. Drain tomatoes, reserving liquid. Add tomato liquid, water, onion, garlic and gravy base to meat in skillet. Cover and simmer for about 1¼ hours or until meat is tender. Uncover and stir in Worcestershire sauce and pepper strips (also mushrooms and wine, if used). Cover and simmer for 5 minutes. If necessary, thicken gravy with a mixture of a little flour and cold water. Add drained tomatoes and cook about 5 minutes more. Serve over hot cooked rice.

Serves 6

Mrs. Owen Youles

Deep Dish Pizza

2	cans biscuits (10 each)			Pizza sauce
1	pound ground chuck		1	package mozzarella cheese

Brown meat. Roll biscuits out with rolling pin. Connect the biscuits together to form crust on bottom and sides of long medium casserole dish. Put meat, pizza sauce, and cheese on top. Cook according to biscuit directions. This is a good, quick dish. You can add anything else on top according to what you like on your pizza.

Jane Sherwood

Pizza-Style Meat Pie

1	pound lean ground beef	1	teaspoon salt
1	medium onion, chopped fine	¼	teaspoon pepper
1	(15-ounce) can tomato sauce	1	(9-inch) unbaked pie shell with high fluted rim
1	egg, slightly beaten	4	ounces mozzarella cheese, sliced
2	tablespoons minced parsley	½	cup grated Parmesan cheese
1	teaspoon dried oregano		

Heat a 10-inch skillet; add the beef and the onions. Cook over moderately low heat using fork to crumble meat into tiny pieces until browned. Remove from heat and pour off fat. Remove from heat and stir into the tomato sauce, egg, parsley, oregano, salt, and pepper. Pour into pie shell. Arrange mozzarella slices over the top. Sprinkle the generous amount of Parmesan cheese all over the pie. Bake at 400 degrees until crust is golden brown, 25 minutes. Let stand for 5 minutes or so to allow filling to settle before cutting.

Serves 4 to 6

Mrs. Bill Gibbons

Rolled Round Steak in Wine

2	round steaks (totaling 3 pounds)	1	tablespoon boiling water
	Salt, pepper, paprika	1	whole raw egg
¼	pound sliced mushrooms		Stuffed olives
	Thinly sliced onions	¼	cup butter or bacon or drippings
	Pimentos	6	whole mushrooms
	Finely rolled breadcrumbs	3	small onions
½	cup melted butter	1	cup red wine

Pound until thin, steaks. Rub in salt, pepper, and plenty of paprika. Overlap steaks on meat board, making 1 large steak. Spread a layer of mushrooms, blanket with a layer of thinly sliced onions. Dot with pimento. Cover with finely rolled breadcrumbs. Then dribble over crumbs the following mixture: ½ cup melted butter, boiling water and egg., beaten together. Arrange stuffed olives in a row on long side of steaks. Begin roll of meat around olives. Tie roll firmly. Flour outside. Brown in butter or bacon drippings in roaster or deep earthenware baker. Place whole mushrooms and onions in roaster and sprinkle all lightly with salt, pepper and paprika. Add wine. Roast meat at 350 degrees oven for about 2 hours. Serve hot or cold.

Serves 6

Mrs. W. G. Amos

Roast in Foil

1	(3-pound) chuck roast	1	package onion soup mix
2	tablespoons meat sauce	1	can mushroom soup

Place meat in center of heavy aluminum foil Brush on sauce. Sprinkle mix; spread on mushroom soup. Wrap in foil. Bake 2½ to 3 hours at 350 degrees.

Mrs. George Hart

Sauerbraten

1	(4- to 6-pound) roast beef	6	whole cloves
2	onions, sliced	12	peppercorns
½	parsnip, sliced	12	juniper berries
2	carrots, sliced	2	teaspoons salt
2	bay leaves	1	quart red wine vinegar

Place above in an earthenware bowl. Pour over this 1-quart red wine vinegar that has been heated to boiling. Let marinate 3 days or more. Turn meat twice a day. Keep in refrigerator. When ready to cook, drain meat and brown it thoroughly in hot fat. Add marinade with vegetables, but not enough to cover meat. Simmer slowly 3 to 4 hours until tender. Remove meat to heated platter.

Gravy

¼	pound butter	1	cup marinade
1	tablespoon sugar	⅔	cup red wine

Melt butter, add sugar, flour to make roux. Let it darken, stirring constantly. Slowly add 1 cup of marinade and ⅔ cup red wine and continue cooking until it is the consistency of heavy cream. Strain.

Mrs. Richard Beckmann

Sirloin Tip Roast or Steak

1	onion chopped fine	1	tablespoon chives
1	clove garlic, minced	1	tablespoon parsley flakes
½	cup real butter	1	tablespoon Worcestershire
1	(2-pound) sirloin tip roast		sauce
	or steak, cut ¼-inch thick,		Salt and pepper to taste
	1x2-inch strips		

Brown onion and garlic in ½ of the butter. Add steak in pieces, few at a time and brown about 1 minute each side. Move meat aside in pan when all cooked, and add chives, parsley, Worcestershire sauce, salt, and pepper with remaining butter. Heat thoroughly and push steak back into sauce and simmer until meat is tender.

Serves 4 to 6

Mrs. A. R. Pitts

Beef Stroganoff

1	cup butter or margarine			Salt to taste
1½	cups finely chopped onion		6	tablespoons tomato paste
1½	cups slice mushrooms		2	teaspoons Worcestershire
1	(3½-pound) top round beef,			sauce
	cut in small strips		½	cup sour cream
6	tablespoons flour		1½	cups cream
3	cups bouillon (or 3 cubes		8	cups cooked rice
	dissolved in 3 cups boiling			
	water)			

Melt ⅓ cup butter in large saucepan. Add onions and sauté until golden brown. Remove and set aside. Use ⅓ cup more butter and sauté mushrooms until lightly browned. Roll beef in flour and brown lightly in remaining butter. Add bouillon, salt and onions. Cover and simmer slowly until beef is tender. Add tomato paste, Worcestershire sauce, sour cream, cream and the mushrooms. Heat thoroughly, but do not let boil. Serve the stroganoff mixture and hot rice in separate dishes.

Serves 10 to 12

Mrs. Ed Garvin

Skid Row Stroganoff

8	ounces uncooked noodles		2	tablespoons flour
1	beef bouillon cube		2	teaspoons salt
1	garlic clove, minced		½	teaspoon paprika
½	cup chopped onion		2	small cans mushrooms
2	tablespoons cooking oil		1	cup sour cream
1	can cream of chicken soup			Chopped chives
1	pound ground beef			

Cook noodles according to package directions in water in which bouillon cube is dissolved. Brown garlic, onions and beef in oil. Add flour, salt paprika and mushrooms. Stir and let cook for 5 minutes. Add soup and simmer until to boiling point. Stir in sour cream and parsley, keeping heat low. Serve over noodles.

Mrs. Ferrell Singleton

Spaghetti

3	pounds ground beef
	Butter
2	large onions, chopped
2	large green peppers, chopped
2-3	cloves garlic, minced
2	cans tomato paste
1	can tomatoes
1	tomato can water
3	tablespoons Worcestershire sauce

	Salt and black pepper to taste
2	bay leaves
1	teaspoon basil
1	tablespoon Italian seasoning
1	teaspoon celery salt
	Mushrooms (optional)
	Pimento stuffed olives (optional)

Cook ground beef in small amount of butter, stirring until lightly browned and pour off grease. Sauté onions, green peppers and garlic in ¼ cup butter in large Dutch oven type container. Add cooked meat and all other ingredients and simmer slowly 4 to 5 hours. Serve over cooked, drained spaghetti noodles and serve with Parmesan cheese.

Mrs. Jack Sullivan

Stay-Abed Stew

1½	pounds stew beef
1	small can tiny English peas
3	pieces celery, sliced
3	carrots, pared and sliced
1	large onion, chopped
2	raw potatoes, pared and cubed

1	teaspoon salt
¼	teaspoon pepper
1	can tomato soup, thinned with ½ can of water
1	bay leaf

Combine all ingredients in this order except bay leaf. Add bay leaf on top of mixture and remove when done. Cook covered at 275 degrees for 5 hours.

Mrs. Joe Stubbs

Swiss Steak

1 (2-pound) round steak, cut into pieces	2 tablespoons butter
Salt and pepper to taste	1 can tomato paste
Flour	1 cup water
Shortening	3 tablespoons wine vinegar
½ cup celery, chopped	1 tablespoon sugar
1 clove garlic	¼-½ cup sherry

Salt, pepper and flour meat. In a skillet, brown meat in shortening. In a large skillet or Dutch oven, sauté celery and garlic in butter. Add remaining ingredients to make sauce. Add browned steak. Cook slowly for 1½ to 2 hours, stirring occasionally.

Mrs. Jack Sullivan

Taghiarena

2 tablespoons olive oil	Salt to taste
1 large onion, chopped	Pepper to taste
2 cloves garlic, minced	1 pound grated sharp Cheddar cheese
1 large green pepper, chopped	2 pounds cooked ground chuck
1 quart stewed tomatoes	1 (8-ounce) package egg noodles, cooked
1 can cream style corn	Grated cheese to top
1 small can ripe olives	
1 large can mushrooms	
2 tablespoons liquid from jar of olive	

Sauté onion, garlic, and green pepper in olive oil. Pour into in large baking dish and add tomatoes, corn, olives, mushrooms, olive liquid, salt, pepper, cheese, and ground chuck. Mix well. Bake at 300 to 325 degrees for 1 hour. Serve over egg noodles. Top with cheese.

Rose Ware

Tamale Pie

¼	cup olive oil	1	tablespoon salt
1½	pounds ground beef	1¼	tablespoons chili powder
2	cloves garlic	¼	teaspoon pepper
1	cup chopped onions	½-¾	cup cornmeal
½	cup chopped green pepper	1	cup water
1	(20-ounce) can tomatoes	1	cup ripe, pitted olives
1	(12-ounce) can whole kernel corn		

In a skillet, brown meat in oil. Add garlic, onions, and green pepper. Cook stirring until onion is golden. Stir in next 5 ingredients. Simmer 5 minutes. Stir in cornmeal mixed with water. Cover and simmer 10 minutes. Add olives then turn into 3-quart casserole dish.

Topping

1½	cups milk	½	cup cornmeal
1	teaspoon salt	1	cup grated American cheese
2	tablespoons margarine	2	eggs, lightly beaten

Heat milk with salt and butter. Slowly stir in ½ cup cornmeal. Cook, stirring until thickened. Remove from heat. Stir in cheese and eggs and pour over meat mixture. Bake 30 to 40 minutes at 350 degrees. May fix day ahead and refrigerate. If so, cook for 1 hour and 20 minutes.

Mrs. C. E. Davis

Corned Beef

	Beef	6-7	peppercorns
1-2	cloves garlic	1	onion, cut in half

Wash off beef. Place in pot with cold water to cover. To water, add garlic, peppercorns and onion. Cover and bring to boil. Simmer 3 hours and 15 minutes. Check at 3 hours with knife. If soft, it's done. Remove any scum while it's cooking. Cut off fat. Let cool in water.

Mrs. Bob Maturi

Corned Beef Hash

1	can corned beef	3	tablespoons bacon drippings
1	medium onion, finely chopped	2	cups water

Combine all ingredients and cook until onions are tender and only a small amount of liquid remains. Salt and pepper to taste. This is good served with cabbage and corn bread.

Mrs. Chandler Blanton

Veal Scaloppini

1	(1-pound) veal round or cutlets in ¼-inch slices Salt and pepper Flour	1	cup mushrooms, thinly sliced
		½	cup olive oil
		½	cup cooking Sauterne or regular Sauterne

Cut veal into 10 to 12 pieces of similar shape and pound very thin; about ⅛-inch wide. Sprinkle with salt and pepper, then flour lightly. In large skillet, cook mushrooms in 2 tablespoons of olive oil until tender, about 4 to 5 minutes. Remove mushrooms and keep warm. Add remaining olive oil to skillet and heat. When hot put in several pieces of veal and brown over high heat, about 1 minute per side. Keep cooked meat warm while browning remainder. When all meat is browned, return mushrooms and meat to pan. Add cooking Sauterne and simmer until meat is tender, about 15 to 30 minutes. Arrange meat and mushrooms on warmed platter. Scrape bottom of pan, stirring to mix pan drippings with Sauterne. Pour over meat.

Serves 4

Mrs. I.H. Tillman, Jr.

New England Boiled Dinner

1 (2- to 3-pound) brisket of
   corned beef
3-4 cubed potatoes

3-4 sliced carrots
2-3 onions
1 cabbage, cut in wedges

Cover meat with water, bring to a boil. Simmer 3 to 4 hours. Add vegetables for last 30 minutes. Season to taste.

Mrs. George Hart

Barbecue Leg of Lamb

Lamb
1 leg of lamb

Garlic salt

Wash and sprinkle leg of lamb with garlic salt. Cook at 300 degrees for 1 hour.

Sauce
1 can tomato paste
1 can vinegar (using tomato
   paste can to measure)
3 cans water (using tomato
   paste can to measure)
1 tablespoon garlic salt
2 garlic cloves, minced

1 teaspoon black pepper
10 heaping teaspoons sugar
2 tablespoons Worcestershire
   sauce
1½ lemons, sliced in rounds
   Tabasco sauce to taste

Combine ingredients and cook slowly until the mixture thickens slightly. Remove lemon peels and pour over leg of lamb and continue cooking in oven, basting occasionally, until lamb is done.

Mrs. Bob Hornbuckle

Asparagus and Ham Casserole

1	can drained asparagus	½	cup breadcrumbs
1	cup cooked, diced ham	¼	cup grated cheese
2	hard-boiled eggs	2	tablespoons lemon juice
2	tablespoons green pepper	½	cup cream or milk
2	tablespoons chopped onion	1	can cream of chicken or
2	tablespoons parsley or		mushroom soup
	parsley flakes	1	tablespoon butter

Grease casserole dish. Place layer of asparagus, layer of ham and eggs. Combine all other ingredients. Combine soup and milk until smooth and pour over mixture in casserole dish. Top with buttered breadcrumbs. Bake 30 minutes at 375 degrees.

Mrs. Edward Willis

Barbecued Spareribs

2	pounds spareribs	1	cup lemon juice
¼	cup chopped onions	2	tablespoons brown sugar
1	tablespoon bacon drippings	1	cup chili sauce
½	cup water	½	teaspoon salt
2	tablespoons vinegar	½	teaspoon paprika
1	tablespoon Worcestershire sauce		

Cut ribs into serving pieces. Place in pan and cover with waxed paper. Bake at 500 degrees for 15 minutes. Reduce heat to 350 degrees. Sauté onions in drippings and add remaining ingredients. Simmer for 20 minutes. Remove paper from meat and pour sauce over it. Bake 1 hour longer, basting frequently.

Serves 4

Barbecued Pork Chops

6	pork chops	½	teaspoon red pepper
	Salt	2	tablespoons Worcestershire
	Pepper		sauce
2	onions, thinly sliced	½	cup catsup
2	tablespoons vinegar	1	teaspoon chili powder
1	teaspoon paprika	1	cup water

Salt and pepper chops. Place in roaster and cover with onions. Combine remaining ingredients to make sauce. Mix well. Pour over chops. Cover and cook 1½ hours at 325 to 350 degrees.

Mrs. Charles Richards

Overnight Broccoli and Ham Strata

12	slices firm textured white bread, crusts removed	1	teaspoon dry mustard
1	pound frozen chopped broccoli, defrosted	1	teaspoon Worcestershire sauce
1	pound sharp Cheddar cheese, shredded	2	tablespoons instant minced onion
2	cups (or 12-ounces) diced cooked ham	½	teaspoon garlic powder
3½	cups milk	⅛	teaspoon cayenne pepper
		6	eggs

Using a 3-inch doughnut cutter, cut a ring from each bread slice, set aside. Cut crusts into cubes and save. Spread broccoli on a paper towel to drain. Do not cook. In a buttered 9x13-inch dish, arrange in layers the bread cubes, ¾ cheese, broccoli, ham, and bread rounds. Top with remaining cheese. Beat together eggs, milk, mustard, Worcestershire, onion, garlic and cayenne until blended. Pour over casserole. Be sure all bread rounds are saturated. Cover and refrigerate 12 hours. Bake at 350 degrees for 1 hour. Cool 15 minutes before cutting into squares.

Serves 12

Sally Moritz

🍴 *Ham and Cheese Fondue*

3	cups cubed ham	3	tablespoons dry mustard
3	cups cubed bread	3	tablespoons melted butter
1	cup cubed sharp Cheddar cheese	4	eggs
		3	cups milk
3	tablespoons flour	3	drops hot sauce

Arrange layers of bread, ham and cheese in a 2-quart casserole dish. Mix flour and mustard, and sprinkle over cheese. Drizzle butter over top. Beat eggs and add milk and hot sauce. Pour over layers, cover and chill for at least 4 hours or overnight. Bake uncovered at 350 degrees for 1 hour.

Linda Miller

Plantation Casserole

2	cups diced cooked ham (chicken or beef)	¼	pound American process cheese, cut into small pieces (optional)
1½	cups cooked, drained peas, lima beans or cut-up carrots	⅓	cup evaporated milk
		¼	cup chopped onion
1	(1-pound) can cram-style corn	1	tablespoon Worcestershire sauce

Mix ham, peas, lima beans, or carrots, corn, cheese, evaporated milk, chopped onion and Worcestershire sauce. Pour into a greased 12x8-inch baking dish. Bake in a 400 degree oven 10 minutes or until bubbly at edges.

Mix well

1	cup biscuit baking mix	½	teaspoon salt
½	cup cornmeal	1	egg
2	tablespoons sugar	⅔	cup evaporated milk

Pour on hot mixture, leaving center uncovered. Spread to edges. Bake 20 minutes or until golden brown.

Serves 6

Mrs. John Bosch

Smithfield Ham

Scrub and wash well with soap and water, 1 Smithfield or country ham, the old-fashioned cured variety. Pour boiling water over ham; cover and leave all day or night. Preheat oven to 500 degrees. Remove water. Place ham on rack and add enough boiling water to cover bottom; cover and close all vents on roaster. Do not remove cover until cooking process is finished. Bake ham 20 minutes. Turn oven off. Allow to remain in oven without opening the oven door for 3 hours. Turn heat to 500 degrees again and leave 15 minutes. Turn off the heat and allow ham to remain in oven for at least 3 hours. It can even be left in overnight. Remove ham from roaster and cut off the rind. Ham is ready to serve or may be glazed if desired.

Mrs. William M. Gabard

Grilled Pork Chops

1	tablespoon soy sauce	1	clove crushed garlic
1	tablespoon sugar	4	pork chops, at least 1-inch
2	tablespoons cider vinegar		thick

Mix soy sauce, sugar, vinegar and garlic. Pour over chops in flat pan and let marinate several hours in refrigerator, turning once or twice. Cook on grill about 12 to 15 inches from coals so will cook slowly for 45 minutes to an hour.

Mrs. Jack Sullivan

Pork Chop Supreme

	Pork chops, thickly sliced	1	tablespoon brown sugar per chop
1	slice onion per chop		
1	slice lemon per chop	1	tablespoon catsup per chop

Place pork chops in a casserole dish. On top of each chop place onion, lemon, brown sugar, and catsup. Cover with aluminum foil. Bake at 350 degrees for 1 hour. Uncover and bake ½ hour longer.

Mrs. Wayne Ellerbee

Neapolitan Pork Chops

6	loin chops, 1-inch thick	1	cup thinly sliced onion
2	tablespoons pure vegetable oil	1	(1-pound) can tomatoes
1	pound fresh button mushrooms	½	teaspoon oregano
1	cup thinly sliced green pepper	1	teaspoon salt
		⅛	teaspoon pepper

Trim fat from chops. Brown on both sides in hot oil in skillet. Remove and reserve. Sauté mushrooms, green pepper, and onion in oil remaining in skillet until tender. Add tomatoes, oregano, salt and pepper; simmer 5 minutes. Add pork chops. Cover and simmer 1 hour or until chops are tender. If thicker sauce is desired, uncover and simmer 15 minutes longer. Serve over rice.

Serves 6

Mrs. John Gayle

Party Bake Pork Chops

4	lean pork chops, 1-inch thick	1	(1 pound, 13-ounce) can tomatoes
4	thin slices onion	½-1	teaspoon salt
¼	cup uncooked rice (not instant)		Pepper

Trim any excess fat from chops. Season chops well on both sides with salt and pepper. Brown on both sides in lightly greased hot skillet. Top each chop with a slice of onion, 1 tablespoon rice, and cover with whole tomatoes. Add any remaining tomatoes and juice to skillet. Be sure to completely saturate rice with juice. Season with salt. Cover tightly, simmer over low heat or bake in foil-covered, (11½x7½x1½-inch) baking dish at 350 degrees for 1½ hours, or until tender.

Serves 4

Christy Kirbo

🎗 *Pork Chops and Dressing*

Pork chops	**Water**
Onion	**Crumbled toast**
Worcestershire sauce	**Mushroom soup**

Brown pork chops. In the same pan with drippings, sauté onions. Add water and Worcestershire sauce. Use own judgment on amount of water. Make dressing of crumbled toast and pour liquid over. Put chops in casserole dish and mound dressing on each one. Pour a can of cream of mushroom soup over all. Bake at 350 degree for approximately 30 minutes.

Sharon Mink

🎗 *Dot's Sausage-Wild Rice Casserole*

1	**pound sausage**	1	**cup white rice**
1	**package long grain, wild rice**		**Chicken broth or bouillon**

Brown sausage, drain. Cook wild rice according to directions on package. Cook white rice in 1-quart boiling water for 15 minutes, drain. Mix sausage, wild rice, and white rice. Place in large casserole dish. When ready to bake, pour a little chicken broth or bouillon over casserole. Bake at 350 degrees for 30 minutes or until heated thoroughly.

Jane Stanaland

St. Paul's Rice Casserole

1	**pound mild pork sausage**	2	**envelopes chicken noodle**
1	**large bell pepper, diced**		**soup mix**
1	**large onion, diced**	½	**cup raw rice**
1	**rib of celery, diced**	4½	**cups water**

Toss and brown sausage. Drain on paper towel; pour off grease. Add and sauté pepper, onion, and celery. Combine soup mix, rice, and water. Boil for 7 minutes. Place all together in casserole dish with ½ to 1 cup slivered almonds. Bake covered at 350 degrees for 1 hour.

Mrs. Dave Wainer

117

Stuffed Pork Chops Calle

6	large pork chops, 1½-inch thick with pocket for stuffing	1	tablespoon Worcestershire sauce
			Dash of Tabasco sauce
½	onion, chopped	1	teaspoon crushed dill seed
½	green pepper, chopped	4	tablespoons butter
1	(4-ounce) can mushrooms	2	cups cooked rice
2	teaspoons garlic salt		

Sauté onion, bell pepper in butter until tender. Add remaining ingredients including rice and allow rice to brown slightly. Pack mixture in pocket of chops and secure with toothpick. Broil on both sides to brown and place in uncovered glass dish at 400 degrees for 30 minutes.

Mrs. Diane Smith

Sweet and Sour Pork

2	pounds lean pork	½	teaspoon salt
2	teaspoons sherry wine	1	clove garlic, crushed
1	tablespoon soy sauce	½	cup oil

Cut pork into 1-inch cubes. Remove all fat. Mix together pork, sherry, soy sauce, and salt. Set aside to marinate for 30 minutes to 1 hour. Heat oil and add crushed garlic. Fry the meat on both sides. Edges should be crisp. Drain on paper towel.

Sauce

⅔	cup sugar	2	tablespoons soy sauce
¼	cup catsup	2	tablespoons cornstarch
⅓	cup pineapple juice	⅓	cup water
⅓	cup cider vinegar	1	cup pineapple chunks

Make sauce by heating first 5 ingredients. Dissolve cornstarch in water. Add to sauce mixture and cook over medium low heat 15 minutes, stirring frequently. Add pineapple chunks and fried pork to sauce and simmer about 30 minutes on low heat until pork is tender. Serve over hot rice and top with Chinese noodles.

Mrs. Jack Sullivan

🦅 *Doves with Orange Sauce Glaze*

12 doves, cleaned
    Juice of 2 lemons
¾ cup Worcestershire sauce
1 teaspoon salt
    Dash of pepper

6 slices bacon, halved
1 (12-ounce) can frozen
    orange juice concentrate,
    thawed and undiluted

Place doves in large bowl. Pour lemon juice over each bird; add Worcestershire sauce, salt and pepper. Cover tightly and marinate several hours, turning to marinate all sides. Remove from marinade. Wrap each bird with bacon, securing with a toothpick. Place in a shallow roasting pan, and pour orange juice concentrate over birds. Bake at 350 degrees for 1 hour, turning birds and basting frequently.

Serves 6 to 12

Ellen Oliver

White Oak Hunting Lodge Quail

2 dozen quail
1 pound butter

1 cup sherry
½ cup currant jelly

Place quail in large flat, glass casserole dish; breast side up. Melt butter and add sherry and jelly. Pour over birds and bake at 250 degree for about 3 hours. Quail will brown and do not dry out. Baste while cooking.

Mrs. Jack Sullivan

Dove or Quail

12-16 dove or quail
    Salt and pepper
1 large apple

3-4 stalks celery
¼ cup sherry
¼ cup more sherry

Salt and pepper dove and brown in butter. Put in heavy pot or skillet. Add enough water to cover. Slice apple and celery and add to dove. Sprinkle a little more salt and pepper over all. Add ¼ cup sherry and bring to boil. Reduce heat to low and steam birds for 1 to 1½ hours. Before serving pour ¼ cup more sherry over dove.

Mrs. Frank Elderidge

Quail with Mushrooms

4	quail	½	cup hot water
4	slices of bacon	1	(3-ounce) can broiled
1	tablespoon butter		mushrooms, drained
	Juice of ½ lemon		

Wipe quail dry inside and out with paper towels. Wrap each bird with a slice of bacon. Put quail in buttered pan and roast at 350 degrees in oven, basting occasionally, about 45 minutes or until tender. Remove quail and add butter, water and lemon juice to drippings in pan, stirring to make a gravy. Add mushrooms. Serve the quail on toast with gravy poured over them.

Mrs. Jack Sullivan

Venison Steak

1	(2- to 3-pound) venison	1	cup water
	steak	4	tablespoons salt
1	cup flour		Black pepper
½	cup vinegar		Garlic salt

Pound steak until tender. Soak in vinegar, water and salt for 1 hour to draw blood and wild taste out of meat. Remove from liquid and dry. Dip in flour, black pepper and garlic salt. Fry in shortening over medium heat until done.

Mrs. Jack Sullivan

Wild Duck

8-10 ducks		**Water**
2	onions, chopped	**Salt, pepper, seasoning salt**
	Bacon drippings	**Sherry (optional)**

Split ducks. Salt, pepper and flour lightly. Brown in bottom of roaster in chopped onion and enough bacon drippings to cover bottom of pan well. When all are browned, add about 1 cup of water and simmer slowly covered for 2 hours or until ducks are very tender. May add ½ cup or so of sherry last 30 minutes of cooking if desired. Also may add more water to keep from sticking.

Note: Ducks frozen in water and thawed in water will be tender.

Mrs. Frank Strickland

Venison Pot Roast

1	(6- to 8-pound) venison roast	1	large carrot, pared and sliced
3-6	slices bacon	1	tablespoon salt
2	cups Burgundy wine	10	whole black peppercorns
½	cup apple cider vinegar	2	bay leaves
2	celery tops	1	clove garlic, crushed
1	medium onion, sliced	1	cup water
4	slices lemon	¼	cup flour
		2	tablespoons salad oil

Wipe roast with damp paper towels. Arrange bacon slices over surface of meat. Combine all remaining ingredients except flour and oil. Pour over roast. Cover and refrigerate for 24 hours, turning occasionally. Remove roast from marinade; Brown roast on all sided in hot oil. Add 1 cup of the marinade and bring to a boil. Reduce heat and simmer, covered for 4 hours or until roast is very tender. Baste occasionally during cooking with pan liquid. Add remaining 1 cup of marinade as needed.

Mrs. Jack Sullivan

Dearing Street Casserole

1	cup celery, minced	2	cups crabmeat
1	small green pepper, minced	2	cans cream mushroom soup
1	small onion, minced		Salt and pepper to taste
1	can mushrooms	1-2	tablespoons butter
2	cups cooked wild rice		Grated Parmesan cheese
2	cups cooked white rice		Buttered crumbs
2	cups whole shrimp		

Sauté celery, green pepper, onion and mushrooms in butter. Mix with cooked rice, shrimp, crab, and mushroom soup. Add salt and pepper. Put in buttered baking dish; sprinkle with cheese and crumbs. Bake in pan of water at 350 degrees for 1 hour.

Serves 12

Julie Budd

Savannah Seafood Casserole

1	pint coffee cream	1	teaspoon Worcestershire
2	tablespoons butter		sauce
2	tablespoons flour	1	teaspoon paprika
1	can artichoke hearts, drained	1	tablespoon lemon juice
1	pound crabmeat	2	tablespoons catsup
1½	pounds cooked and peeled		Sherry to taste
	shrimp		

Make a sauce from cream, butter and flour. Mix with remaining ingredients and bake at 350 degrees until well heated and bubbly.

Serves 8 to 12

Mrs. Howard Dasher (Mary)

Crab Casserole

1	can mushroom soup, undiluted	1	cup sliced celery
¾	cup sherry	¼	cup finely chopped onion
½	cup almonds	1	(3-ounce) can Chinese noodles
1	can water chestnuts		Butter
1	large can sliced mushrooms, drained		Buttered breadcrumbs
	Dash Worcestershire sauce		Slivered almonds
1	pound (or 2 cans) crabmeat	2	tablespoons cream

Combine soup and sherry. Mix with almonds, chestnuts, mushrooms, Worcestershire sauce, crabmeat, celery, and onion. Butter baking dish. Line with part of noodles and mix rest into mixture. Sprinkle buttered crumbs and slivered almonds on top. Dot with butter. Add cream. Bake 30 minutes at 350 degrees.

Mrs. D.S. Wainer

Seafood Casserole Supreme

2	pounds boiled and peeled shrimp	1	box chicken Rice-A-Roni
2	pounds lump crabmeat	1	cup sour cream
2	pounds sautéed scallops	1	cup mayonnaise
		1	cup grated Cheddar cheese

Prepare seafood. Cook Rice-A-Roni as box directions suggest. Mix sour cream and mayonnaise with Rice-A-Roni, and then add all seafood and mix. Put in 3-quart casserole dish. Top mixture with cheese and bake at 350 degrees for 30 minutes.

Serves 12 to 16

Sue Cox

Crabmeat and Hollandaise

½	stick butter	1	generous dash Tabasco sauce
1	cup fresh white lump crabmeat	½	tablespoon lemon juice
1	hard-boiled egg, grated	1½	cups Hollandaise sauce
2	tablespoons sherry	4	pieces toast

Melt butter, add crabmeat, grated egg and seasonings. Heat thoroughly. Place squares of toast in individual ramekins. Cover with crabmeat, top with Hollandaise sauce. Brown under broiler. Serve immediately.

Serves 4

Mrs. Marshall Parks

Crab Mornae

½	cup butter	2	cups milk
3	tablespoons flour	1	pound fresh crabmeat
2	teaspoons white pepper		Grated cheese
1	teaspoon mace (optional)		

Use first 5 ingredients to make a white sauce and then add crabmeat. Top with cheese and bake at 350 degree until bubbly.

Mrs. Clarence Paine

Deviled Crab

1	pound fresh crabmeat	1	teaspoon prepared mustard
1½	cups milk	1	teaspoon lemon juice
	Butter, the size of an egg	3	hard-boiled eggs, grated
2½	tablespoons flour	1	cup breadcrumbs
1	teaspoon horseradish		Salt to taste
1	teaspoon Worcestershire sauce		

Make white sauce with butter, flour and milk. Add all other ingredients except breadcrumbs. Fill crab shells or casserole dish. Lightly brown breadcrumbs. Fill crab shells or casserole dish. Lightly brown breadcrumbs in ½ stick butter. Sprinkle over crab. Bake at 350 degrees for 30 minutes.

Mrs. Walton Carter

Poached Trout Marinier

4	(½-pound) fillets of trout	2	cups milk
	Barley	½	teaspoon salt
	Wine and vinegar or lemon juice (optional)	¼	teaspoon cayenne pepper
½	cup butter	⅓	cup white wine
1	cup finely chopped shallots	2	egg yolks, beaten
3	tablespoons flour		Paprika

Poach trout in salted water. Cover fish with barley. Wine and vinegar or lemon juice may be added. Melt butter in a 9-inch skillet. Sauté shallots until tender. Blend in flour and cook slowly 3 to 4 minutes, stirring constantly. Stir in milk. Add salt, pepper and wine. Cook about 10 minutes. Add trout and heat thoroughly. Remove from heat and stir in egg yolks. Place pieces warm trout in serving dish and spoon hot sauce over top. Sprinkle with paprika and heat under broiler until piping hot.

Serves 4

Mrs. Clarence Paine

Crab Pie

1	pound crabmeat	2	tablespoons Worcestershire sauce
2	cups milk		
3	cups cubed bread	2	tablespoons onion, chopped fine
1	tablespoon melted butter		
1	tablespoon mustard	1	teaspoon salt and pepper
2	tablespoons mayonnaise		

Mix all ingredients well. Turn into buttered dish. Place margarine on top. Bake in 350 degree oven for 25 to 30 minutes.

Mrs. Grady Durden

Court Bouillon

1	tablespoon shortening	1	can tomatoes
2	tablespoons flour	1	quart water
	Thyme		Parsley
1	large onion, finely chopped	1	green pepper, chopped
1	clove garlic	1	fish fillet, red snapper or bass
2	bay leaves		Salt and pepper

Combine all ingredients, except fish, salt, and pepper, to make sauce. Simmer for ½ an hour. Salt and pepper the fish. Lay fish in sauce. Simmer 15 minutes.

Mrs. Clarence Paine

Baked Shrimp

1	clove garlic	½	stick butter
1	pound cleaned broiled shrimp	4	saltine crackers

Chop garlic over shrimp and butter in a baking dish. Crumble crackers over shrimp. Bake at 350 degrees for 20 minutes or until hot an bubbly.

Mrs. Richard Beckman

Baked Fish

1 cup chopped onion	Dash celery salt
2 tablespoons butter	Salt and pepper
½ cup catsup	1 medium dill pickle, finely
1 can consommé	chopped
Dash soy sauce	1 (6-pound) white fish or red
1 teaspoon prepared mustard	snapper

Brown onion in butter. Add catsup, consommé, soy sauce, mustard, celery salt, salt and pepper. Simmer 10 minutes and add pickle. Pour over fish. Bake at 375 degrees for 25 minutes or until fish flakes.

Mrs. D. L. Burns

Chinese Skewered Shrimp

2 pounds large shrimp	⅓ cup sherry
17 ounces water chestnuts	Finely chopped ginger,
Several strips bacon	garlic, or fresh herbs
⅓ cup soy sauce	(optional)
⅓ cup olive oil	

Shell and devein shrimp. Thinly slice water chestnuts and bore hole in each to slide on skewers without cracking. Cut bacon in 1-inch squares. Soak shrimp several hours in marinade. Ginger, garlic or fresh herbs may be added. Thread shrimp on metal skewers alternating with chestnuts and bacon. Grill over hot coals, turning and basting with the marinade several times. Serve on a bed of rice garnished with fresh tomatoes.

Serves 4

Mrs. Richard Beckmann

Shrimp Creole

1	green pepper, chopped	1	tablespoon Worcestershire
1½	cups celery		sauce
1	onion, chopped	1	dash of Tabasco sauce
3	tablespoons bacon		Pinch of oregano
	drippings	3	tablespoons flour
1	lemon, juice and rind	2	pounds raw shrimp
1	(30-ounce) can tomatoes		

Brown pepper, celery and onion in bacon drippings. Add all other ingredients except flour and shrimp. Cook about 20 minutes. Mix flour with just enough water to make a paste and add to above mixture. Cook until thickened. Add shrimp 10 minutes before serving.

Mrs. Christie Patterson

Shrimp and Cheese Casserole

6	slices white bread	¼	cup butter, melted
1	pound or more cooked,	3	whole, beaten eggs
	peeled shrimp	½	teaspoon dry mustard
½	pound Old English cheese,		Salt
	coarsely grated	1	pint milk

Remove crust from bread, break into small pieces. Arrange shrimp, bread, and cheese in layers in greased casserole dish. Pour melted butter over this mixture. Beat eggs well, add mustard, salt, and then milk, slowly. Pour milk mixture over ingredients in casserole dish. Let stand overnight in refrigerator. Bake covered, 1 hour in a 350 degrees oven.

Serves 4

Mrs. Howard Dasher (Mary)

127

🍤 *Golden Shrimp*

6-8	slices day old bread; trimmed, buttered, and cubed	1½	cups milk
2	cups cooked shrimp	3	eggs
1	(3-ounce) can mushrooms	½	teaspoon dry mustard
1	can tomatoes	½	teaspoon salt
½	pound sharp cheese, grated		Pepper
			Paprika

Blend shrimp, mushrooms, tomatoes, ½ of bread cubes and cheese. Put in casserole dish. Blend milk, egg, and seasoning. Pour over shrimp mixture. Bake at 325 degrees for 45 to 50 minutes.

Martha Grow

Shrimp Curry

1	cup milk	½	cup chopped apple
1	package flaked coconut	¼	cup chopped celery
2	cups water	½	teaspoon Worcestershire sauce
1	tablespoon lemon juice		Light cream
1	teaspoon salt	1	teaspoon curry powder
1	pound fresh shrimp in the shells	½	teaspoon salt
2	tablespoons butter	½	teaspoon flour
1	clove garlic, minced	½	teaspoon powdered ginger
½	cup chopped onion	¼	teaspoon pepper
1	tomato, peeled and chopped		

Scald milk and pour over coconut. Let stand 20 minutes. Drain. Reserve coconut milk. In a saucepan, bring water, lemon juice and salt to a boil. Add shrimp. Cover and simmer for 5 minutes or until shrimp turns pink. Remove shrimp from liquid. Cool, shell and devein shrimp. Melt butter in skillet and sauté garlic, and onion until golden and soft. Add tomato, apple, celery, and Worcestershire sauce. Add enough light cream to the coconut milk to make 1½ cups. Stir into skillet. Cover and bring to boil. Blend curry powder, salt, flour, ginger and pepper with enough water to make a paste. Stir into coconut milk then cover. Simmer about 20 minutes over low heat until vegetables are tender, stirring occasionally. Add shrimp; cook 5 minutes longer. Serve on rice.

Mrs. William M. Gabard

Shrimp Casserole #1

2 cups cooked rice
1 pound New York state cheese, grated
1 can tomato soup
1 tablespoon Worcestershire sauce
  Salt
1 medium onion, chopped and cooked until soft in butter
1 cup celery, chopped
1 green pepper, chopped
1 (4-ounce) can mushrooms and juice
2 pounds cooked and cleaned shrimp

Mix rice and cheese. Add soup, 1 tablespoon Worcestershire, salt, onions, celery and green pepper, mushrooms, and shrimp. Put into buttered casserole dish and sprinkle with cheese. Cook 40 minutes at 350 degrees.

Mrs. Avalon Griffin

Shrimp Casserole #2

2½ pounds large shrimp, shelled and deveined
1 tablespoon lemon juice
3 tablespoons salad oil
¼ cup minced green pepper
¼ cup minced onion
2 tablespoons butter
¾ cup cooked rice
1 teaspoon salt
⅛ teaspoon pepper
⅛ teaspoon mace
  Dash cayenne
1 can tomato soup, undiluted
1 cup heavy cream
½ cup sherry
¾ cup, slivered, blanched almonds

Cook shrimp in boiling, salted water for 5 minutes. Drain. Cut in halves lengthwise. Sprinkle with lemon juice and salad oil. Sauté green pepper and onion 5 minutes in butter. Mix all ingredients well and place in casserole dish. Reserve a few shrimp and almonds for top. Bake, uncovered 35 minutes at 350 degrees. Place reserved almonds and shrimp on top. Bake about 20 minutes longer.

Serves 6 to 8

Mrs. Henry Brice

Shrimp Delight

1½-2	pounds boiled shrimp	1	cup chopped onion
2	cans cream of mushroom soup	1	tablespoon Worcestershire sauce
6	slices buttered toast, crumbled		Salt and pepper
1	cup mayonnaise	3	hard-boiled eggs
2	small jars pimentos	½	cup slivered almonds

Combine all except 2 slices of toast. Put into buttered casserole dish. Crumble reserved toast on top. Bake at 350 degrees for 20 to 30 minutes.

Mrs. J. Edward Willis

Shrimp Gumbo

5	tablespoons bacon drippings	1	teaspoon pepper
6	tablespoons flour	1	large package frozen okra
2	medium onions, chopped	2	pounds shrimp
1½	cups chopped celery	1	can crabmeat (optional)
1	clove garlic	1	pint small oysters (optional)
2	(20-ounce) cans tomatoes	3	tablespoons Worcestershire sauce
1	can tomato sauce		Tabasco sauce and red pepper to taste
2-3	cups water		
3	teaspoons salt		

Make a golden roux with drippings and flour using heavy deep skillet. Add onions, celery and garlic and brown. Add tomatoes, tomato sauce, water, salt and pepper. Simmer for 1 hour. Add okra and seafood. Cook 20 minutes longer. Add Worcestershire and other seasoning. Serve over hot rice, or as a heavy soup with hard bread.

Serves 8

Mrs. Owen Youles

Shrimp Valencia

1½	pounds jumbo raw shrimp, shelled deveined	2	large cloves garlic, sliced
	Lime or lemon juice		Semi-stale breadcrumbs (Cuban bread is best)
2	sticks butter		Sauterne

Rinse shrimp in cold water and lime or lemon juice. Drain well. Early in day, melt butter, add garlic and set aside. About 15 minutes before serving, roll shrimp in semi-stale breadcrumbs. Sauté in melted butter, turning carefully. When done, add ½ to ¾ cup good Sauterne, heating thoroughly. Do not overcook or shrimp will be tough. Remove garlic. Serve immediately with saffron rice and Cuban or French bread. Serve generous amount of sauce.

Mrs. John Bosch

Minced Oysters

1	quart standard oysters		Dry mustard
2	packages soda crackers		Salt
1½	sticks butter		Pepper
1	medium onion, minced		Catsup
	Tabasco sauce	1½	cups milk
	Worcestershire sauce		

Cut oyster 3 times with scissors. Crush soda crackers into crumbs. Melt butter in heavy pan. Add oysters and onion, Season to taste with Tabasco sauce, Worcestershire sauce, dry mustard, salt, pepper and a little catsup. Add milk and crumbs. Butter casserole dish and pour mixture into it. It should be a little soupy. Add more milk if needed. Bake at 350 degrees for 20 to 25 minutes.

Serves 16

Mrs. Conner Thomson

Shrimp Fried Rice

5	strips bacon	3	cups cooked rice
2	bunches spring onions, chopped	1¼	pounds cooked, peeled shrimp, chopped
1	medium green pepper, chopped		Soy sauce to taste

Fry bacon crisp; drain. Add chopped onions and green pepper. Sauté slowly for about 15 minutes. Add rice and shrimp. Cook approximately 25 minutes, stirring or turning with large spoon or spatula. Sprinkle with soy sauce, about 4 times while cooking. When ready to serve, crumble bacon and stir in.

Mrs. Dave Wainer

Shrimp Pilau

2	pounds raw shrimp	1	cup finely diced onion
1	full cup finely chopped white bacon	2	cups rice
			Salt and pepper to taste

Boil cleaned shrimp in a small amount of water until just pink. Finish out liquid with enough water to make 3 cups. Cook bacon and onion over low heat until tender, not brown. Add shrimp, liquid, bacon and onion to rice. Cook 2 hours in double boiler. At end of first hour, lift from sides with fork. Season with salt and black pepper at end of first hour.

Mrs. Howard Dasher (Mary)

Tuna Burgers

1	(6½-ounce) can tuna	¼	cup mayonnaise
1	cup chopped celery		Salt and pepper to taste
½	cup diced American cheese	6	hamburger buns
1	small onion, minced		Soft butter

Preheat oven to 350 degrees. Mix tuna, celery, cheese, onion, mayonnaise, salt, and pepper. Spread 6 split hamburger buns with soft butter and fill with mixture. Wrap in aluminum foil. Bake 15 minutes.

Serves 6

Mrs. Mickey Anthony

Lobster and Chicken Cantonese Dinner

1   clove garlic, minced
¼   cup butter
1   (5-ounce) can fancy water chestnuts, drained and sliced
1   (5-ounce) can fancy bamboo shoots, drained
¼   pound sliced fresh mushrooms
1   (10-ounce) package frozen peas, slightly thawed
¼   cup cold water
¼   cup cornstarch
1   tablespoon soy sauce
1   teaspoon brown gravy
3   cups chicken broth
1½ teaspoons salt
1   (6½-ounce) can lobster or 1 package cooked lobster tails
2   chicken breasts; skinned, boiled and sliced
1   (3-ounce) can Chow Mein noodles
2   eggs, hard-boiled and chopped

Cook garlic in butter for 1 minute. Add water chestnuts, bamboo shoots, mushrooms and peas. Cook 3 minutes. Combine water, cornstarch, soy sauce, brown gravy, chicken broth and salt. Add to vegetable mixture. Cook over moderate heat until thickened, stirring consistently. Fold in lobster and chicken, heat thoroughly. Serve over Chow Mein noodles. Garnish with chopped eggs. Serve over Chinese rice with sweet and sour sauce.

Chinese Fried Rice
2   tablespoons salad oil
2   cups chopped onion
2   cups cooked rice
2   eggs
½   teaspoon salt
1   tablespoon soy sauce
    Green pepper (optional)
    Cooked shrimp (optional)

Fry onions in oil. Sauté rice 2 minutes; add eggs, salt and soy sauce. Beat together. Fry until brown on high heat, turning with a spoon. Green pepper and/or cooked shrimp may be added.

Sweet 'n Sour Sauce
¾   cup sugar
¼   cup soy sauce
2   tablespoons cornstarch
½   cup vinegar
1   small can crushed pineapple

Combine ingredients. Cook until thickened.

Mrs. A. R. Pitts

Salmon Loaf

1	large can salmon	1	cup dry breadcrumbs
1¼	cups grated cheese	¼	cup diced onion
1	egg	½	teaspoon salt
½	cup evaporated milk		

Preheat oven to 350 degrees. Combine above ingredients and shape into a loaf. Bake 45 minutes.

Mrs. Benny Mitcham

Foolproof Salmon Croquettes

2	(6½-ounce) cans salmon	1	egg
3	tablespoons minced onion		Soda crackers
	Salt and pepper to taste		Shortening

Combine salmon, onion, salt, pepper, and egg. Shape croquettes into desired shapes. Roll each croquette in a bowl of soda cracker crumbs. Fry in shortening until golden brown.

Mrs. Frank J. Eldridge (Gail)

Scalloped Oysters

1	quart milk	1	box soda crackers, crushed
	Salt and pepper	½	pound butter
1	quart oysters		

Heat milk just to boiling point. Quickly add salt and pepper and oysters. Remove from heat immediately. Put a thin layer of cracker crumbs in a casserole. Take oysters out of milk and place on cracker crumbs. Add another layer of cracker crumbs. Pour melted butter over top. Cook in oven at 325 degrees for 20 minutes. Eat immediately.

Mrs. Christie Patterson

Brunswick Stew

3	pounds chicken (may use pork and/or veal also)	1	can lima beans
1	pound onions	1½	bottles catsup
3	pounds potatoes	1	bottle Worcestershire sauce
2	cans tomatoes	½	cup vinegar
2	cans corn (or 2 packages frozen corn)	¾	cup lemon juice
		2	teaspoons Tabasco sauce
1	can English peas	2	tablespoons salt
			Black pepper

Cook meat until well done. Grind and set aside. Put onion and potatoes through food grinder. Add to broth. Cook until well done. Add meat and other ingredients. Cook on low heat until well done and thick, 2 to 3 hours. Serve hot or cool. Pour into container and freeze.

Makes 5 to 6 quarts

Mrs. John Wiggins

Chicken Breast Supreme

4	individual chicken breasts, boned but not skinned	2	egg whites
		1	cup fine breadcrumbs
3-4	ounces chopped cooked chicken liver or 1 can goose liver spread	½	cup butter
		4	ounces ripe olives, chopped
	Salt and pepper	2	ounces Madeira wine
½	cup rich chicken stock		Flour

With a flat knife, spread the chicken liver between the skin and meat of each breast. Season with salt and pepper, roll in flour, then dip in egg whites, slightly beaten and coat with the breadcrumbs. Sauté in butter, skin side down first until golden brown. Reduce heat, cover and cook slowly for about 10 minutes. Remove chicken to warm platter. Add 1 tablespoon flour to pan and lightly brown. Add chicken stock and chopped olives. Let simmer until slightly thick. Add wine and remove from heat. Pour sauce over chicken breasts and serve at once.

Bud King of the Valdosta Country Club

Arroz Con Pollo

1	(4-pound) frying chicken, cut up	2	chicken bouillon cubes
	Salt	1½	cups water
	Pepper	1¼	cups uncooked rice
	Paprika	1	bay leaf
¼	cup olive oil	¼	teaspoon saffron
½	cup finely chopped onion	½	teaspoon dried oregano leaves
2	cloves garlic, minced	1¼	teaspoons salt
1	medium-sized green pepper, chopped	1	(10-ounce) package frozen peas, partially thawed
1	(1 pound, 12-ounce) can stewed tomatoes	2	pimentos, cut in strips

Wash and dry chicken. Sprinkle lightly with salt, pepper and paprika. Heat oil in skillet. Brown chicken on all sides. Remove chicken and place in 3½- to 4-quart casserole dish. Add onion, garlic and green pepper to skillet and cook until tender. Add tomatoes and bouillon cubes. Cook and stir about 5 minutes. Stir in water, rice, bay leaf, saffron, oregano and the 1¼ teaspoonful of salt. Pour over chicken. Cover and bake in 350 degrees oven 25 minutes. Remove from oven and stir to mix rice and sauce. Add additional water if rice seems dry. Return to oven and bake 20 minutes. Add peas and stir into rice mixture. Bake 15 minutes. Garnish with pimento strips.

Mrs. James M. Allen

Chicken and Almond Casserole

1	cup cooked chicken, chopped	2	hard-boiled eggs, chopped
1	cup finely chopped celery	½	cup slivered almonds
½	cup mayonnaise	1	teaspoon minced onion
1	can cream of chicken soup, undiluted	⅓	cup cracker crumbs

Combine all ingredients, toss lightly and pour into casserole. Top with crumbled potato chips. Bake at 350 degrees for 20 minutes.

Serves 6

Mrs. J.C. Sherwood

Chicken with Almonds

3	chicken breasts, halved	½	cup slivered almonds
1	can cream of chicken soup	1¼	cups uncooked rice
1	can cream of mushroom soup	¼	cup grated cheese
½	cup butter	1	can cream of celery soup

Mix together undiluted soups, melted butter and almonds. Set aside 1 cup of this mixture to baste chicken. Add rice to remaining mixture and pour into 2-quart oven dish. Place chicken breasts on top of mixture. Bake at 325 degrees, about 2 hours. Baste chicken at 15 to 20 minute intervals. Near end of baking time, sprinkle with cheese and allow to brown lightly.

Serves 6

Mrs. Quentin Lawson

Creamy Baked Chicken

1	broiler	1	cup biscuit mix
1	can cream of chicken soup	¼	cup yellow cornmeal
1	can mushroom soup	3	tablespoons milk
½	cup milk		

Cut chicken into serving pieces. Arrange in buttered 2½-quart casserole dish. Combine ½ chicken soup and all of mushroom soup. Add milk and mix well. Pour over chicken. Cover. Bake at 350 degrees for 30 minutes. Stir and bake 30 minutes more. Combine biscuit mix, cornmeal, 3 tablespoons milk, and remaining chicken soup. Drop batter in mounds on top of chicken mixture. Bake for 15 minutes.

Mrs. Bill Gibbons

Chicken Breast Sauté

4-6	**chicken breasts**	¼	**teaspoon pepper**
¼	**cup butter**	1	**chicken bouillon cube**
1	**minced clove garlic**	1	**cup hot water**
1	**small onion, minced**	¼	**cup dry white wine**
2	**tablespoons flour**		**Snipped parsley**
½	**teaspoon salt**		

Sauté chicken in butter until well browned. Add onion and garlic. Cook 5 minutes. In small bowl combine flour, salt and pepper, slowly stirring in bouillon cube dissolved in 1 cup hot water. Pour over browned chicken, add wine, cover and cook slowly for 1 hour. Garnish with parsley.

Mrs. Marshall Parks

Oriental Chicken Casserole

2	**big fryers or 1 (5-pound) hen**	2	**package French style frozen string beans**
2	**cans mushroom soup**	2	**(20-ounce) cans bean sprouts**
1	**can chicken broth**	2	**cans fried onion rings**
2	**tablespoons soy sauce**		
1	**can water chestnuts**		

Cook chicken and remove meat from bones. Put into buttered casserole dish. Mix mushroom soup, chicken broth and soy sauce together to make a sauce. Layer chicken, sliced water chestnuts, green beans, bean sprouts, and onion rings. Cover with half the sauce. Repeat the above layers again, and then cover with rest of sauce. Bake at 325 degrees for 1 hour. Can be made 24 hours ahead. Freezes well.

Serves 12 to 14

Dean Brooks

Chicken Casserole #1

2	cups cooked chicken		**Salt**
1	cup cooked rice		**Pepper**
1	cup celery, finely chopped	½	cup slivered almonds
2	tablespoons onion, finely chopped	1	cup corn flake crumbs, crumbled
1	can cream chicken soup	2	tablespoons melted butter
¾	cup mayonnaise		

Combine chicken, rice, celery, onion, soup, mayonnaise and salt and pepper to taste. Pour into casserole dish. Sprinkle almonds over top, and then corn flake crumbs. Pour melted butter over this. Bake 45 minutes at 325 degrees.

Linda Miller

Chicken Casserole #2

5	chicken breasts, cooked and diced	1	cup diced celery
1	cup cooked white rice	1	teaspoon salt
½	cup toasted almonds	½	grated onion
1	can pimento, drained	1	teaspoon pepper
2	tablespoons lemon juice	3	hard-boiled eggs, sliced
1	(8-ounce) can water chestnuts	1	can cream of chicken soup, undiluted
¾	cup mayonnaise	¾	can grated cheese
		1	can onion rings

Mix all ingredients except cheese and onion rings in casserole dish. Top with cheese. Bake at 350 degrees for 20 minutes. Then crumble onion rings on top and bake about 10 more minutes.

Serves 10

Beverly Edwards

🐝 *Chicken Casserole #3*

1	package herb stuffing mix	½	cup mayonnaise
1	stick butter	¾	teaspoon salt
1	cup chicken broth		Pepper
2½	cups chopped chicken	2	eggs
1½	cups chopped green onions	1½	cups milk
½	cup celery	1	can mushroom soup

In large casserole dish, spread ½ package stuffing mix. Melt butter in chicken broth. Pour over dressing. Mix chicken, onion, celery, mayonnaise, salt and pepper. Spread over butter and broth. Beat 2 eggs with milk; pour over. Cover casserole with foil and refrigerate overnight. Before cooking, remove casserole from refrigerator and let sit out until dish is at room temperature. Spread mushroom soup over casserole. Then top with remainder of dressing mix. Bake for 1 hour at 350 degrees.

Gloria Anderson

Chicken Casserole #4

6	chicken breasts, boned	1½	cans undiluted cream of mushroom soup
	Bacon		
1	jar chipped beef	1	cup sour cream
			Fresh mushrooms

Wrap each breast with strip of bacon. Place each in baking dish with a piece of chipped beef under each. Mix mushroom soup with sour cream. Pour over chicken. Dot with fresh mushrooms. Bake at 350 degrees for 1½ hours or more.

Mrs. D.S. Wainer

Chicken Casserole #5

1	large hen	4	hard-boiled eggs, diced
½	cup chicken fat		Salt
½	cup flour		Pepper
1	cup milk		Worcestershire sauce
½	cup celery		Lemon juice
½	cup finely diced onion	1	(8-ounce) package bite-sized
1	small jar pimentos, diced		pasta
1	can mushrooms, sliced		Buttery cheese cracker
1	can tiny English peas		crumbs

Boil hen. When tender, remove chicken from bones and cut in pieces about 1-inch thick. Save chicken and stock. Make sauce of chicken fat and flour. Blend and add half milk and 1 cup chicken stock. Add celery and onion. Cook until tender, then add the pimentos, mushrooms, peas, eggs, and small chicken pieces. Season to taste with salt, pepper, Worcestershire sauce, and lemon juice. Cook pasta in left over chicken stock. Drain and add to sauce. Fold in large pieces of chicken. Pour into casserole dish. Cover with cracker crumbs. Heat in at 325 to 350 degrees until bubbly.

Serves 10 to 12

Mrs. T. C. Ashley

Cordon Bleu Chicken Breasts

2	large whole chicken breasts, cut in halved	4	slices Provolone cheese
		1	egg, slightly beaten
¼	pound paper thin cooked ham	2	tablespoons butter
		¼	cup dry breadcrumbs

Have breasts cut in halves boned and skinned. Flatten each breast, put a slice of ham and a slice of cheese on each piece. Roll up from narrow end and secure with toothpicks. Melt butter in shallow pan. Dip each breast in egg and then roll breasts in breadcrumbs. Place in melted butter, turning gently to drench both sides. Bake at 375 degrees approximately 30 minutes. Turn after 15 minutes of baking.

Serves 4

Mrs. John Bosch

Chicken 'n Cream

4-5	skinless chicken breast halves	2	slices uncooked bacon, diced
2	tablespoons butter	½	cup sherry
	Sprinkling of parsley	½	pint heavy cream
	Sprinkling of thyme	4	cloves garlic
	Sprinkling of bay leaf	1	can mushrooms, drained
	Salt and pepper to taste	1	onion, diced

Brown chicken in butter. Add seasonings, bacon, sherry, cream, and garlic. Cover and cook slowly for 20 minutes. Sauté mushrooms and onion in butter. Add to first mixture. Serve with rice.

Mrs. Linda Singleton

Chicken and Dressing Casserole

1	(8-ounce) package cornbread dressing or stuffing mix	½	cup melted margarine
		½	cup flour
		¼	teaspoon salt
1	cup water	1	dash pepper
1	stick margarine, melted	4	cups chicken broth
3	cups cubed cooked chicken	6	eggs, slightly beaten

In 3-quart glass baking dish, combine stuffing mix with water and 1 stick margarine, and spread evenly in dish. Top with cubed chicken. In large saucepan add ½ cup margarine and brown the flour to make a roux. Add salt and pepper. Add chicken broth and cook until sauce thickens. Pour 1 cup sauce into beaten eggs, stirring constantly, then pour egg mixture back into sauce and blend well. Pour over chicken. Bake at 325 degrees for 45 minutes. Cut into squares and serve with giblet gravy.

Serves 12

May use turkey instead of chicken.

Teresa Steinberg

Chicken Chow Mein #1

2	medium green peppers, cut lengthwise in 8ths	1	package onion soup mix
1½	cups celery, sliced	2	cups bean sprouts
2	tablespoons butter	2	cups chicken broth
2½	cups diced cooked chicken	2	tablespoons cornstarch
		2-3	tablespoons soy sauce

Cook peppers and celery in butter until tender. Add other ingredients and cook 15 to 20 minutes more. Serve over rice or Chinese noodles and may add slivered almonds on top.

Mrs. Charles E. Layton

Chicken Chow Mein #2

¼	cup butter	2	cups leftover chicken, cut in thin strips
1	cup finely diced onions		
2	cups finely diced celery	1	teaspoons salt
1½	cups hot water	1	dash pepper
1	can Chinese mixed vegetables or bean sprouts, drained		

Melt butter and add onions. Fry 3 minutes. Add celery and water and cook covered 5 minutes. Add Chinese vegetables and mix well. Add meat and seasoning. Mix well. Just before serving, add thickening. Then, serve hot over rice or with chow mein noodles.

Thickening

2	tablespoons cold water	1	tablespoon soy sauce
2	tablespoons cornstarch	1	teaspoon sugar

Combine to make thickening.

Marsha Rudolph

143

🦃 Chicken Cashew Casserole

1 large onion, diced	3 drops Tabasco sauce
1 cup celery, diced	Pepper
Butter	2 cups cooked chicken
1 can mushroom soup	1 can bean sprouts
⅓ cup chicken broth	1 can chow·mein noodles
¼ teaspoon soy sauce	⅓ can cashew nuts

Sauté onion and celery in butter. Add soup, broth, soy sauce, Tabasco, pepper, chicken and bean sprouts. Simmer a few minutes. Pour into 1-quart casserole dish. Sprinkle with noodles and nuts. Bake at 350 degrees for 30 minutes.

Serves 6

Betty Jean Daugharty

Chicken Country Captain

2 large fryers, cut into frying size pieces	1 teaspoon thyme
	½ teaspoon black pepper
2 teaspoons cooking oil	1 large can tomatoes
3 onions, chopped	1 cup currants
3 green peppers, finely chopped	1 can mushrooms
	1 cup dry red wine
1 teaspoon butter	1 cup raw rice
1 clove garlic, minced	1 cup blanched almonds,
1 teaspoon salt	toasted and salted
1 teaspoon curry powder	

Brown chicken in hot cooking oil. Sauté onions and peppers in butter. Add garlic, salt, curry, thyme, pepper and tomatoes. Simmer 15 minutes. Add currants, mushrooms and wine. Pour this over chicken, which has been placed in large roasting pan, and cook in oven at 350 degrees for 1 hour. Cook rice as directed on package. When ready to serve, arrange rice in center of large serving platter. Sprinkle rice with toasted almonds. Lay chicken on rice. Pour sauce over chicken.

Mrs. I. H. Tillman, Jr.

🎋 Chicken and Kraut

8	boned chicken breast halves, cut in half	¾	pound Swiss cheese, grated
1	(30-ounce) can chopped sauerkraut, drained	1	(8-ounce) bottle Thousand Island dressing

Layer bottom of baking dish with chicken. Put drained kraut over chicken. Spread half of cheese over chicken. Pour dressing over cheese. Add another layer of chicken and cover with remaining cheese. Bake at 325 degrees for 2 hours.

Can be prepared a day ahead.

Nancy Parris

Aunt Willie's Chicken Dish

6	large chicken breasts		Garlic to taste
2	cups sour cream	4	teaspoons salt
4	teaspoons Worcestershire sauce	½	teaspoon pepper
¼	cup lemon juice	1¾	cups packaged dry breadcrumbs
4	teaspoons celery salt	½	cup butter
2	teaspoons paprika	⅓	cup shortening

Cut chicken breasts in halves and wipe with damp paper towel. In large bowl, combine sour cream, Worcestershire sauce, lemon juice, celery salt, paprika, garlic, salt and pepper. Add chicken to this mixture, coating well. Let stand overnight in refrigerator. Next day, preheat oven to 350 degrees, remove chicken from sour cream mixture. Roll in crumbs coating evenly, and arrange in shallow baking pan. Melt butter and shortening and spoon half over chicken. Bake, uncovered, 45 minutes. Spoon rest of butter and shortening over chicken and bake 10 or 15 minutes more, or until chicken is tender.

Serves 12

Mrs. Howard Dasher (Mary)

Chicken Divine

2	(10-ounce) packages frozen broccoli	½	teaspoon curry powder
3	whole chicken breasts	½	cup shredded American cheese or sharp Cheddar cheese
2	cans cream of chicken soup		
1	cup mayonnaise	½	cup soft breadcrumbs
2	teaspoons lemon juice	1	tablespoon melted butter

Arrange cooked broccoli and then cooked, boned, and skinless chicken in layers in greased shallow baking dish. Combine next 4 ingredients and pour over chicken. Sprinkle cheese on top. Mix breadcrumbs and melted butter. Sprinkle of cheese. Bake at 350 degrees for 25 to 30 minutes.

Mrs. Chandler Blanton

Chicken Loaf

1	(6-pound or more) hen		Salt, red and black pepper, and Worcestershire sauce to taste
1½	sticks butter		
½	cup flour, browned in oven		
1	quart milk	9	eggs, beaten
1	cup chicken stock		

Cook hen in salted water. Grind meat from thighs, drumsticks, and wings. Cut breasts. Make cream sauce of butter, flour, milk, chicken stock and season to taste with salt, pepper, and Worcestershire sauce. Add ground and chopped chicken. Mix well. Add eggs to sauce and chicken mixture. Pour into 2 (2-quart) buttered mold. Set mold in pan of water. Bake at 350 degrees for about 1 hour, until firm. Turn out of molds, sprinkle with paprika, and spoon mushroom sauce over molds.

Mushroom Sauce

2	medium cans of mushrooms		Red pepper, salt and Worcestershire sauce to taste
	Butter		
2	cans of mushroom soup		

Brown mushrooms in butter. Add to soup. Heat and season with red pepper, salt and Worcestershire sauce.

Serves 16

Mrs. J. K. Bland, Jr.

June's Easy Chicken

2	fryers, quartered	1	stick butter
1	small bottle Durkee's dressing		Juice of 1½ lemons

Clean chicken, place skin side up in casserole dish. Heat Durkee's, butter, and lemon juice. Pour over chicken and cover with sauce. Bake uncovered 1½ hours at 350 degrees.

Mrs. Walton Carter

Chicken Spaghetti

1	hen	1	can tomato paste
1	(8-ounce) package spaghetti	3	tablespoons chili powder
2	tablespoons butter	1	large can mushrooms
1	small onion, chopped and sautéed		Salt and pepper
1	green pepper, sautéed	1	cup grated Parmesan cheese

Boil hen in plenty of water until meat falls off bone. Cook spaghetti in water that chicken was cooked in. Combine butter, onion, green pepper, tomato paste, chili powder, mushrooms, salt, and pepper. Simmer 1 hour. Cut chicken in small pieces. Add chicken and spaghetti to sauce. Add cheese just before serving.

Mrs. Frank Strickland

Chicken with Pecans

1	fryer, cut top	1	teaspoon paprika
½	cup evaporated milk	½	cup finely chopped pecans
1	cup biscuit mix	½	teaspoon poultry seasoning
1½	teaspoons salt	½	cup melted margarine

Dip chicken pieces in evaporated milk. Mix dry ingredients. Coat dipped chicken with dry mixture. Place in shallow baking pan. Pour melted margarine over chicken. Bake uncovered at 375 degrees for 1 hour.

Mrs. Tom Smith, Jr.

Chicken Devoni

Broccoli, chopped	**Blue cheese**
Chicken, cooked	**Buttered breadcrumbs**
White sauce	**Parmesan cheese, grated**

Line casserole with cooked, chopped broccoli and top with sliced, cooked chicken. Cover with white sauce to which has been added blue cheese to suit to your taste. Cover with buttered breadcrumbs and top with grated parmesan cheese. Bake at 350 degrees until bubbly.

Mrs. C. W. Warner

Biscuit Crust for Chicken Pie

2½ **cups sifted flour**	½ **cup shortening**
3 **teaspoons baking powder**	¾ **cup milk**
1 **teaspoon salt**	

Make a soft dough. Knead softly on a floured board. Roll out ¼-inch thick. Cut with round biscuit cutter. Brush with cream or butter for browning. Place over chicken pie filling in large baking dish. Bake at 400 degrees until browned.

Mrs. Marshall Parks

Chicken Pie

1 **chicken boiled, deboned**	**Pepper**
1¾ **cups chicken broth**	1 **stick butter**
1 **can chicken or celery soup**	1 **cup self-rising flour**
Salt	¾ **cup milk**

Place chicken in bottom of 9x13-inch casserole dish. Pour chicken broth, cream of chicken or celery soup, salt and pepper, if needed, over chicken. In separate bowl, mix butter, flour, and milk. Pour mixture over casserole dish contents. Bake at 350 to 375 degrees for 40 minutes or until brown.

Jane Rainey

Party Chicken Bake

½	envelope Italian dressing mix	1	(4-ounce) container whipped
2	tablespoons butter, melted		cream cheese with chives
4-6	chicken breasts	½	cup Sauterne
1	can cream of mushroom soup	1	cup instant rice

Reserve ½ teaspoon salad dressing mix. In large skillet combine dressing mix with butter. Add chicken and brown slowly. Place in 12x7½x2-inch baking dish. Blend soup and cream cheese. Stir in Sauterne. Spoon over chicken. Bake uncovered at 325 degrees for 1 hour, basting once or twice. Garnish with parsley. Prepare rice according to package directions, adding reserved salad dressing mix to water.

Serves 4 to 6

Mrs. J. Edward Willis

Two Layer Chicken Pie

1	(3½-pound) hen, boiled		Salt and pepper to taste
3	cups chicken broth	8	tablespoons flour
2½	cups milk	4	hard-boiled eggs
¼	pound butter	1	pie pastry, sliced

Remove bones and skin from chicken. Cut into chunks. Heat broth, milk, butter and seasonings to boiling point. Thicken with flour mixed to a smooth paste with water. Cook a couple of minutes. Arrange half of chicken and eggs in a greased casserole, 13x9x2½-inches. Add half the liquid and top with pastry strips. Brown in a 450 degree oven. Top with the remaining chicken, eggs and liquid, and cover with pastry crust. Bake at 350 degrees for 30 to 45 minutes.

Serves 10 to 12

Mrs. Arthur Smith

🪶 *Chicken and Stuffing Bake*

2	cups cubed, cooked chicken	½	cup milk
1	can cream mushroom soup	1	package stuffing
1	cup grated Cheddar cheese		

Mix chicken, soup, cheese and milk together and pour into shallow 2-quart casserole dish. Prepare stuffing according to package directions and sprinkle over chicken mixture. Bake at 350 degrees for about 45 minutes until lightly browned. Add more chicken, cheese and milk for larger casserole.

Gayle Mosby

🪶 *Chicken Soufflé*

	Thinly sliced bread with crusts removed	2	cups milk
4	cups cooked chopped chicken		Salt
			Small jar pimentos
	Mayonnaise	1	small can mushrooms
	Thinly sliced Cheddar cheese	1	can mushroom soup
		1	can celery soup
4	eggs	1	small can water chestnuts
			Breadcrumbs

Line a buttered, flat, 3-quart baking dish with slices of bread. Cover with 4 cups cooked, bite-size pieces of chicken. Cover chicken with a very thin layer of mayonnaise. Add layer of thinly sliced Cheddar cheese. Beat 4 eggs with 2 cups of milk and a little salt. Pour over and fork mixture down to bread. Mix 1 can of mushroom soup, celery soup, and chopped pimento. Add small can mushrooms and a can sliced water chestnuts. Spread over top. Cover with foil and refrigerate overnight. Bake 1 hour at 325 degrees. Sprinkle with breadcrumbs and bake 15 additional minutes.

Serves 10 to 12

Anne Plageman

Chicken and Pork Caribbean

1	frying chicken, cut up (or 6 choice pieces)	1	can tomatoes
6	pork chops	½	cup raisins
	Salt and pepper	¾	cup green stuffed olives, drained
1	small onion, sliced	½	teaspoon oregano
2	cloves garlic, finely chopped	½	cup water
¼-½ cup olive oil or salad oil			

Salt and pepper chicken and pork chops. Brown well in a large skillet, which has a cover. Remove meat, sauté onions and garlic in oil until soft. Replace chicken and pork. Add remaining ingredients. Bring to a boil; cover and simmer for 45 minutes to 1 hour. Serve with rice.

Mrs. John Bosch

Polynesian Chicken

1	(3½-ounce) can pineapple chunks	1	sliced onion
½	cup margarine	1	sliced green pepper
1	(3- to 4-pound) fryer, disjointed (or 8 breasts)	1	can sliced mushrooms
1	(7-ounce) can shrimp, drained	½	cup sliced stuffed olives
		1	can tomato soup

Drain pineapple. Reserve juice. Melt margarine in broiler pan. Arrange chicken in pan with skin side down. Bake 30 minutes at 425 degrees. Then add to chicken the pineapple, shrimp, onion, peppers, mushrooms, and olives. Combine soup with pineapple juice. Pour over chicken. Cover pan with foil. Bake 30 more minutes. Remove foil and bake 15 minutes longer. Serve with rice.

Serves 6 to 8

Marci Mathis

151

Chicken Loaf and Sauce

1	hen	1	cup cooked rice
	Onion	1	teaspoon salt
	Celery	½	teaspoon paprika
	Salt	½	teaspoon red pepper
	Pepper	4	eggs, beaten
1	tablespoon parsley	1¼	pints chicken stock
1	cup breadcrumbs		

Chop and cook hen, season to taste with onion, celery, salt and pepper while cooking. Mix cooked hen with remaining ingredients. Cook in 2 greased loaf pans for 45 minutes at 350 degrees. Should be crusty brown.

Sauce

½	stick butter	1	large can mushrooms
¼	cup flour	¼	teaspoon paprika
1	pint chicken stock	¼	cup cream
2	egg yolks	2	teaspoons lemon juice
	Salt and pepper to taste		

Melt butter; add flour and chicken stock. Cook until thick. Add mushrooms and other ingredients, adding egg yolks last. Serve over slices of chicken loaf.

Mrs. Joyce Mixon

Pressed Chicken

2	envelopes gelatin	1	teaspoon chopped pickles
1	cup hot chicken broth	2	teaspoons vegetable relish
1	pint mayonnaise	¼	cup green olives
1	(5- to 6-pound) hen, cooked and diced		Juice of ½ lemon
			Salt and pepper to taste
2	cups diced celery	1	cup almonds, chopped
4	hard-boiled eggs, chopped		

Dissolve gelatin in ½ cup cold water. Pour 1 cup hot broth into gelatin. Cool. Add mayonnaise and rest of ingredients. Place in loaf pan and chill in refrigerator.

Serves 12

Mrs. O.J. Taylor

Paella

2	cloves garlic, minced	1	(1½-pound) Boston Butt,
1	Spanish or Bermuda		cut into chunks
	onion, chopped	¼	teaspoon saffron threads
1	green pepper, diced	1½	cups long grain rice
¼-½	cup olive oil	3	canned pimentos, diced
	Salt and pepper	1½	pounds fresh or frozen
6-8	pieces selected chicken		shrimp; peeled, deveined,
			and well drained

In a small skillet sauté garlic, onion and green pepper in a small amount of olive oil until soft, but not brown. Put aside. Salt chicken and pork and brown in olive oil in a Dutch oven or large pot. After browning all pieces, cover with water and place lid on pot and simmer until done and tender. Remove 1 cup of the hot stock in which the chicken and pork have cooked and add saffron to it. Allow to stand for about 15 minutes. Strain this cup of stock into a large pot and discard saffron threads. Add 2 more cups of stock, making a total of 3 cups. If you do not have sufficient stock to make 3 cups, add water. To the 3 cups of stock, add the onion, garlic, green pepper, the rice, pimentos, shrimp and pork. May choose to add 1 teaspoon salt and taste. If the broth has retained very much salt from the chicken and pork the salt may not be necessary. Stir this complete mixture carefully and brink to boil, being careful so as not to scorch the bottom. Arrange the pieces of the cooked chicken on top. Cover and lower heat to simmer. Cook 25 minutes. Do not stir during cooking process.

Mrs. John Bosch

Chicken with Oysters

1	(3-pound) chicken, cut in	1	teaspoon herb seasoning
	pieces	1	teaspoon monosodium
	Salt and pepper to taste		glutamate
½	stick butter	⅔	cup cream
1	cup consommé	1	pint drained oysters

Brown seasoned chicken in butter. Pour consommé, herb seasoning, and MSG over chicken. Cover and bake at 375 degrees for 40 minutes. Before serving, add cream and oysters. Bake 10 to 15 minutes. Serve over wild rice.

Mrs. William M. Gabard

153

Lemon Barbeque Chicken

Lemon Barbeque Sauce

½   teaspoon salt
1   peeled clove garlic
¼   cup salad oil
½   cup lemon juice

½   teaspoon pepper
¼   teaspoon dried thyme
2   tablespoons grated onion

Mash salt and garlic in bowl. Add remaining ingredients. Chill 24 hours.

Makes ¾ cup

Chicken

Chicken
Salt

Pepper
Flour

Salt and pepper chicken, dust lightly with flour. Brown pieces of chicken. Place chicken in glass baking dish. Pour sauce over chicken. Cook at 375 degrees about 1 hour, turning and basting often.

Mrs. Harry Cooper

Chicken and Oyster Dressing

4   whole eggs
1   cup cooked rice
1½   cups breadcrumbs
2   cups crushed saltines

1   pint oysters
Chicken stock, with chicken bits
Salt and pepper

Beat eggs until light and fluffy. Mix rice, breadcrumbs and crackers. Add eggs to dry ingredients. Add oysters to above. Use chicken stock to make a soupy mixture. Season to taste. Butter baking pan. Fill and cook at 350 degrees for 45 minutes.

Mrs. P.K. Moore

Chicken Royal

4	small whole chicken breasts	½	teaspoon salt
¾	cup flour	⅛	teaspoon pepper
¼	teaspoon paprika		

Herb Stuffing

2	cups breadcrumbs, toasted	⅛	teaspoon pepper
1	teaspoon onion	2	teaspoons melted butter
½	teaspoon salt	¼	cup hot water
¼	teaspoon poultry seasoning		

Combine flour and seasonings in bag. Add chicken and shake. Fill each breast with stuffing. Skewer with toothpicks. Dip in melted butter and place in baking dish. Bake at 325 degrees for 45 minutes. Turn and bake 45 minutes longer. Serve with sauce.

Sauce

½	pint sour cream	1	(10-ounce) can cream of
2	teaspoons parsley		mushroom soup, undiluted

Combine and heat slowly.

Mrs. Marshall Parks

Turkey Gumbo

1	large onion, chopped	Left over ham
1	large clove garlic	Fresh country link pork
½	bell pepper, chopped	sausage
2	cans chopped okra	Left over turkey
	Turkey stock	Salt, pepper and Tabasco
	Turkey gravy	sauce to taste
1	large can tomatoes	

Combine onion, garlic, bell pepper, and okra. Cook until okra starts to separate. Add stock, gravy and tomatoes. Add ham. Fry sausage until brown and put in gumbo. Add turkey, let simmer. Add salt, pepper and a few drops of Tabasco sauce. Serve over hot rice in soup bowl.

Mrs. Clarence Paine

Chicken Tetrazzini #1

1   **(3-pound) chicken, cooked and cooled in stock and cut in medium pieces**
1   **box small egg noodles**
1   **cup chopped celery**
1   **medium onion, finely diced**
    Butter

1   **can mushroom soup**
½   **can milk**
½   **cup sliced stuffed olives**
    Salt, pepper and
    Worcestershire sauce
    Grated cheese

Cook chicken, cool, cut up. Boil noodles in chicken stock according to directions on box. Fry celery, onion until light brown in butter. Mix soup with ½ can milk. Heat well and add celery, onions, olives, and chicken. Season to taste with salt, pepper and Worcestershire sauce. Place in 2-quart casserole, first a layer of noodles, then chicken and sauce. Top with grated cheese and dot with butter. Bake at 325 degrees for about 30 minutes.

Serves 8

Mrs. John Anderson

Chicken Tetrazzini #2

1   **large chicken**
1   **package egg noodles**
1   **stick margarine**
3   **medium onions, diced**
1   **green pepper, diced**

1   **cup celery, diced**
1   **small can mushrooms**
1½ **cups milk**
½   **pound cheese**
1   **can mushroom soup**

Boil chicken, remove from broth and when cool, remove bones. Add sufficient water to broth to cook noodles. Melt margarine in large skillet and sauté onions, pepper, and celery. In sauce pan, mix mushrooms and liquid from can of mushrooms and milk. Add skillet mixture. Mix well and bring back to boil. Add cheese, soup, noodles and chicken, stirring gently. Pour into 2-quart casserole dish and bake at 325 degrees for 45 minutes or until top is slightly browned.

Jean Fowler

Creamed Eggs Chartres

1 cup finely shredded white onion	¼ teaspoon cayenne pepper
⅓ cup butter	4 hard-boiled eggs, peeled and sliced (reserving 4 center slices for garnish)
¼ cup flour	
2 cups milk	
1 egg yolk	2 tablespoons Parmesan cheese
¼ teaspoon salt	1 tablespoon paprika

In skillet over medium heat, sauté onion in butter until transparent. Stir in flour, cook 3 to 5 minutes. Blend in milk and egg yolk (add yolk to a little milk, first). Add salt and pepper and cook, stirring constantly until thick. Remove from heat, add sliced eggs. Mix lightly. Spoon into 2 (8-ounce) casserole dishes and sprinkle lightly with paprika and Parmesan cheese mixed together. Heat thoroughly at 350 degrees. Garnish with egg slices.

Serves 2

Mrs. Geneva M. Morris

Creamed Eggs

½ tablespoon diced green bell pepper	¼ teaspoon salt
	Small jar mushrooms, chopped
¼ cup butter	
¾ cup flour	Small jar pimentos, chopped
1 quart milk	
1 tablespoon minced onions	¼ cup ripe olives, chopped
⅛ teaspoon pepper	9 hard-boiled eggs
⅛ teaspoon celery salt	

Sauté pepper in half of the butter, set aside. Melt the rest of the butter in another pan. Add flour and remove form heat. Add the milk and simmer until thickened. Add all other ingredients. Add eggs last. Heat to boiling. Serve on toast.

Mrs. Lawrence Alvarez

🎽 *Breakfast Casserole*

1	pound regular or hot sausage	1	teaspoon salt
6	eggs	1	teaspoon dry mustard
2	cups milk	4	slices cubed bread
		1	cup grated sharp cheese

Cook sausage until done, breaking it into bits as you cook it. Drain and set aside. Beat eggs; add milk, salt and mustard. Into a greased baking dish, layer the bread, sausage and cheese. Pour egg mixture over these ingredients. Refrigerate overnight. Bake at 350 degrees for 45 minutes.

Anne Plageman

🎽 *Blender Cheese Soufflé*

8	ounces crumbled sharp Cheddar cheese	4	eggs
10	slices buttered bread, minus crusts	2	cups milk
		1	tablespoon salt
		½	tablespoon dry mustard

Put ½ of all ingredients in blender and mix on high-until well blended. Then put other ½ of ingredients into blender and mix. Pour into greased casserole dish. Cook uncovered for 1 hour at 350 degrees.

Jane Sherwood

🎽 *Cheese Omelet*

6	eggs	3	tablespoons margarine
2	tablespoons grated Parmesan cheese	½	cup grated Cheddar cheese
½	teaspoon salt	2	tablespoons cream
1	tablespoon water		Parmesan cheese to top
			Parsley

Beat eggs, 2 tablespoons Parmesan cheese, salt, and 1 tablespoon water until just combined. Heat skillet, add margarine. Turn mixture into skillet. Sprinkle with grated cheese and cream. Cook over medium heat. Run spatula around edge, tilt pan. Fold in half. Sprinkle with Parmesan and parsley.

Jane McLane

Cheese Strata

8	slices white bread	4	beaten eggs
	Butter	1½	cups milk
	American cheese		Salt and pepper to taste
1	cup grated sharp Cheddar cheese		

Trim crusts from white bread. Butter both sides of bread and make 4 cheese sandwiches. Put in square glass dish. Sprinkle with grated cheese. Mix eggs with milk. Add salt and pepper. Pour over sandwiches. Refrigerate several hours or overnight. Bake at 350 degrees for 45 minutes.

Serves 6 to 8

Mrs. Omer Franklin

Creamed Stuffed Eggs

4	hard-boiled eggs	1	small can deviled ham
1	tablespoon butter		Cheese sauce

Cut eggs in halves, while hot and remove yolks. Mash yolks with butter and deviled ham. Restuff eggs. Make a cheese sauce in a large skillet. Turn stuffed eggs down into sauce. Warm and serve over buttered toast.

Serves 2

Mrs. Bill Lester

Curried Deviled Eggs

6	eggs, hard-boiled cooled, and shelled	3	slices bacon, crumbled
¼	teaspoon mustard	¼	teaspoon salt, or to taste
3	tablespoons mayonnaise or salad dressing	¼	teaspoon curry powder

Cut eggs in halves lengthwise. With spoon, carefully remove yolks and mash. Mix with remaining ingredients. Pile mixture onto egg whites.

Makes 12 halves

Mrs. C.W. Warner

Curried Eggs

1½ pounds mushrooms, sliced
2-3 tablespoons butter
6 cups light cream sauce
¾ cup grated Parmesan cheese
4½ teaspoons curry powder
6 tablespoons chopped pimentos

6 tablespoons chili sauce
Salt and pepper to taste
6 tablespoons sliced water chestnuts
15 hard-boiled eggs, peeled and quartered
Breadcrumbs
Butter

Sauté mushrooms in butter. Prepare cream sauce. Season with cheese, curry powder, pimentos, chili sauce, salt and pepper. Bring sauce to boil and add mushrooms, water chestnuts, and eggs. Pour into baking dish, top with breadcrumbs, and dot with butter. Place under broiler until crumbs brown.

Serves 12

Mrs. Henry Brice

Eggs Continental

¾ cup fine soft breadcrumbs
4 hard-boiled eggs, sliced
3 slices bacon, diced
¼ pound fresh mushrooms sliced (or 1 can mushrooms)
½ pint sour cream

2 tablespoons minced parsley or chives
¼ teaspoon salt
¼ teaspoon paprika
½ cup grated cheese

Line 8-inch pie plate with the breadcrumbs. Place sliced eggs in a layer over the crumbs. Meanwhile fry the bacon until crisp. About 5 minutes before the bacon is done, add the mushrooms and sauté until just softened. Drain off fat, add bacon and mushrooms to sour cream, parsley or chives, salt and paprika. Mix thoroughly and spread over eggs. Top with grated cheese and sprinkle with paprika. Bake at 350 degrees for 15 to 20 minutes, or until cheese is melted and sauce is bubbly.

Mrs. Howard Dasher (Mary)

Eggs Benedict ~
Quick Version of Old Classic

8	large buttered toast rounds	8	poached eggs
2	(3-ounce) cans sliced mushrooms	1	(10½-ounce) can cheese soup

Place 2 toast rounds on each plate. Drain mushrooms and divide evenly between the toast rounds. Top with a poached egg. Heat the cheese soup over low heat, stirring constantly until bubbly. Spoon over the poached eggs. Serve immediately.

Serves 4

Mrs. C. W. Warner

Mushroom Quiche

2	green onions, finely chopped	½	teaspoon salt
1	tablespoon butter		Freshly ground black pepper
1	cup small fresh mushrooms, thinly sliced	1	egg, whole
		1	egg yolk
2	teaspoons lemon juice	¾	cup half-and-half
1	tablespoon finely chopped fresh parsley	¼	cup Parmesan cheese
		1	(8-inch) pie shell, baked

In a skillet, sauté onions in butter until soft, not brown. Add mushrooms to skillet along with lemon juice and toss over moderate heat for about 3 minutes until softened. Remove from heat and stir in finely chopped parsley, salt, and pepper to taste. Combine whole egg, egg yolk, half-and-half, and Parmesan cheese. Beat with fork until thoroughly blended. Spread base of pie shell with mushroom mixture. Fill it with cream mixture, pouring it gently over the back of a tablespoon to avoid disturbing mushrooms and onions. Transfer pie shell on a baking sheet to the oven. At 350 degrees, bake for 25 to 30 minutes until filling is well puffed and set, with a rich golden color on top. Serve immediately.

Serves 4

Note: Recipe for filling, doubled, will fill a quiche dish and may have to cook a little longer.

Suzanne Sullivan

Impossible Quiche

12	slices bacon, crisply fried and crumbled	½	cup biscuit/pancake baking mix
1	cup shredded cheese	4	eggs
⅓	cup finely chopped onion	¼	teaspoon salt
2	cups milk	⅛	teaspoon pepper

Preheat oven to 350 degrees. Lightly grease a 9- or 10-inch pie pan. Sprinkle bacon, cheese, and onion evenly over bottom of pan. Place remaining ingredients in blender. Cover and blend remaining ingredients on high speed 1 minute. Pour into pie pan. Bake at 350 degrees for 50 to 55 minutes or until golden brown. Let stand 5 minutes before cutting.

Donna Newbern

Quiche Lorraine

1	pie pastry		Pepper
4	eggs	1	pound bacon
2	cups thin cream	1	small onion, minced
	Pinch cayenne	1	cup grated Swiss cheese
	Pinch sugar		

Line a 10-inch pie plate with pastry. Prick bottom and chill. Beat eggs and cream until blended. Add seasoning and stir. Cook bacon and break into bits. Sauté onion. Put bacon and onion, then cheese, then egg mixture into pie shell. Bake at 450 degrees for 12 minutes, then 325 degrees for 15 minutes.

Mrs. Marshall Parks

Sides

Vegetables

Apple-Cheese Casserole 165

Scalloped Apples 165

Spicy Glazed Apple Ring 165

French Artichokes 166

Artichoke Ramaki 166

Asparagus Delight 166

Asparagus Casserole 167

Spiced Beets 167

Barbequed Butter Beans 167

Baked Beans 168

Mexican Bean Rarebit 168

Pinto Beans 168

Mrs. Everett's Baked Beans 169

Conversation Bean Pie 169

Broccoli Casserole #1 170

Broccoli Casserole #2 170

Broccoli Casserole #3 170

Broccoli Casserole #4 171

Broccoli and Cauliflower 171

Broccoli and
    Sour Cream Casserole 171

Cabbage and Tomatoes 172

Scalloped Cabbage 172

Cabbage-Stir Fried 173

Sweet and Sour Red Cabbage 173

Marinated Carrots 173

Carrot Casserole 174

Celery Casserole 174

Carrot Ring 175

Glazed Carrots 175

Cranberry Soufflé 175

Corn Soufflé 176

Curried Fruit 176

Scalloped Eggplant 176

Eggplant Casserole #1 177

Eggplant Casserole #2 177

Eggplant Casserole #3 177

Eggplant Soufflé #1 178

Eggplant Soufflé #2 178

Eggplant Casserole Patrice 179

Green Bean and Corn Casserole 179

Green Bean Casserole #1 180

Green Bean Casserole #2 180

Green Bean Casserole #3 181

Green Bean Casserole #4 181

Green Bean Casserole #5 182

French Green Bean Casserole 182

Cold Green Beans 182

Green Beans with Onions 183

Mushroom Casserole 183

Baked Stuffed Onions 184

Onion Pie 184

Onion-Celery-Almond Casserole 185

French Fried Onion Rings 185

Hot Cheese Pineapple 185

English Pea Casserole 186

Aunt Ruth's Creole Peas 186

Deviled Peas 187

Epicurean Peas 187

Broiled Peaches 187

Duke's Special ~
    John Wayne's Favorite! 188

Spinach Casserole 188

Acorn Squash 189

Spinach Soufflé 189

Spinach and Artichoke Casserole 189

Baked Squash 190

Squash Casserole #1 190

Squash Casserole #2 191

Squash Casserole #3 191

Squash Casserole #4 192

Squash Soufflé #1 192

Squash Soufflé #2 193

Escalloped Tomatoes 193

Vegetables continued

Tomato Casserole 193

Stuffed Tomatoes 194

Mixed Vegetable Mornay 194

Tomatoes Au Gratin 195

Goldie's Turnips 195

Vegetable Casserole 195

Zucchini 196

Grits

Grits Casserole #1 196

Grits Casserole #2 197

Baked Hominy Bread 197

Pasta

Pasta Casserole Marie-Blanche 197

Macaroni and Cheese 198

Macaroni Casserole 198

Potatoes

Potatoes with Cheese 198

Potato Casserole 199

Scalloped Potatoes #1 199

Scalloped Potatoes #2 199

Potato Topper for Baked Potatoes 200

Sweet Potato Soufflé #1 200

Sweet Potato Soufflé #2 200

Sweet Potato Casserole #1 201

Sweet Potato Casserole #2 201

Rice

Brown Rice 202

Mother's Rice Casserole 202

Rice Casserole 202

Green Chili Pepper
    Rice Casserole 203

🌿 *Apple-Cheese Casserole*

1 stick margarine	½ pound Cheddar cheese, grated
¾ cup flour	(or processed cheese loaf)
1 cup sugar	1 can sliced, unsweetened
	apples

Blend margarine and flour until crumbly. Add sugar and cheese, mixing until well blended. Put apples in buttered casserole and cover with cheese mixture. Bake in preheated oven 30 to 45 minutes at 350 degrees.

Rosemary Brannen

🌿 *Scalloped Apples*

4 cups diced apples	½ cup butter
¾ cup sugar	3 cups breadcrumbs or cubed
Cinnamon, nutmeg, or	bread
other spices to taste	

Combine apples, sugar, and spices. Mix butter and bread. Place alternate layers in baking dish beginning with apples and ending with crumbs on top. Cover and bake at 350 degrees for 30 minutes. Remove cover and brown for about 5 minutes.

Serves 6

Kitty Fricks

Spicy Glazed Apple Ring

1 cup sugar	2 red apples; washed, cored
¼ teaspoon nutmeg	and sliced into ¾-inch thick
½ cup water	rounds
	Food coloring of choice
	(optional)

Combine sugar, nutmeg and water in saucepan. Bring to a boil and boil 10 minutes. Dip apple rounds, 3 or 4 at a time, into the sugar syrup. Cook 3 to 4 minutes, until tender, turning once. Drain on waxed paper. Food coloring (preferably red) may be used to color apple rings.

This dish is to be used as a garnish around meat dishes.

Mrs. Wynona Parramore

French Artichokes

6	artichokes	2	tablespoons vinegar
1	quart cold water	1	teaspoon salt

Cut the coarse outer leaves from 6 artichokes and wash in cold water mixed with vinegar. Drain and put into boiling water with salt. Trim artichoke tops if needed. Cook until outer leaves are tender. Remove from burner and stand artichokes upside down to drain. When cold turn right side up. Spread leaves apart and scoop out heart and discard. Marinate several times during the day with Italian dressing or serve right side up with drawn butter or Hollandaise sauce.

Mrs. C. W. Warner

 Artichoke Ramaki

1	can artichoke hearts, drained and sliced into halves or quarters		Onion salt
		8	slices of bacon, cut in half

Sprinkle artichoke pieces with onion salt. Wrap ½ slice bacon around each artichoke piece. Broil 6 inches from heat about 8 minutes, turning once.

Serves 8 to 16

This can be prepared and refrigerated until ready to broil.

Beverly Moye

Asparagus Delight

	Butter	1	cup cheese, grated
1	garlic clove, split	1	cup nuts, broken
1	can long green asparagus		Buttered breadcrumbs
½	cup cream		

Butter a shallow casserole dish that has been rubbed with garlic clove. Arrange drained asparagus in dish. Pour enough cream over asparagus to slightly cover. Pour cheese and nuts over top, then breadcrumbs over all. Bake at 400 degrees for 30 to 40 minutes, or until bubbly and brown.

Makes 5 to 6 servings

Mrs. C.W. Warner

Asparagus Casserole

1	can asparagus	½	cup chopped almonds
1	bag of potato chips	1	can cream of mushroom soup

In a baking dish layer asparagus, potato chips, almonds, then repeat. Pour mushroom soup over top. Bake 15 minutes at 375 degrees.

Patty Castleberry

Spiced Beets

1	can sliced beets (or fresh beets)	1	teaspoon mustard seed
¾	cup tarragon vinegar	¼	teaspoon salt
½	cup sugar	1	Pinch of powdered cloves
1	teaspoon cinnamon		Several thinly sliced small white onions

One can of sliced beets cooked a short time in their juice. Combine all remaining ingredients, except onions, to make dressing. Simmer dressing for 5 minutes. Remove beets from juice. Put a layer of beets, a layer of onions in a covered dish. Pour the hot dressing over the onions and beets. Cover. Refrigerate to cool.

Mrs. Maxwell Oliver

Barbequed Butter Beans

1	(1-pound) can butter beans	1	medium-size onion, finely chopped
2	tablespoons brown sugar		
1	(10½-ounce) can tomato puree or paste	4	slices bacon, chopped in small pieces
			Salt and pepper to taste

Mix above ingredients in casserole dish. Bake at 325 degrees or cook on low heat on stovetop.

Baked Beans

2	(1-pound) cans pork and beans	1	tablespoon Worcestershire sauce
¼	cup plus 1 teaspoon maple syrup		Strips of bacon
¼	cup plus 1 teaspoon light brown sugar		Onion slices

Combine all ingredients except bacon and onion slices. Pour into baking dish. Cover mixture with onion slices, then with bacon strips. Bake at 325 degrees for 2 to 2½ hours.

Mrs. John Bosch

Mexican Bean Rarebit

¼	pound butter	1	can red kidney beans
½	pound processed cheese	1	green pepper, diced
1	teaspoon chili powder		

Melt butter and cheese in double boiler. Add chili powder, beans and pepper. Allow mixture to get slightly warm.

Mrs. Michael Kaiser

Pinto Beans

1	stalk celery, diced	2	cans pinto beans
1	large onion, diced	¼	cup molasses
1	bell pepper, diced	½	cup chili sauce or catsup
1	clove garlic, diced	¼	teaspoon dry mustard
	Bacon drippings		

Sauté celery, onion, bell pepper and garlic clove in bacon drippings. Mix with remaining ingredients in bean pot or casserole dish with enough liquid to cover. Bake at 300 degrees covered for 2½ hours. Remove, cover, and bake an additional 1½ hours.

Serves 6 to 8

Mrs. Quentin Lawson

Mrs. Everett's Baked Beans

1	small bag dried beans	1	tablespoon prepared
1	quart salted water		mustard
3	tablespoons bacon	1	cup packed brown sugar
	drippings	1	teaspoon paprika
1	cup chili sauce	2	tablespoons Worcestershire
1	cup catsup		sauce
1	medium onion, grated	2	tablespoons soy sauce
			Strips of bacon

Soak beans in cold water overnight. Next day boil in salted water with 3 tablespoons bacon drippings. When beans are tender, drain off most of the liquid. Add remaining ingredients, except bacon. Put all in large baking dish. Cover top with bacon strips and bake at 250 degrees for 3 hours.

Mrs. I.H. Tillman, Jr.

Conversation Bean Pie

1	(28-ounce) can Boston-style	2	cups milk
	baked beans	3	tablespoons melted butter
3	eggs, well beaten	½	cup dark brown sugar
1	teaspoon cinnamon	½	cup white sugar
¼	teaspoon ginger	2	teaspoons vanilla
¼	teaspoon nutmeg	2	(9-inch) pie pastry shells,
¼	teaspoon black pepper		unbaked

Remove pieces of pork from beans. Pour in blender or push through sieve and combine with eggs, cinnamon, ginger, nutmeg, pepper, milk, butter, and sugars. Flavor with vanilla. Pour into 2 pie shells and bake at 375 degrees for about 30 minutes or until a knife inserted in the center comes out clean.

Mrs. Earl Taylor

Broccoli Casserole #1

1	**(10-ounce) package frozen broccoli**	1	**can cream of mushroom soup**
¼	**cup minced onion**	¾	**cup milk**
2	**tablespoons butter**	¼	**cup blue cheese (1¼ ounces)**

Place broccoli in casserole dish. Sauté onion in butter, stir in soup and milk, blending well. Add cheese and stir until cheese melts. Pour over broccoli and bake at 350 degrees for 30 to 40 minutes.

Mrs. Fred Dodson

Broccoli Casserole #2

2	**(10-ounce) packages frozen broccoli, cooked**	¾	**cup sour cream**
1	**(10½-ounce) can mushroom soup**	1	**cup diced celery**
		½	**teaspoon pepper**
1	**(2-ounce) jar pimento**	1	**teaspoon salt**
			Grated cheese to top

Mix all ingredients together and put in casserole dish. Top with grated cheese. Bake at 350 degrees for 20 to 25 minutes.

Mrs. John Rudolph

Broccoli Casserole #3

2	**(10-ounce) packages frozen or fresh broccoli, cooked until tender**	1	**can cream of mushroom soup**
3	**eggs beaten**	1	**cup mayonnaise**
		1	**cup sharp Cheddar cheese**

Mix all of the ingredients in a large casserole dish. Place the dish in a pan of boiling water, covering ½ of the depth of the casserole dish. Bake uncovered 1 hour at 350 degrees.

Dorothy Chandler

🍴 *Broccoli Casserole #4*

2	packages frozen broccoli, chopped	1	medium onion, finely chopped
2	eggs, well beaten	1	stick butter, melted
½	cup grated cheese		Round, buttery crackers
½	cup mayonnaise		

Cook broccoli. Mix remaining ingredients and put into casserole. Sprinkle with crushed round, buttery crackers. Bake at 325 degrees for 30 minutes.

Serves 8

Marilyn Henderson

Broccoli and Cauliflower

4	boxes frozen broccoli	1	can cream of celery soup
3	boxes frozen cauliflower (optional: may use broccoli only)	1	can cream of asparagus soup
1	pint sour cream		Grated sharp Cheddar cheese

Cook frozen vegetables as directed on package. Mix sour cream and soups. Add vegetables to cream mixture and put in large casserole. Top with grated cheese. Bake.

Mrs. James L. Dowling, Jr.

Broccoli and Sour Cream Casserole

1	package chopped broccoli	¼	cup pimento
1	cup sour cream	1	cup chopped celery
1	can cream of mushroom soup	½	cup slivered almonds
			Grated cheese

Slightly cook broccoli. Combine with sour cream, soup, pimento, celery and almonds and top with cheese. Bake at 350 degrees for 20 to 25 minutes.

Mrs. Hugh Van Horn

Cabbage and Tomatoes

½	cup chopped onion	¾	teaspoon salt
4	tablespoons butter, separated	½	teaspoon sugar
3	tablespoons flour	¼	teaspoon pepper
2	cups canned tomatoes	6	cups finely shredded cabbage
2	teaspoons Worcestershire sauce	3	slices bread, cubed
		¼	pound processed cheese, cubed

Sauté onion until tender in 3 tablespoons of butter, blend in flour, stir until smooth. Add tomatoes, Worcestershire sauce, salt, sugar and pepper. Cook cabbage in a little salted water for 5 minutes. Brown bread cubes in 1 tablespoon of butter. Arrange layer of cabbage, tomato mixture, bread and cheese in 2-quart casserole dish. Finish with bread and cheese on top. Bake at 375 degrees oven for 30 minutes.

Mrs. Maxwell Oliver

Scalloped Cabbage

1	medium cabbage	¼	cup pimentos, minced
½	stick butter	1	cup grated cheese
3	tablespoons flour	6	slices fried bacon, crumbled
2½	cups milk		Buttered crumbs

Discard outer leaves of cabbage, and chop into big pieces. Drop into boiling water and boil 8 minutes only, covered. For cream sauce, melt butter then add flour and milk. Stir until thick. Place cabbage in long buttered baking dish. Pour cream sauce over this. Top with pimentos, cheese, and bacon. Top with buttered crumbs. Bake at 275 degrees for 1 hour.

Julie Budd

🐾 *Cabbage-Stir Fried*

1	small cabbage head	1	tablespoon salt
2	tablespoons oil	½	tablespoon sugar

Quarter and core cabbage. Cut into small chunks. Sprinkle with water. Heat pan, add oil and cabbage. Stir-fry 2 minutes, lower heat if cabbage starts to brown. Add salt and sugar mix. Add 2 tablespoons water and cook covered for about 2 more minutes. Toss well.

Jane McLane

Sweet and Sour Red Cabbage

1	medium cooking apple with peel, chopped	1	medium-sized red cabbage, shredded
1	medium onion	1	cup sugar
1	tablespoon bacon drippings	½	cup vinegar
			Pinch of salt

Sauté apple and onion in bacon drippings. Add cabbage, sugar, vinegar and salt. Simmer for 1 hour.

Mrs. Richard Beckmann and Peggy Durden

Marinated Carrots

1	bunch carrots, sliced	1	can cream of tomato soup
½	scant cup oil	1	onion, chopped
½	scant cup vinegar	1	bell pepper, chopped
½	scant cup sugar		

Parboil carrots until tender. Marinate in remaining ingredients. Chill overnight.

Mrs. Robert Scruggs

Carrot Casserole

12 carrots	2 cups milk
¼ cup butter	⅛ teaspoon pepper
1 small onion, chopped	¼ teaspoon celery salt
¼ cup flour	2 cups grated mild Cheddar
1 teaspoon salt	cheese
¼ teaspoon dry mustard	3 cups buttered breadcrumbs

Pare and slice carrots and cook in saucepan in small amount of water until just tender. Drain. Add butter and onion to carrots in saucepan and cook gently 2 to 3 minutes. For sauce, mix flour, salt and mustard, stirring well and add milk gradually, stirring until smooth. Add pepper and celery salt. In 2-quart casserole dish, put layer of carrots, layer of cheese, etc. ending with cheese. Pour on sauce. Top with breadcrumbs. Bake uncovered at 325 degrees for 25 minutes, or until breadcrumbs are brown.

Mrs. A. R. Pitts

Celery Casserole

3 cups celery, chopped	½ cup sliced mushrooms
1 small can water chestnuts, sliced	½ cup crushed croutons
¼ cup slivered almonds	¼ cup cream

Cream Sauce

3 tablespoons butter	1 cup chicken broth
3 tablespoons flour	⅛ tablespoon curry powder
¾ cup cream	

Cook celery 5 minutes, then drain. Layer celery, almonds, water chestnuts and mushrooms. Pour cream sauce over this. Sprinkle ½ cup crushed croutons on top. Dribble ¼ cup cream over this. Bake 35 minutes at 325 degrees. One layer of onions may also be added.

Sara Holt

Carrot Ring

1	cup shortening	1	tablespoon lemon juice
¾	cup light brown sugar	1½	cups flour
¼	cup white sugar	1	tablespoon baking powder
4	eggs	½	tablespoon baking soda
2	cups grated carrots	1	tablespoon cinnamon
1	tablespoon water	½	tablespoon salt

Combine shortening, sugars and eggs. Mix well. Add carrots, water and lemon juice. Sift dry ingredients; add to first mixture. Pour into well-greased mold or Bundt pan. Bake at 350 degrees for 45 minutes. Let stand 5 minutes. Turn out onto serving plate. Add green peas to center and trim outside with broccoli.

Serves 8 to 10

Frances Golivesky

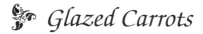

Glazed Carrots

1	pound carrots	2	tablespoons sugar
	Salt to taste	4	thin lemon slices
3	tablespoons butter		

Cook carrots in salted water, drain. Melt butter; add sugar, lemon slices, and carrots. Cook over medium heat until tender or desired texture.

Serves 4

Jerry Powers

Cranberry Soufflé

2	cups fresh cranberries	1	cup oatmeal
2	cups chopped apples	¾	cup chopped pecans
¾	cup brown sugar	1	stick butter, melted
¾	cup sugar		

Alternate cranberries, apples, brown and white sugar, oatmeal and nuts in a buttered dish. Repeat. Pour melted butter over all of it. Bake 45 to 60 minutes at 350 degrees.

Barbara Griffin

Corn Soufflé

5	tablespoons sugar	2	cups whole kernel corn
½	cup flour	¼	cup butter, melted
1	teaspoon salt	1	quart milk
4	eggs, beaten		

Mix sugar, flour and salt. Add eggs, corn, and butter. Stir well then add milk. To bake, pour corn mixture into a buttered shallow pan so that the mixture is not more than 2 inches deep. Bake at 350 degrees and after 15 minutes insert a spatula and lift the corn carefully from the bottom on all parts of the pan. Do not stir. Repeat the process in 10 minutes, then allow to brown.

Mrs. Arthur Smith

Curried Fruit

1	(20-ounce) can pear halves		Maraschino cherries
1	(20-ounce) can peach halves	½	cup butter
1	can pineapple chunks or half slices	1	cup light brown sugar
2	cups plums or prunes	4	teaspoons curry powder

Drain and dry fruit. In a flat casserole dish, layer butter, brown sugar and curry powder and arrange fruit over it. Bake at 350 degrees for 45 to 60 minutes.

Mrs. Grady Durden

Scalloped Eggplant

2	medium eggplant, peeled and cut in ⅔-inch cubes	1	small onion, chopped
2	tablespoons melted butter	1	cup dry breadcrumbs or crushed crackers
	Salt and pepper to taste	½	cup grated Cheddar cheese
1	egg, beaten	½	cup buttered breadcrumbs

Cook eggplant until tender. Drain thoroughly. Add butter, salt, pepper, egg, onion and dry breadcrumbs. Mix well. Place in greased baking dish. Cover with grated cheese, then buttered breadcrumbs. Bake at 375 degrees for about 25 minutes.

Makes 6 servings

Mrs. R.C. Elliott

Eggplant Casserole #1

2	pound eggplant	¼	teaspoon pepper
2	onions	2	eggs
½	stick butter	¾	cup cream
1	teaspoon salt	1	cup cornbread dressing mix

Stew eggplant and onions until tender. Drain, add butter, salt, pepper, eggs, cream and dressing mix. Place in casserole dish and top with ½ cup grated cheese. Bake at 350 degrees for 20 to 25 minutes.

Substitute squash for eggplant.

Mrs. L.O. Smith

Eggplant Casserole #2

1	large eggplant, cubed and cooked until tender	1	tablespoon onion juice
1½	cups cream sauce	1	teaspoon salt
2	cups grated cheese	2	eggs, beaten slightly
1	tablespoon catsup	2	cups breadcrumbs

Combine all ingredients. Pour into buttered casserole dish and cook slowly for about an hour. Top with extra breadcrumbs before baking if desired.

Mrs. James Noell, Jr.

Eggplant Casserole #3

1	eggplant, sliced		Salt and pepper to taste
	Fresh or canned tomatoes	1	can cream of mushroom soup
1	large onion, sliced	6	ounces sharp cheese, grated

Slice eggplant and tomatoes. Drain tomatoes if canned. Slice onion. Alternate layers of eggplant, tomatoes, and onion in a casserole dish. Season with salt and pepper. Top with undiluted mushroom soup. Use 2 cans, depending on size of eggplant. Sprinkle cheese on top of casserole. Bake at 325 degrees for 1 hour.

Barbara Griffin

Eggplant Soufflé #1

2	medium eggplant, peeled	¾	cup soft breadcrumbs
2	tablespoons butter	2	tablespoons grated onion
2	tablespoons flour	1	tablespoon catsup
1	cup milk	1	teaspoon salt
½	cup grated cheese	2	eggs, separated

Cut eggplant into small pieces. Cook until tender. Mash fine and set aside. Melt butter; add flour and blend until smooth. Add milk, eggplant, cheese, breadcrumbs, onion, catsup, salt and beaten egg yolks. Fold in beaten egg whites. Bake in buttered baking dish at 350 to 375 degrees for 35 to 40 minutes.

Makes 8 servings

Mrs. R. C. Elliott

Eggplant Soufflé #2

1	large eggplant (or 2 medium ones)		Salt, pepper, Worcestershire sauce and nutmeg to taste
2	eggs		
¼	cup milk	1	tablespoon butter
	Juice of 1 small onion (or to taste)		Crushed butter flavored crackers

Peel and slice eggplant and soak in salt water about 45 minutes. Drain and boil in fresh water. When done, drain well and mash fine. Beat eggs and combine with milk. Add this and all seasonings to eggplant. Put in buttered casserole dish and top with finely crushed butter flavored crackers, dotted with extra butter. Bake at 325 degrees for 30 to 40 minutes or until knife put into center comes out dry.

Mrs. Maxwell Oliver

Eggplant Casserole Patrice

1	eggplant		Salt and pepper
4	medium tomatoes		Sugar
2	green bell peppers, chopped	¾	pound Cheddar cheese,
1	large onion, chopped		sliced
	Garlic salt		

Slice unpeeled eggplant in 1½-inch slices and parboil for a few minutes. Put layer of eggplant in large flat casserole dish, then layer of tomatoes. Sprinkle with bell pepper, onion and seasonings. Cover with cheese, repeat layers. Cover and bake at 400 degrees for 30 minutes. Remove cover, reduce heat to 350 degrees and bake 30 minutes more.

Ingrid Carroll

Green Bean and Corn Casserole

1	can French style green beans, drained	½	cup grated cheese
1	can shoe-peg corn, drained	1	cup cream of celery soup
½	cup chopped onion	½	cup sour cream

Mix the above ingredients together and pour into 2 (2-quart) casserole dishes. Cover with topping.

Topping

1	sleeve round, butter crackers	¾	cup melted margarine

Bake at 350 for 30 minutes.

Sharon Coleman

180

Green Bean Casserole #1

	Green beans, fresh or canned	⅓	**cup milk**
1	**can cream of chicken soup**		**Canned French fried onion rings**

Place green beans in casserole dish. Blend soup with milk. Pour over beans. Top with onion rings. Bake at 400 degrees until bubbly, about 15 minutes.

Mrs. A.B. Smith

Green Bean Casserole #2

2	**cans whole green beans**	**2**	**tablespoons parsley flakes**
½	**cup thinly sliced onions**	**3**	**tablespoons butter**

Cook beans with chosen seasoning for 30 minutes. Drain. Cook onions and parsley in butter on low heat for about 5 minutes. Pour into casserole dish.

Sauce

3	**tablespoons butter**	**½**	**pint sour cream**
2	**tablespoons flour**		**Grated rind of 1 lemon**

Toss beans in sauce. Place in casserole dish.

Topping

¾	**cup soda crackers, crumbled**	**¾**	**cup sharp Cheddar cheese, grated**
¾	**stick butter**		

Blend crackers, butter and cheese together. Pour topping over casserole. Bake 30 minutes at 325 degrees.

Mrs. Walton Carter

Green Bean Casserole #3

3	cans French style green beans	1	tablespoon sugar
2	tablespoons butter	1	small onion
2	tablespoons flour	1	pint sour cream
1	teaspoon salt	½	pound cheese, grated
¼	teaspoon pepper	2	cups corn flakes

Drain beans. Combine butter, flour, salt, pepper, sugar, onions and sour cream in saucepan. Cook and stir until thick. Combine beans with sauce and pour into greased casserole dish. Cover with grated cheese. Crush corn flakes, add butter, and sprinkle on top casserole. Bake 20 to 30 minutes at 400 degrees.

Mrs. Ed Willis

Green Bean Casserole #4

½	cup butter	1	teaspoon seasoned salt flavor enhancer
¼	cup flour	¾	pound cheese grated, or sliced
2	cups milk		
1	large onion, thinly sliced	3	cans green beans
2	cans sliced mushrooms	2	medium cans sliced water chestnuts
½	teaspoon hot pepper sauce		
2	teaspoons soy sauce	½	can slivered almonds
1	teaspoon salt		Breadcrumbs
½	teaspoon pepper		Parmesan cheese

Make white sauce of butter, flour, and milk. Brown onions and mushrooms lightly and add. Add seasonings, then cheese. Add beans and nuts last. Sprinkle with breadcrumbs and Parmesan cheese. Bake at 375 degrees for 20 minutes.

Serves 12

Mrs. C. C. Varnedoe

Green Bean Casserole #5

2	tablespoons butter	2	cans French style green beans
2	tablespoons flour		Salt and pepper
½	pint sour cream		Sliced Swiss cheese
1	medium onion, grated	1	can French fried onions

Make white sauce with butter, flour and sour cream; add onions and beans. Salt and pepper to taste. Put into buttered 1-quart casserole dish and put slices of Swiss cheese on top. Bake about 20 minutes at 350 to 375 degrees, until bubbly, then add French fried onions and brown about 5 to 10 minutes.

Leigh Smith

French Green Bean Casserole

2	packages frozen French style green beans	1	can cream of mushrooms soup grated sharp cheese
1	can bean sprouts	1	can French fried onion rings chopped onion (optional)
1	can water chestnuts		

Prepare beans according to package directions and drain. Drain bean sprouts and water chestnuts. Chop chestnuts, and then mix beans, bean sprouts, chestnuts and onion (if used). Spread in alternate layers with the soup and grated cheese. Top with onion rings. Bake at 300 degrees for 20 to 30 minutes.

Mrs. Blake Ellis

Cold Green Beans

2	cans whole green beans	½	cup sugar
1	onion, sliced	¼	cup water
	Seasoned salt flavor enhancer	3	teaspoons salad oil
½	cup white vinegar		Salt

Spread layers of beans and onion, sprinkled with seasoned salt flavor enhancer, in bowl. Combine vinegar, sugar, water, oil and salt to make syrup. Boil 2 minutes. Cool. Pour over beans and onions. Refrigerate at least overnight.

Mrs. Bill Keller

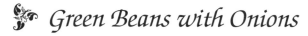

Green Beans with Onions

2	packages French style green beans, frozen	2	tablespoons chopped garlic
½	cup butter	3	tablespoons dry white wine
½	cup slivered almonds	½	tablespoon salt
2	tablespoons brown sugar	¼	tablespoon pepper
		1	large jar small onions

Prepare beans according to directions. Drain. Melt butter in skillet with tight lid. Stir in almonds, sugar, garlic, wine and seasonings. Add drained onions and simmer 20 to 30 minutes, coating onions well. Pour over hot beans.

Serves 6

Betty Dow Templeton

Mushroom Casserole

8	slices bread, trimmed and broken	½	cup mayonnaise
1	pound fresh mushrooms, sautéed	1	tablespoon salt
		½	tablespoon pepper
½	cup chopped onion	2	eggs
½	cup chopped celery	1½	cups milk
½	cup chopped green pepper	1	can mushroom soup
			Grated cheese

Place half the breadcrumbs in bottom of casserole dish. Combine mushrooms with onion, celery, green peppers, mayonnaise, salt and pepper. Pour mushroom mixture over breadcrumbs, and put remaining bread over top. Combine beaten eggs with milk. Pour over casserole and let stand in refrigerator overnight. Before baking pour 1 can mushroom soup over top of casserole. Bake at 325 degrees for 50 minutes. Sprinkle grated cheese over top of casserole 10 minutes before removing from the oven.

Teresa Minchew

Baked Stuffed Onions

6-8	large white Bermuda or Vidalia onions	2	tablespoons parsley
2	quarts water	1	tablespoon marjoram
1	cube beef bullion	½	tablespoon paprika
1	cup chopped mushrooms	1	tablespoon salt
4	strips bacon, cooked crisp and chopped fine	⅛	tablespoon pepper
		2	tablespoons bacon drippings
1	cup breadcrumbs	3	tablespoons butter, melted

Slice thin slice off top of onions and peel. Boil onions in water and bullion cube until just tender. Remove centers, leaving about one quarter of onions. Invert and cool. Measure chopped onion centers to 1 cup. Add other ingredients and mix with bacon drippings and melted butter. Stuff onion shells with mixture. Bake about 20 minutes at 350 degrees.

Mrs. Joe M. Taylor

Onion Pie

1	cup butter cracker crumbs	¾	teaspoon salt
½	stick melted butter		Dash of coarse ground black pepper
2	cups thin sliced white onions	¼	cup grated sharp Cheddar cheese
2	tablespoons butter		Paprika
2	eggs		Parsley
¾	cup milk		

Mix cracker crumbs with ½ stick melted butter. Press into 8-inch pie plate. Sauté onion in 2 tablespoons butter until clear, but not brown. Spoon into cracker crust. Beat eggs with milk, salt and pepper. Pour over onions. Sprinkle cheese. Sprinkle paprika. Bake at 350 degrees for 30 minutes. Test with knife, when comes out clean, its ready. Garnish with parsley.

Mrs. Jim Owens

Onion-Celery-Almond Casserole

1	cup diced celery	½	cup blanched, slivered
2	jars boiled onions		almonds
1½-2	cups white sauce		Parmesan cheese
			Paprika

Cook celery in a little boiling salted water until tender. Drain. Drain onions. Make white sauce and season well. Layer onions, celery, and almonds in a buttered casserole dish. Cover with sauce. Sprinkle with Parmesan and paprika. Bake at 350 degrees until bubbly and brown.

Mrs. Henry T. Brice, Jr.

French Fried Onion Rings

1	large white onion	1	can condensed milk

Slice onion and chill in ice or ice water. Dip each ring in canned milk and then in flour and fry in deep fat until golden brown. These will stay crisp.

Mrs. Chandler Blanton

Hot Cheese Pineapple

2	cans pineapple chunks, drain and reserve juice	½	cup sugar
		1	pound mild Cheddar cheese
½	cup flour	1	tablespoon lemon juice

Coat pineapple chunks with flour and sugar. Layer pineapple and cheese. Pour ½ cup pineapple juice and lemon juice over this. Bake 1 hour at 325 degrees.

Peggy Gayle

English Pea Casserole

1	small onion, chopped	1	can asparagus, drain and
½	cup chopped celery		reserve juice
1	can tiny English peas, drain	1	can tomato sauce
	and reserve juice	1	can cream of mushroom soup
			Crumbled saltines

Add onion and celery to asparagus and pea liquid. Cook about 20 to 30 minutes. Layer peas and asparagus in casserole dish. Add tomato sauce and mushroom soup. Add onion and celery and some of liquid. Crumble saltine crackers and mix some with casserole. Top with additional crumbled saltines. Bake 400 degrees for 30 minutes.

Phyllis Drury

Aunt Ruth's Creole Peas

8	slices bacon	1½	cups celery, chopped
2	cans tiny English peas	1-2	large onions, chopped
2	cups white sauce	2	cans tomato soup, undiluted
	Tabasco sauce, to taste	6	hard-boiled eggs
1	tablespoon sugar	1	cup grated cheese
1	green pepper, chopped		

Fry bacon and drain on paper towel. Reserve about half bacon drippings and cook onion, pepper and celery in it until tender, but not brown. Add a little water if necessary. Make white sauce and season rather highly with Tabasco sauce. Add sugar. Mix together, pepper, celery, onions, white sauce and tomato soup. In a casserole dish, place a layer of peas, layer of above mixture, sliced eggs and crumbled bacon. Repeat, putting a layer of mixture on top. Sprinkle grated cheese over this. Bake at 325 degrees for 30 to 40 minutes.

Serves 10 to 12

Mrs. Henry T. Brice, Jr.

Deviled Peas

1	cup celery	1	cup grated sharp cheese
1	bell pepper, finely chopped	1	can mushroom soup
	Bacon drippings	1	can tomato soup
1	can English peas	½	cup chili sauce
1	can mushrooms	3	hard-boiled eggs, sliced
1	can pimiento		Breadcrumbs

Cook celery and bell pepper in bacon drippings until tender. Mix with other vegetables. Melt cheese in soups. Add chili sauce and eggs to soup mixture. Make layers of sauce and vegetables in large baking dish. Top with breadcrumbs and heat through.

Mrs. Jesse Parrott

Epicurean Peas

4	slices bacon	1	(20-ounce) can English
1	medium onion, chopped		peas, drained
	Bacon grease	2	tablespoons butter
1	tablespoon flour		Salt to taste
1	cup light cream or milk	¼	teaspoon pepper
		1	can mushrooms

Cook bacon. Crumble when crisp and set aside. Brown onion in bacon grease. Stir flour and milk until thickened. Add remaining ingredients including crumbled bacon. Bake at 350 degrees in greased casserole dish for about 20 minutes.

Mrs. Archie Griffin

 Broiled Peaches

1	can peach halves	Grape jelly
	Butter	Ground cinnamon
	Red raspberry jelly	Sugar

Drain peaches. Place peach halves, cut side up in a shallow baking pan. Dot centers with butter. Fill the centers with a little raspberry and grape jelly (half-and-half). Mix cinnamon and sugar together and sprinkle over peaches. Heat in 300 degrees or higher until juice bubbles in center, about 30 minutes.

Caroline Harris

🌿 *Duke's Special ~ John Wayne's Favorite!*

2	cans green chili peppers	⅔	cup evaporated milk
1	pound Monterey Jack cheese, shredded	⅓	teaspoon salt
1	pound Cheddar cheese, shredded	1	tablespoon flour
4	eggs, separated	⅛	teaspoon pepper
			Sliced tomatoes

Preheat oven to 325 degrees. Combine chilies and cheeses. Turn into well-buttered 12x8x2-inch casserole dish. Beat egg whites until they forms moist peaks. In a separate bowl combine egg yolks, milk, salt, flour, and pepper. Mix well. Fold egg whites into yolk mixture gently. Pour this mixture over cheese chili mixture, and with fork cut into mixture. Bake 30 minutes, remove from oven. Arrange sliced tomatoes over topping around edge of casserole. Bake 20 minutes longer or until knife inserted in center comes out clean. Garnish with sprinklings of chopped chilies.

Martha Grow

Spinach Casserole

2	packages frozen, chopped spinach	Salt and pepper
		Seasoned breadcrumbs
3	ounces cream cheese	Paprika
½	stick butter	1 can fried onion rings

Boil spinach approximately 10 minutes in salted water, drain and blend with butter and cream cheese in a blender or mixer. Salt and pepper to taste and pour into a buttered casserole dish and sprinkle a generous layer of breadcrumbs on top. Bake at 400 degrees until crumbs are brown, about 45 minutes. Sprinkle paprika over the outer edge of the casserole and pile canned onion rings in the middle of casserole just before serving. Warm the onion rings in the oven at low temperature for few minutes before garnishing the casserole.

Katherine A. Holmes

🌿 *Spinach Soufflé*

1	package frozen chopped spinach	¼	pound Cheddar cheese, cubed
3	eggs	¼	pound American cheese, cubed
4	tablespoons flour	1	pound cottage cheese
¼	cup butter		
	Salt and pepper to taste		

Cook spinach in boiling water. Drain and cool. Beat eggs; add spinach, flour, butter, salt and pepper, stirring to blend while adding the ingredients. Fold in cubed cheeses and cottage cheese. Bake 1 hour at 350 degrees.

This can be baked ahead and frozen.

Sue Bentley

🌿 *Spinach and Artichoke Casserole*

2	(10-ounce) packages, frozen spinach	1	tablespoon lemon juice
½	cup butter, melted	1	cup artichoke hearts, drained
1	(8-ounce) package cream cheese		Cracker crumbs
			Parmesan cheese

Grease casserole dish. Cook spinach according to directions. To cooked spinach add butter, cream cheese and lemon juice. Blend together. Place artichokes on bottom of casserole dish. Add spinach mixture. Top with cracker crumbs and Parmesan cheese. Dot with butter. Bake at 350 degrees for 25 minutes.

Betty Jean Daugharty

Acorn Squash

1	acorn squash, halved and seeded	2	tablespoons brown sugar
2	tablespoons chopped onion	1	tablespoon
			Salt and nutmeg to taste

Fill each squash half with 1 tablespoon of onion, 1 tablespoon brown sugar and ½ tablespoon butter. Salt and nutmeg to taste. Put a little water in bottom of baking pan and bake at 350 degrees for 1 hour and 15 minutes or until tender.

Mrs. John Rudolph

Baked Squash

Select 8 to 10 small tender yellow crookneck squash. Wash and cut necks off. Boil whole until just tender. Drain. Cut in halves lengthwise and scoop out inside, reserving shells to stuff. Mix what you have scooped out with.

1	beaten egg	1	teaspoon salt (or to taste)
1	cup sharp grated cheese	1	teaspoon parsley
2	tablespoons grated onion		(or to taste)
1	teaspoon salt (or to taste)		

Stuff shells of squash, which have been placed on cookie tin with above mixture and top with buttered cracker crumbs. Bake at 350 degrees until hot and slightly brown, 20 to 30 minutes.

Mrs. Marie Crockett

Squash Casserole #1

2	onions	1	small jar pimentos
2	carrots		Celery salt, to taste
3	pounds squash		Oregano, to taste
2	teaspoons salt		Pepper, to taste
1	can cream of chicken soup	1	stick butter
1	small carton sour cream	1	cup bread dressing mix

Slice onions, carrots, and squash; salt and cook with small amount of water. Combine soup, sour cream, and pimentos. Season with celery salt, oregano and pepper. Melt 1 stick butter in hot drained squash and add cream mixture and bread dressing mix. Put into 2 small dishes or 1 large flat casserole dish and top with a little dry dressing mix. Bake at 350 degrees for 30 minutes.

Mrs. Joyce Mixson

Squash Casserole #2

¾	stick butter	1	teaspoon salt
1	cup evaporated milk	½	teaspoon pepper
2	cups breadcrumbs	2	eggs
2	cups cooked squash, mashed	1	cup chopped onion
		1	cup grated Cheddar cheese

Melt butter in hot milk and pour over breadcrumbs. Mix well and add to mashed squash. Add seasonings. Beat eggs and then add eggs and onions to mixture. Pour into greased 2-quart baking dish. Top with cheese. Bake at 375 degrees for about 40 minutes.

Serves 6

Mrs. E.G. Barham

Squash Casserole #3

2	pounds squash	½	cup mayonnaise
½	cup chopped onion	½	cup pimentos
¼	cup chopped bell pepper	1	tablespoon sugar
	Soda crackers	½	cup nuts
½	stick butter	½	cup grated sharp cheese
2	eggs		

Cook squash, onion, and bell pepper in salted water until tender. Drain and mash. Add a few soda crackers and butter with all other ingredients except cheese. Top with cheese. Place in shallow dish. Dot with butter. Bake 30 to 40 minutes at 350 degrees.

Judy DeMott

Squash Casserole #4

2	pounds squash, chopped	1	(8-ounce) carton sour cream
1	onion, chopped	½	cup melted butter
½	tablespoon salt	1	(8-ounce) package herb
1	tablespoon pepper		seasoned stuffing mix
1	can cream of chicken soup		

Combine squash, onion, and seasonings. Cook until tender. Drain squash. Pour into casserole dish with remaining ingredients except stuffing mix. Add stuffing mix on top. Bake until bubbly and brown at 325 degrees for approximately 30 minutes.

Jean Bynum

Squash Soufflé #1

½	cup finely chopped onion	4	tablespoons chopped
4	tablespoons butter		pimentos
4	pounds yellow or white	1	tablespoon salt
	squash	¼	teaspoon pepper
1½	cups fine breadcrumbs	2	eggs, beaten

Sauté onion in the butter until tender and light brown. Wash and slice squash. Cook in boiling, salted water until tender. Drain and put through food chopper, electric blender, or food mill. Add sautéed onion, breadcrumbs, pimentos and seasonings. Add eggs and beat thoroughly. Pour into a well-buttered casserole dish and cook at 350 degrees for 30 minutes.

Mrs. Sam L. Harvey, Jr.

Squash Soufflé #2

1	can squash (may use fresh cooked squash)
1	cup white sauce
1	tablespoon grated onion
¼	teaspoon prepared mustard
¼	cup sugar
	Salt and pepper
2	eggs
	Breadcrumbs

Drain squash. Mash up and mix with white sauce, grated onion, mustard, sugar, salt and pepper to taste. Beat eggs and fold in. Place in casserole and top with breadcrumbs. Bake at 350 degrees about 30 minutes or until done.

Serves 5

Mrs. Arthur McLane

Escalloped Tomatoes

1	small onion, chopped
¼	cup butter
1¼	cups dry breadcrumbs
½	cup brown sugar
1	(20-ounce) can tomatoes
1	teaspoon salt
⅛	teaspoon pepper

Sauté onion in butter, using an iron frying pan. Add breadcrumbs and sugar; cook slowly. Stir in tomatoes and seasoning. Place mixture in buttered shallow pan and bake 45 minutes at 325 to 350 degrees.

Mrs. Arthur Smith

Tomato Casserole

1	can tomato sauce
1	large can tomatoes
½	cup chopped onions
4-5	slices buttered dry toast, broken into pieces
1	cup chopped celery
1	tablespoon sugar
¾	cup shredded cheese
⅓	cup chopped bell pepper

Mix all together and top with extra cheese and extra toast crumbs. Bake at 350 degrees for 45 minutes.

Mike Vallotton

Stuffed Tomatoes

6	tomatoes	1	tablespoon onion juice
6	slices bacon, crisp and crumbled	½	tablespoon salt
¼	cup chopped celery	½	cup grated cheese
⅛	tablespoon pepper	2	tablespoons butter
1	cup soft breadcrumbs	¼	cup water

Wash but do not peel tomatoes. Cut top from each and scoop out centers. Combine tomato pulp with bacon, celery, pepper, breadcrumbs, onion juice, salt, and half the cheese. Fill tomatoes with mixture, cover with remaining cheese and dot with butter. Place in shallow baking dish with water. Bake at 300 degrees for 30 minutes.

Serves 6

Joy Puckett

Mixed Vegetable Mornay

2	packages frozen mixed vegetables	¼	teaspoon salt
¼	cup water	⅛	teaspoon garlic salt
1	teaspoon salt		Pinch of nutmeg
¼	teaspoon garlic salt		Pinch of thyme
3	tablespoons melted butter, separated	2	cups reserved vegetable liquid and milk
¼	cup butter	¼	cup grated Parmesan cheese
¼	cup flour		

Cook vegetables until tender in water. Drain; reserve liquid for sauce. Add salt, garlic salt and 2 tablespoons of butter to vegetables; mix lightly. Put in greased baking dish. Top with Mornay Sauce. To make sauce: Melt butter. Blend in flour, salt, garlic salt and spices until smooth. Add liquid and cook over low heat, stirring constantly until mixture comes to a boil and thickens. Add cheese; stir until melted. After topping vegetable mixture with Mornay Sauce, combine breadcrumbs with rest of butter and sprinkle over sauce. Bake in 350 degrees oven for 30 minutes.

Mrs. James M. Allen

Tomatoes Au Gratin

2	(20-ounce) cans tomatoes	½	heaping cup grated
½	cup breadcrumbs		Parmesan cheese
1	teaspoon basil	½	scant cup breadcrumbs
	Salt and pepper to taste	2	scant tablespoons olive oil

Drain off about ½ cup of juice from each of the 2 cans of tomatoes. Put tomatoes and remaining juice into a baking dish and stir into them ½ cup of breadcrumbs, basil, and salt and pepper to taste. Mix together, Parmesan cheese and ½ cup of breadcrumbs. Spread over the top of the tomatoes. Dot with olive oil. Bake for 20 minutes in a 375 degrees oven.

Mrs. Ed Blalock

Goldie's Turnips

1	bunch of turnips	Salt to taste
1	piece of ham hock or fresh pork	

Season with salt to taste. Use a big pot. Put 3½ to 4 cups of water in it, and boil meat for 30 minutes. Wash bunch of turnips well while meat is boiling. Put turnips into pot. When you bring to a boil, turn turnips over and stir and turn heat down to medium. Salt. Cook at least 1½ hours, covered.

Mrs. John Rudolph

Vegetable Casserole

2	packages lima beans	1	medium onion, chopped
2	packages French style green beans	1	teaspoon prepared mustard
		1	teaspoon lemon juice
2	packages peas	1	teaspoon Worcestershire sauce
1½	cups mayonnaise		
3	hard-boiled eggs, grated		Dash of garlic

Cook the Lima beans, green beans, and peas separately. When done mix with mayonnaise, eggs, onion, mustard, lemon juice, Worcestershire sauce and garlic. Bake in 2 large casserole dishes until thoroughly heated.

Mrs. Bob Hornbuckle

Zucchini

3	pounds zucchini, parboiled and cut in 1-inch rounds
1	medium onion
¼	bell pepper
1	small garlic clove, chopped
1	tablespoon butter
1	tablespoon bacon drippings
1	can tomatoes
	Flour or cornstarch
	Grated Parmesan cheese

Quarter zucchini in salty water until tender when pierced with a fork. Do not overcook. To make sauce combine onion, pepper and garlic over low heat in butter and bacon drippings. Cook until tender. Add tomatoes and heat thoroughly, then thicken with flour or cornstarch. Squash should be done by this time. Drain and turn into a baking dish. Pour sauce over squash and top with grated Parmesan cheese. Bake in 375 degree oven until bubbly.

Mrs. D.L. Burns

Grits Casserole #1

1½	cups regular grits
6	cups boiling water
2	tablespoons seasoned salt
1	tablespoon onion salt
1	tablespoon garlic salt
¾	tablespoon Worcestershire sauce
½	cup butter
3	eggs, beaten
½	pound Cheddar cheese
1	roll garlic cheese
	Red pepper and paprika
	Corn flakes

Cook grits in boiling water 5 minutes. Stir in salts, Worcestershire sauce, and butter. Stir eggs into grits. Add cheeses. Pour into a 2-quart soufflé dish. Sprinkle red pepper and paprika on top. Top with Corn Flakes. Cover and refrigerate overnight. Bake at 350 degrees for 1½ hours.

Serves 12 to 16

Susan Crago

Grits Casserole #2

1	cup raw grits	1	roll garlic cheese
4	cups water	2	eggs, beaten
1	teaspoon salt	1	cup milk
1	stick butter		Corn flakes

Cook grits in water with salt. When done, add butter and cheese to grits. Stir until melted. Add eggs and milk. Pour into deep casserole dish and cover with crushed corn flakes. Bake at 350 degrees for 40 minutes.

Mrs. Joyce Mixson

Baked Hominy Bread

1	cup grits	½	cup or so milk
3	eggs, beaten		Salt and pepper to taste
1	cup grated New York sharp Cheddar cheese		Breadcrumbs

Cook grits as directed. When done mash with fork and add beaten eggs, cheese, milk, salt, pepper and some breadcrumbs to thicken. It should be consistency of mashed potatoes. Top with more grated cheese and breadcrumbs. Bake at 400 degrees for 30 minutes.

Mrs. Marie Crockett

Pasta Casserole Marie-Blanche

1	cup cream style cottage cheese	⅓	cup chopped chives
1	cup sour cream	¾	(8-ounce) package angel hair pasta, cooked and drained
½	teaspoon salt		
½	teaspoon red pepper	1	tablespoon butter

Combine cottage cheese, sour cream, salt, pepper and chives, then add noodles. Pour into buttered 2-quart casserole dish and dot top with 1 tablespoon butter. Bake about 20 minutes or until it bubbles at 350 degrees.

Mrs. Jerry Purvis

🍴 *Macaroni and Cheese*

1	can cream of mushroom soup
½	cup mayonnaise
2	cups grated sharp Cheddar cheese
1	tablespoon grated onion
2	tablespoons snipped fresh parsley
1	(7-ounce) package macaroni, cooked and drained
½	cup crushed cheese crackers

Combine mushroom soup, mayonnaise, cheese, onion, and parsley. Mix with macaroni and place in a greased shallow 2-quart baking dish. Top with crushed crackers. Bake at 350 degrees for 35 to 40 minutes.

Serves 6 to 8

Teresa Minchew

🍴 *Macaroni Casserole*

1	box macaroni, cooked and drained
2	cans mushroom soup
1	soup can of milk
1	medium can mushrooms, drained
1	small jar pimentos
1	bell pepper
1	onion
¾	cup mayonnaise
½	pound sharp grated cheese
	Crackers
	Melted butter

Mix all ingredients together, except crackers. Crush crackers, mix with melted butter and put on top. Bake at 350 degrees for approximately 30 minutes.

Sharon Mink

Potatoes with Cheese

6	large potatoes
12	ounces Cheddar cheese
2	tablespoons grated onion
	Salt and pepper

Boil potatoes whole, not peeled. When tender, drain and cool. Peel potatoes and grate potatoes. Grate cheese. Toss onion and potatoes together. Butter a 1-quart casserole dish and arrange alternate layers of cheese and potatoes with salt and pepper. Bake at 350 degrees for 40 minutes.

Mrs. Buddy Webb

🌿 *Potato Casserole*

2	pounds frozen hash brown potatoes, crumbled
1	can cream of chicken soup
1	stick butter, melted
½	cup chopped onion
2	cups shredded sharp cheese
1	cup sour cream
1	tablespoon salt
	Buttered corn flakes

Combine all ingredients except corn flakes. Turn into casserole dish. Top with buttered corn flakes. Cook 1 hour at 350 degrees.

Serves 10 to 12

Sally Moritz

Scalloped Potatoes #1

½	green pepper
1	onion
1	jar pimentos
6	Irish potatoes, thinly sliced
	Salt and pepper to taste
1	can mushroom soup
½	can whole milk (use soup can to measure)
	Shredded Cheddar cheese

Grate the pepper and onion. Mix with pimentos. In large casserole dish, place layer of sliced potatoes, layer of pepper-onion mixture, ending with potatoes. Heat soup and milk in a saucepan and pour over potatoes. Cover with cheese and bake at 375 degrees until potatoes are tender.

Mrs. Ed Garvin

Scalloped Potatoes #2

1	can Cheddar cheese soup
½	cup milk
4	cups thinly sliced potatoes
1	small onion, thinly sliced
1	tablespoon butter
	Paprika

Stir cheese soup until smooth, gradually add milk. In buttered 1½-quart casserole dish, arrange alternate layers of potatoes, onion and sauce plus salt and pepper. Dot top with butter. Sprinkle generously with paprika. Cover and bake at 375 degrees for 1 hour. Uncover and bake 15 minutes more.

Mrs. Jack Sullivan

Potato Topper for Baked Potatoes

1	cup shredded sharp Cheddar cheese
½	cup sour cream

¼   cup soft butter
2   tablespoons chopped green onion

Blend above ingredients. Serve at room temperature.

Makes 1 cup

Mrs. Joe C. Stubbs

Sweet Potato Soufflé #1

3   well beaten eggs
1   cup milk
3   cups mashed sweet potatoes (baked fresh, peeled and mashed or from can)
1   stick butter
Cinnamon and nutmeg

Grated lemon peel or
1 teaspoon fresh orange juice
1   cup sugar
Pecans
Raisins
Marshmallows

Mix eggs and milk with mashed sweet potatoes. Then add butter, cinnamon and nutmeg to taste, lemon peel or orange juice and sugar. Beat these ingredients together and place in casserole dish. On top of the mixture, place pecans and raisins. Bake for 30 minutes at 350 degrees. Just before removing from oven, spread marshmallows on top of the casserole and let them melt.

Mrs. Marie Crockett

Sweet Potato Soufflé #2

3   cups cooked sweet potatoes
¼   teaspoon salt
2   tablespoons butter
¼   teaspoon walnut flavoring
2   eggs

⅓   cup undiluted evaporated milk
1   cup sugar
½   cup pecans or walnuts
2-3 large marshmallows

Mash potatoes, add salt, butter and walnut flavoring. Beat with mixer until light and fluffy, adding eggs, one at a time. Add milk and sugar gradually. Add nuts and 2 or 3 marshmallows. Pour in greased baking dish and garnish with extra marshmallows. Bake 30 minutes at 350 degrees.

Mrs. John Rudolph

Sweet Potato Casserole #1

1	cup sugar	⅓	stick margarine, melted
3	cups mashed sweet potatoes	½	tablespoon salt
½	cup milk	1	tablespoon vanilla
2	eggs		

Mix and pour into greased casserole dish.

Topping

1	cup brown sugar	⅓	stick butter, melted
½	cup flour	1	cup pecans

Bake at 350 degrees for 30 minutes. 15 minutes covered and 15 minutes uncovered.

Sheila Myddleton

Sweet Potato Casserole #2

2	cups mashed sweet potatoes	½	cup milk
1	cup light brown sugar	1	cup coconut
½	cup crushed pineapple	1	egg
1	tablespoon vanilla	3	tablespoons butter
½	cup nuts		

Mix above ingredients and bake at 300 degrees for 20 or 30 minutes.

Topping

2	tablespoons flour	3	tablespoons corn syrup
⅓	cup brown sugar	2	tablespoons butter
½	cup nuts		

Mix and put on top of casserole. Bake a few minutes longer.

Peggy Gayle

Brown Rice

2	cups rice	1	small can mushrooms with
2	tablespoons beef flavoring		juice
2	cups hot water	¼	teaspoon salt
1	onion, chopped		

Brown rice in dry iron skillet. Place in casserole dish. Make beef bouillon from beef flavoring and water. Pour over rice. Brown onion in butter and add mushrooms, juice and salt, mixing well. Bake uncovered for 20 minutes at 400 degrees.

Mrs. Avalon Griffin

Mother's Rice Casserole

1	cup raw rice	1	can cream of mushroom soup
½	stick butter, melted	1	small can mushrooms,
1	can consommé		drained

Combine all ingredients. Bake at 350 degrees Bake covered for 30 minutes, stir and leave uncovered for 30 minutes more.

Joy Puckett

Rice Casserole

2	packages instant noodle	1	bell pepper
	soup mix	1	large onion
½	cup raw rice	2	stalks celery
4½	cups water	1	stick butter

Boil soup mix and rice in water for 7 minutes. Cook pepper, onion and celery in butter until tender. Place all in covered casserole dish and bake 1 hour at 350 degrees.

Serves 8

Mrs. Courtney B. Foy

℘ *Green Chili Pepper Rice Casserole*

1 cup chopped onion	½ teaspoon salt
¼ cup butter	⅛ teaspoon pepper
4 cups cooked rice	2 cups grated sharp cheese
1 cup sour cream	2 (4-ounce) cans green chili
1 cup cream style cottage	peppers
cheese	Chopped parsley
1 large bay leaf, crumbled	

In large skillet, sauté onion in hot butter until golden brown. Remove from heat; stir in rice, sour cream, cottage cheese, bay leaf, salt and pepper. Toss to mix well. Layer half of rice mixture in buttered baking dish. Then half of drained peppers (cut up, leaving seeds) sprinkle with half of cheese. Repeat. Bake at 375 degrees uncovered for 25 minutes. Sprinkle with chopped parsley.

Carol Woodall

Breads

Breads

Angel Biscuit 207
Biscuits 207
Apricot Bread 207
Banana Bread #1 208
Banana Bread #2 208
Banana Bread #3 208
Banana Nut Muffins 209
Bran Muffins 209
Caraway Sticks 210
Cheese Biscuits 210
Cinnamon Swirls 210
Corn Bread 211
Owendaw Corn Bread 211
Sour Cream Corn Bread 211
Corn Muffins 212
Mexican Corn Bread 212
Corn Fritters 212
Cranberry Bread 213
Cranberry Banana Bread 213
Double Braided Bread 214
Crescent Poppy Seed Rolls 214
Date Muffins 215
Dill Bread 215
Doughnuts 215
Icebox Rolls 216

Herbed Cheese Bread 216
Homemade Bread 217
Hot Cakes 217
Granny's Muffins 218
Hush Puppies #1 218
Hush Puppies #2 218
Irish Soda Bread 219
Six Week Muffins 219
Magic Muffins 219
Prune Muffins 220
Rye Bread Casserole 220
Sesame Bread 220
Rye Batter's Bread 221
Spoon Bread 221
Sweet Potato Biscuits 221
Quick Yeast Rolls 222
Marge's Onion Sesame Bread 222
Virginia Spoon Bread 222
Sally Lunn 223
Yeast Rolls 223
No-Knead Rolls 223
Waffles #1 224
Waffles #2 224
Freezer Yeast Rolls 224

Angel Biscuit

5	cups flour	¼	cup sugar
3	teaspoons baking powder	1	cup shortening
1	teaspoon soda	2	cups buttermilk
1	teaspoon salt	2	tablespoons warm water
1	package dry yeast		

Sift and measure flour. Sift again with dry ingredients, using a large bowl. Cut in shortening. Add buttermilk and yeast dissolved in warm water. Mix well. Roll out on floured board. Cut and cook on greased pan at 425 degrees for 15 minutes. Biscuits are best if started in cold oven. Dough will keep well in refrigerator for up to 2 weeks. After cutting refrigerated dough, let sit at room temperature about 10 to 15 minutes before cooking for best results.

Mrs. Quentin Lawson

 # Biscuits

1	cup self-rising flour	½	cup sour cream
1	stick butter		

Combine all ingredients. Bake 10 minutes at 400 degrees

Beverly Edwards

Apricot Bread

2	cups dried apricots, cut into pieces	2	eggs
1	cup boiling water	3	cups flour
4	tablespoons butter	2	teaspoons baking powder
1½	cups sugar	½	teaspoon salt
		1	cup nuts

Cover apricots with boiling water and let stand for 15 minutes. Cream the butter and sugar. Add eggs, the apricots and the water they are in. Sift flour, baking powder and salt. Stir into apricot mixture. Add nuts. Pour into 1 large or 2 small loaf pans, greased. Bake at 325 degrees for 1 hour.

Mrs. Diane Smith

Banana Bread #1

1¾ cups sifted all-purpose flour	⅔ cup sugar
¼ teaspoon soda	2 eggs, beaten
½ teaspoon salt	1 cup mashed bananas
⅓ cup butter	

Sift flour, baking soda, and salt. Cream butter and sugar until light and creamy. Add eggs and beat well. Add flour mixture alternately with bananas, beating smooth after each addition. Turn into greased 9x5x3-inch loaf pan. Bake for 1 hour and 10 minutes in 350 degree oven.

Mrs. Richard Beckman

Banana Bread #2

½ cup butter	1 teaspoon soda
1 cup sugar	1 teaspoon salt
2 eggs	1 cup pecans, chopped
3 bananas, mashed	8 dates, cut in small pieces
2 cups flour	

Cream butter and sugar. Fold in eggs. Add mashed bananas. Sift and beat in dry ingredients. Add nuts and dates. Turn into greased loaf pan and let stand 20 minutes. Bake at 350 degrees for 50 minutes.

Mrs. Jack Sullivan

Banana Bread #3

3 ripe bananas	½ cup butter
2 tablespoons lemon juice	1 cup sugar
2 cups flour	2 eggs
1 tablespoon soda	½ cup chopped nuts

Mash bananas with lemon juice. Set aside. Sift flour and soda, set aside. Cream butter and sugar. Add eggs, banana mixture, and flour mixture. Fold in nuts. Bake in greased loaf pan at 350 degrees for 40 minutes.

Sue Ellen Patterson

Banana Nut Muffins

½ cup margarine, softened	3 ripe mashed bananas
¾ cup sugar	1¼ cups all-purpose flour
2 eggs, beaten	½ teaspoon soda

Combine margarine and sugar. Beat until light and fluffy; add eggs and beat well. Stir in bananas; combine flour and soda. Add to creamed mixture, stirring just enough to moisten dry ingredients. Fill muffin pans ⅔ full. Bake at 350 degrees for 25 minutes or until done. Serve hot.

Makes 15 muffins

Carol Barker

Bran Muffins

3 cups bran cereal, divided	2½ teaspoons soda
1 cup boiling water	2 eggs, beaten
½ cup salad oil	2 cups buttermilk
2½ cups all-purpose flour	1 cup seedless raisins
1 teaspoon salt	(optional)
1½ cups sugar	

Combine 1 cup cereal, boiling water, and salad oil. Mix well; set aside. Combine flour, salt, sugar, soda, and remaining cereal. Add eggs and buttermilk; mix well. Stir in cereal, oil mixture; add raisins, if desired. Spoon batter into well-greased muffin tins, and bake at 400 degrees for 15 to 20 minutes. Serve hot.

Makes 2½ dozen muffins weeks.

Muffin batter can be stored in the refrigerator for 6

Jean Fowler

Caraway Sticks

1	package refrigerated biscuits	1½	cups crisp rice cereal, coarsely crushed
	Milk	2	tablespoons caraway seed
		2	teaspoons salt

Cut biscuits in halves. Roll each part into a pencil thin stick. Brush with milk. Mix cereal crumbs, seed and salt. Roll sticks into mixture. Bake on greased cookie sheet about 10 minutes at 450 degrees.

Makes 20

Mrs. Loyce Turner

Cheese Biscuits

1	stick butter	½	teaspoon red pepper
1	cup sharp New York cheese, shredded	1	cup flour
1	teaspoon salt		Pecan halves

Cream butter. Add shredded cheese, salt, pepper and flour. Roll into small balls. Press 1 pecan half on top of each ball. Bake at 350 degrees for 15 minutes.

Mrs. Doug Jones

Cinnamon Swirls

¼	cup butter	2	tablespoons butter, melted
1⅓	cups sifted flour	¼	cup sugar
¼	teaspoon salt	1	teaspoon cinnamon
3-4	tablespoons cold water		

Cut butter into flour and salt. Sprinkle water over mixture: stir with fork until dough holds together. Form into a square; flatten to ½-inch. Roll out on floured surface to 12-inch square. Brush with melted butter. Combine sugar and cinnamon; sprinkle over dough. Roll up; seal edges. Chill 30 minutes. Cut into ¼-inch slices, Place on ungreased cookie sheets. Bake at 400 degrees for 12 to 15 minutes until a delicate brown.

Mrs. C. E. Davis

Corn Bread

1	egg	½	cup sweet milk
½	teaspoon soda	½	cup buttermilk
1	teaspoon salt		Water ground cornmeal

Beat egg with soda and salt. Add both milks. Add enough cornmeal to make a thin batter. Heat an iron skillet with 1 tablespoon bacon drippings in 400 degree oven. Cook until light brown.

Iron corn stick pans or iron muffin pans may be used.

Mrs. Richard Beckman

Owendaw Corn Bread

2	cups cooked hominy grits, salted for serving	2	cups milk
4	tablespoons butter	1	cup cornmeal
4	eggs	1	teaspoon salt

Stir butter into hot hominy. Beat eggs until light and add to the hominy, then add milk and then cornmeal. Add salt last. Pour this thin batter into a well-greased casserole dish, and bake at 375 degrees for 1½ hours or until center is firm.

This spoon bread will wait up to an hour's extra cooking. It does not fall.

Mrs. Joyce Mixson

Sour Cream Corn Bread

1	cup self-rising cornmeal	½	cup cream style corn
2	eggs, slightly beaten	1	cup sour cream
½	cup cooking oil		

Preheat oven to 450 degrees. Mix first 4 ingredients. Fold in sour cream last and mix well. Pour into preheated skillet and bake until golden brown. Let cool for 5 minutes before cutting.

Lyn Dickey

Corn Muffins

½ cup sifted flour
⅛ cup sugar
½ teaspoon, baking powder
   (omit if using self-rising
   flour)
1½ tablespoons melted
   shortening or butter

¼ teaspoon, baking soda
½ cup cornmeal
1 egg, unbeaten
½ teaspoon salt
½ cup buttermilk

Preheat oven to 425 degrees. Grease muffin tins and preheat. Mix well. Fill pans ¾ full. Bake at 450 degrees about 25 minutes.

Mrs. John Anderson

Mexican Corn Bread

2 eggs
¾ cup milk
1 can cream style corn
⅓ cup melted shortening

1 cup cornmeal
½ teaspoon, salt
½ teaspoon soda
2 teaspoons baking powder

Spread half of the batter in a greased 8x8x2- or 9x9x1½-inch pan Sprinkle with grated sharp Cheddar cheese. Remove seeds from and mash a small can of chili peppers and spread in a layer over the cheese. Add another layer of grated cheese, then the remaining half of the batter. Top with grated cheese, using ½ pound of cheese in all. Bake 30 to 40 minutes in at 400 degrees.

Use a 9x9x1½-inch pan for a thinner bread.

Mrs. Joyce Mixon

Corn Fritters

1⅓ cups sifted flour
2 teaspoons baking powder
½ teaspoon salt

1 egg
1 small can cream style corn

Mix dry ingredients together. Add well beaten egg and corn. Drop teaspoon in deep hot cooking oil and drain on paper. Serve hot.

Mrs. I. H. Tillman, Jr.

Cranberry Bread

2	cups sifted flour	2	tablespoons cooking oil, added to juice for total of ¾ cup liquid
1	cup sugar		
1½	teaspoons baking powder		
½	teaspoon soda	1	egg, beaten
1	teaspoon salt	½	cup nuts
1	orange, juice and grated rind	2	cups cranberries, ground up

Combine and sift dry ingredients. Add remaining ingredients. Bake 1 hour at 350 degrees.

Mrs. Clarence Paine

Cranberry Banana Bread

⅓	cup shortening	¼	tablespoon soda
⅔	cup sugar	½	cup coarsely chopped nuts
2	eggs	1	cup mashed bananas
1¾	cups sifted enriched flour	1	cup drained fresh cooked cranberries
2	teaspoons baking powder		
½	tablespoon salt		

Cream shortening with sugar; add eggs. Beat well after each. Combine dry ingredients. Add nuts. Add flour mix alternately with bananas to cream mixture. Beat well after each addition. Fold in cranberries. Pour into greased 18½x4½x2½-inch loaf pan. Bake at 350 degrees for 60 to 65 minutes. Cool before slicing. This freezes well.

Mrs. Wayne Ellerbee

Crescent Poppy Seed Rolls

2   tablespoons, sugar
6   tablespoons soft shortening
    or margarine
1   teaspoon salt
1½ cups lukewarm milk
2   cakes compressed yeast

4⅓ cups all-purpose flour,
    sifted
    Soft butter to top
    Egg whites
    Poppy seeds

Mix first 3 ingredients until smooth. Stir milk. Crumble in 2 cakes compressed yeast. Stir until dissolved. Beat flour in with spoon. Scrape dough from sides of bowl, and cover with damp cloth. Let rise until double, about 30 minutes. Shape as crescents by rolling dough ¼-inch thick in a 12-inch circle, spreading with soft butter, and cutting into 16 pie-shaped pieces. Then beginning at rounded edge, roll up and place on pan, point underneath. Place on greased baking sheet, brush with egg whites and sprinkle with poppy seed. Cover, let rise until double, about 15 minutes. Bake at 425 degrees for 12 to 15 minutes until golden brown.

Makes 1⅔ dozen

Mrs. Mike Kaiser

Double Braided Bread

3   tablespoons sugar
1   package yeast
2   teaspoons salt
6   cups all-purpose flour,
    separated

2   cups water
3   tablespoons butter
1   egg
1   tablespoon water

Preheat oven to 350 degrees. Combine sugar, yeast, salt, and 2 cups of flour in mixing bowl. Heat 2 cups water and butter until very warm. Gradually beat liquid into dry ingredients until blended. Beat on medium speed for 2 minutes. Beat in ¾ cup flour. Beat 2 minutes with wooden spoon. Stir in enough flour to make soft dough (about 2½ to 3 cups). Knead about 10 minutes. Shape into a ball. Place in greased bowl, turning so top is greased. Cover and let rise in warm place until doubled for about 1 hour. Punch down. Let rest for 15 minutes. Using ⅔ of dough, make 3 (15-inch) lengths; braid with remaining dough. Make smaller braided loaf; place on top of large loaf. Place on greased cookie sheet, cover, let rise about 1 hour. Beat 1 egg with 1 tablespoon water and lightly brush bread mixture. Bake 40 minutes at 350 degrees. Cool on wire rack.

Ginger Paulk

Date Muffins

¼	cup butter	1	cup chopped dates
1	cup sugar	1	cup chopped nuts
3	eggs	2	heaping tablespoons flour

Cream butter and sugar. Add beaten eggs. Fold in dates and nuts that have been dredged in flour. Bake in greased muffin tins at 350 degrees for 15 minutes. Turn off oven and leave 20 to 30 minutes before removing.

Mrs. Walton Carter

Dill Bread

1	package yeast	1	tablespoon butter
¼	cup warm water	2	teaspoons salt
1	cup cottage cheese, heated to lukewarm	¼	teaspoon soda
		1	egg
2	tablespoons sugar	2	teaspoons dill seed
1	tablespoon minced onion		

Soften yeast in warm water. Add to cottage cheese. Add remaining ingredients. Add 2¼ to 2½ cups sifted flour. Mix well. Cover and let rise about an hour. Pour into 8-inch greased loaf pan. Let rise another hour. Cook at 350 degrees for 45 to 50 minutes.

Mrs. John Wiggins

Doughnuts

2	eggs	2	teaspoons baking powder
1	cup sugar	½	teaspoon salt
½	sweet cream	1	teaspoon nutmeg
1	cup buttermilk		Flour
1	teaspoon baking soda		

Mix first 8 ingredients in order and add flour to make soft dough. Chill dough, pat out (do not roll). Cut and fry in deep fat.

Mrs. Bill Lester

Herbed Cheese Bread

1	cup buttermilk	5	cups sifted regular flour
2	tablespoons sugar	1½	cups grated cheese
2½	teaspoons salt	1	egg
1	tablespoon shortening	½	cup chopped parsley
1	envelope yeast	1	tablespoon Italian seasoning
1	cup very warm water	½	teaspoon, onion salt
½	teaspoons baking soda		

Scald buttermilk with sugar, salt and shortening. Cool to lukewarm. Sprinkle yeast into very warm water, Stir until dissolved then stir into cooled buttermilk mixture. Stir soda into 2 cups of the flour. Beat into buttermilk-yeast mixture to form a smooth soft dough. Beat in cheese and gradually beat in remaining 3 cups flour. Turn out onto floured board and knead until smooth and elastic. Place in large greased bowl. Turn to coat all over with shortening. Cover with towel. Let rise 1 hour or until double in bulk. When dough has risen, mix egg with parsley, Italian seasoning and onion salt. Punch dough down, knead, and divide in half. Roll out, half at a time into a rectangle, 18x6 inches. Spread with half of egg mixture, and roll up, jelly-roll fashion. Place each loaf, seam side down, in a greased loaf pan, 9x5x3 inches. Cover. Let rise again, about 1 hour or until double. Preheat oven to 350 degrees. Bake about 45 minutes or until loaves sound hollow when tapped. Remove from pans, brush tops with margarine and cool on racks.

Makes 2 loaves

Mrs. Henry Brice

Icebox Rolls

5	cups self-rising flour	2	cups lukewarm water
2	packages yeast	⅔	cup vegetable oil
½	cup sugar		

Dissolve yeast, sugar in lukewarm water. Add vegetable oil and mix. Add flour More flour may be necessary for a smooth ball of dough. Place in refrigerator and cover with damp cloth. Roll out and let rise for 1 hour. Bake at 400 degrees until lightly browned or about 10 minutes. Recipe may be halved.

Mrs. John J. Anderson

Homemade Bread

1 cup hot water	1 package yeast
1 teaspoon salt	¼ cup warm water
¼ cup sugar	4 cups sifted flour
4 tablespoons shortening	1 egg, beaten
1 teaspoon sugar	

Pour water over salt, ¼ cup sugar and shortening. Let cool while preparing water, 1 teaspoon sugar and yeast. In ¼ cup warm water, add 1 teaspoon sugar and yeast. Let stand. Grease 2 (9x7x2¼-inch) loaf pans. Mix shortening mixture with yeast mixture. Add egg and flour to shortening-yeast mixture, adding 1 cup of flour at a time and mixing well with a wooden spoon. If dough is too stiff, don't add all of the fourth cup of flour. Grease top of batter with small amount of shortening and let rise 1 hour. Cover the bowl with cloth or waxed paper while rising, and keep in a warm place. After the bread has risen, remove from the bowl and place it onto a floured board. Knead the dough lightly and shape it into one roll. To flatten and roll is the easiest method. Divide the roll in two by pinching at the middle. Shape each section by flattening and then rolling, making 2 loaves. Place in loaf pans. Do not grease tops of loaves for the second rising time. Let rise 1 hour. Bake 15 minutes at 450 degrees on rack, lowered just below center oven level. If tops brown too quickly, place loose foil over it. Remove after 15 minutes, butter tops and return for 5 minutes. Dough should double in bulk on each rising. The weather may require adjusting the necessary rising time. It will take less time in summer, more in winter. Bread should not be sealed in plastic until completely cool because the loaves will sweat.

Mrs. Henry C. Cannon

Hot Cakes

1 cup sifted flour	½ cup milk
2 teaspoons baking powder	2 tablespoons melted butter
2 tablespoons sugar	1 egg
½ teaspoon salt	

Sift flour, baking powder, sugar and salt. Add milk, butter and egg. Add more milk if necessary to make batter thin enough to pour.

Mrs. Grady Durden

Hush Puppies #1

1½ cups cornmeal	2 teaspoons baking powder
1 cup flour	1 small onion, grated
1 teaspoon sugar	1¼ cups buttermilk
1 teaspoon salt	1 egg
¼ teaspoon baking soda	

Mix together cornmeal, flour, sugar, salt, soda and baking powder. Add grated onion, buttermilk and egg. Drop by spoonfuls into hot grease.

Mrs. E. G. Barham

Hush Puppies #2

1 cup finely ground, white cornmeal	2 slices cooked bacon, crumbled
	Bacon grease, from above cooked slices
1 teaspoon baking soda	
2 tablespoons flour	1 small onion, grated
½ teaspoon, salt	1 egg
2 tablespoons brown sugar	Buttermilk

Sift dry ingredients into mixing bowl. Add bacon, bacon grease and grated onion. Mix well. Add egg, unbeaten and stir it in. Then add only enough buttermilk so that 2 teaspoons batter per Hush Puppy can be loosely manipulated into balls. Drop into moderately hot deep fat. They should be only about 1½ inches in diameter, when cooked.

These go well with sausage for Sunday breakfast.

Mrs. Bill Lester

Granny's Muffins

1 cup milk	1 teaspoon salt
2 eggs	1 tablespoon shortening
3 tablespoons sugar	2 teaspoons baking powder
2 cups flour	

Mix and bake in muffin tins at 325 degrees until done.

Makes 1 dozen

Mrs. Clarence Paine

Irish Soda Bread

Your own regular 2 cup flour biscuit recipe	**¼ teaspoon soda**
Buttermilk	**1 cup white raisins**
	1 tablespoon caraway seed

Mix biscuit recipe, using buttermilk and ¼ teaspoon soda. Add 1 cup white raisins and 1 tablespoon caraway seed. Knead about 20 strokes. Put in greased frying pan. Bake 30 minutes at 350 degrees increasing to 400 degrees for at least 5 minutes. Cut in wedges and serve with hot tea.

Mrs. George Hart

Six Week Muffins

1	**(15-ounce) box raisin bran cereal**	2	**teaspoons salt**
3	**cups sugar**	4	**eggs**
5	**cups all-purpose flour**	1	**quart buttermilk**
5	**teaspoons flour**	1	**cup corn or safflower oil**

Mix raisin bran cereal, sugar, all-purpose flour, flour, and salt in a large bowl. Mix remaining ingredients and add to the cereal mixture. Bake 15 minutes at 400 degrees in greased muffin tins. This mix may be stored in the refrigerator up to six weeks.

Ellen Oliver

Magic Muffins

4	**cups biscuit mix**	2	**eggs, beaten**
½	**cup sugar**	1½	**cups milk**
¼	**cup margarine, melted**		

Combine all ingredients in a medium bowl, stirring just until moistened. Spoon batter into greased muffin pans, filling ⅔ full. Bake 15 to 20 minutes at 400 degrees.

Makes 20 muffins

Sally Moritz

❧ *Sesame Bread*

1	cup water	1	stick butter
2	cups biscuit baking mix		Sesame seeds

Mix water and biscuit mix together. Melt the butter; pour ½ butter in the bread pan, then the mix, then the rest of the butter on top. Sprinkle sesame seeds on top. Bake at 450 degrees for 15 to 20 minutes.

Sharon Mink

Prune Muffins

1	cup butter	½	cup coconut (optional)
1½	cups sugar	½	teaspoon soda added to
2	eggs		¼ cup prune juice
2	cups flour	1	teaspoon baking powder
1	cup stewed prunes	¾	teaspoon cinnamon
1	cup nuts	¾	teaspoon nutmeg
¾	teaspoon cloves	¾	teaspoon allspice

Bake at 350 degrees for 30 minutes. Will keep in refrigerator for a week.

Mrs. John W. Lastinger and Mrs. Millie Knowles

Rye Bread Casserole

1	stick butter	3	eggs
10	slices rye bread	3	cups milk
	Brown mustard	1	tablespoon Worcestershire
¾	pound sharp Cheddar cheese, grated		sauce

Melt butter. Spread bread with butter on one side and mustard on the other, then break into small pieces. Put in casserole dish and stir in grated cheese. Beat eggs and add milk and Worcestershire sauce. Pour over bread and cheese and refrigerate overnight. Bake at 375 degrees for 40 minutes.

Mrs. Clement Green

Rye Batter's Bread

1¼	cups warm water	2¾	cups unsifted white flour
1	package yeast	2	teaspoons salt
2	tablespoons honey	1	tablespoon caraway seeds
2	tablespoons margarine	1	cup unsifted rye flour

Put warm water in mixing bowl, sprinkle in yeast and stir. Add honey, margarine, 1 cup white flour, salt, seeds, and rye flour. Blend to mix, beat 2 minutes at medium speed. Add remaining flour; blend in with spoon. Cover and let rise in warm place until doubled (about 30 minutes). Punch down and beat 25 strokes. Spread evenly in greased 9x5x3-inch loaf pan. Cover and let rise about 40 minutes. Bake at 375 degrees for 45 to 50 minutes.

Ginger Paulk

Spoon Bread

1	cup boiling water	1	heaping tablespoon butter, melted
1	cup milk		
1	cup sifted cornmeal	1	teaspoon salt
2	eggs	1	scant teaspoon sugar

Boil water and milk together. Add cornmeal. Cook until mushy. Cool. Beat in eggs, butter, salt and sugar. Put into greased hot baking dish. Bake at 350 degrees for 1 hour.

Serves 6

Mrs. Alex Wainer

Sweet Potato Biscuits

1	cup flour	1	cup mashed, cooked sweet potatoes
3	tablespoons baking powder		
½	teaspoon salt	¾	cup milk
4	tablespoons shortening		

Sift together flour, baking powder and salt. Add shortening, potatoes and milk. Make dough stiff enough to roll. Bake in hot oven about 20 minutes.

Marge's Onion Sesame Bread

2	packages, yeast	4	cups prepared biscuit mix
⅓	cup very warm water	¼	cup melted butter
1	(10½-ounce) can onion	¼	cup or more grated cheese
	soup, undiluted	4	teaspoons sesame seeds

Sprinkle yeast onto very warm water and stir until dissolved. Stir in soup. Pour mixture into prepared biscuit mix and mix until blended. Pour melted butter into 12x8x2-inch pan. Sprinkle pan with sesame seed. Spread batter over pan evenly. Sprinkle with grated cheese and remaining sesame seeds. Cover with towel and let rise in warm place, about ½ hour or until doubled. Bake at 400 degrees for about 25 minutes.

Can be made ahead and toasted.

Serves 8

Mrs. Henry Brice

Virginia Spoon Bread

1	package dry yeast	¾	cup cooking oil
2	cups warm water	1	beaten egg
2	tablespoons sugar	4	cups self-rising flour

Dissolve yeast in warm water. Cream sugar with oil in large bowl and add beaten egg, mixing well. Add dissolved yeast, then flour and stir until well mixed. Store in airtight container in refrigerator. Spoon into well greased muffin tins. Bake at 350 degrees for about 20 minutes or until lightly browned. This dough will keep very well for several days so you can use as needed, returning balance to refrigerator.

Dee Broadfoot

Quick Yeast Rolls

3	cups flour	¼	teaspoon soda
1	tablespoon sugar	1	tablespoon baking powder
1	cup buttermilk	1	yeast dissolved in ¼ cup
2	tablespoons shortening		warm water

Make up as biscuits. Let rise about 1 hour before baking.

Mrs. Bill Keller and Mrs. Nettle Keller
of Valdosta

Sally Lunn

4	tablespoons shortening	4	teaspoons baking powder
4	tablespoons sugar	1	egg, well beaten
1	teaspoon salt	¾	cup milk
2	cups flour		

Cream shortening, sugar and salt. Sift flour and baking powder together. Add egg to shortening and sugar mixture. Add flour mixture and milk alternately to shortening and sugar mixture, making a smooth batter. Bake in hot oven for 25 minutes. Can be baked in well-greased loaf pan, round tube or salad mold.

Mrs. Walton Carter

Yeast Rolls

2	packages dry yeast	⅔	cup cooking oil
⅓	cup sugar	5½	cups self rising flour
2	cups warm water		

Mix yeast and sugar together. Dissolve in warm water. Add cooking oil. Sift flour into liquid mixture. Stir well, then roll out and cut. Put a pat of butter on each roll before baking. Bake at 400 to 450 degrees for about 15 minutes or until turns a golden brown.

Substitute 1 cup of cornmeal for 1 cup of the flour.

Mrs. J.C. Sherwood

No-Knead Rolls

2	cups sweet milk, scalded and cooled	½	cup shortening
3	cups plain flour	2	cups flour
1	package yeast	1	teaspoon, salt
⅓	cup sugar	1	teaspoon baking powder
		⅔	teaspoon soda

Mix first 5 ingredients. Let rise until double, and then add remaining ingredients. Refrigerate at least 1 hour. Roll out and cut as desired. Let rise double. Let rise double again. Bake at 325 degrees.

Mrs. Bill Keller and Mrs. Roswell Garrett
of Columbus, Georgia

Waffles #1

2	cups self-rising flour	1	egg
½	teaspoon soda	¼	cup melted shortening
1	tablespoon sugar	1½	cups buttermilk

Sift flour, measure. Sift flour, soda and sugar. Beat egg. Add shortening and buttermilk and add to dry ingredients. Mix smooth. Bake.

Makes 4 waffles

Mrs. Bill Keller

Waffles #2

2	eggs	1	teaspoon salt
1	cup vegetable oil	1	tablespoon sugar
½	cup milk	¾	cup water
2	cups flour	4	teaspoons baking powder

Beat eggs. Add oil and beat until smooth. Add milk. Sift dry ingredients and add alternately with water. Beat until smooth adding baking powder last. Bake.

Mrs. Joe C. Stubbs

Freezer Yeast Rolls

3	packages dry yeast	3	teaspoons salt
2	cups warm water	1	cup shortening
½	cup sugar	6	cups sifted flour

Dissolve yeast in warm water. Add sugar, salt and shortening. Stir well. Add a little flour at a time until all is used. Place dough in greased bowl, cover, and let rise 1½ hours. Roll out about ¼-inch thickness. Cut and fold in halves. Quick-freeze on cookie sheet. When frozen, place in bags in freezer. When ready for use, remove from bags onto greased cookie sheet. Let rise 3 hours. Bake at 425 degrees for 20 minutes or until brown.

Makes 3 dozen

Mrs. M. M. Harris

Cakes

1-2-3-4 Cake 229
Amalgamation Cake 229
Angel Cake 230
Apple Walnut Cake 230
Apple Cake 231
Apricot Cake 231
Apple Spice Cake 232
Brown Sugar Pound Cake 232
Butter Pecan Cake 233
Butter Sponge Cake 233
Carrot Cake #1 234
Butter Peanut Cake 234
Carrot Cake #2 235
Chocolate Layer Cake 235
Cheese Cake #1 236
Cheese Cake #2 236
Chocolate Cheese Cake 237
Company Cake 237
Chocolate Pound Cake 238
Cranberry Confection Cupcakes 238
Coconut Cake ~ Old Recipe 239
Crunch Cake 239
Cupcakes 240
Date Cake 240
Dark Fruit Cake 241
Date Nut Loaf 241
Devil's Food Cake 242
French Coffee Cake 242
Dutch Cocoa Cream Cake 243
Fruit Cake #1 244
Fruit Cake #2 244
Fruit Cake #3 245
Japanese Fruit Cake 245
Franklin Nut Cake 246
Seventeen-Pound Fruit Cake 246
Top of Stove Fruit Cake 247

White Fruit Cake 247
Fudge Cake or Pie 248
Jelly Roll 248
Tunnel of Fudge Cake 249
Jam Cake 249
German Chocolate Cake 250
Lane Cake 251
Lemon Cheese Cake #2 252
Lemon Cheese Cake #1 252
Marble Cake 253
Oatmeal Cake 253
Mayonnaise Cake 254
Orange Cake 254
Orange Coconut Cake 255
Orange Layer Cake 255
Orange Slice Cake 256
Pineapple Chiffon Cake, Quickie 256
Pecan Whiskey Cake 257
Pumpkin Cake 257
Pineapple Upside Down Cake 258
Pound Cake 258
Mrs. Hensley's
    Delicious Pound Cake 259
Hershey Pound Cake 259
Whipping Cream Pound Cake 259
Peach Brandy Pound Cake 260
Red Cake 260
Sour Cream Pound Cake 261
Sour Cream Nut Cake 261
Shortcake 262
Sweet Potato Cake 262
Strawberry-Pecan Cake 263
Strawberry Cake 263
Sour Cream Chocolate Cake 264
White Chocolate Cake 264

Frostings, Icings, Fillings & Sauces

Caramel Frosting #1 265
Caramel Frosting #2 265
Fudge Icing 265
White Frosting 266
Buttermilk Icing 266
Chocolate Frosting 266
White Icing 266

Milk Chocolate Icing 267
Burnt Sugar Caramel Filling 267
Lemon Cheese Filling 267
Chocolate Sauce 268
Chocolate Sauce For Ice Cream 268
Chocolate Sauce for Hot Fudge Cake 268

Pies

Deep Dish Apple Pie 269
Apple Pie "Henri" 269
Blackberry Pie #1 270
Blackberry Pie #2 270
Black Bottom Pie 270
Caramel Banana Pie 271
Sour Cherry Pie 271
Chess Pie 272
Lemon Chess Pie 272
Southern Chess Pie 272
Chocolate Pie 273
French Silk Chocolate Pie 273
Chocolate Almond Pie 273
German Chocolate Pie 274
Coconut Cream Pie 274
Cream Cheese Pie 275
Japanese Fruit Pies 275
Graham Cracker Pie 276
Different Lemon Pie 276
Old-Fashioned Lemon Pie 276

Lemon Luscious Pie 277
Lime Meringue Pie 277
Key Lime Pie 278
Macaroon Pie 278
Pecan Pie ~
    Silver Springs Coffee Shop 278
Open Sesame Pie 279
Blue Ribbon Peach Pie 280
Down South Pecan Pie 280
Sour Cream Pecan Pie 281
Praline Pie 281
Southern Pecan Pie 282
Patton House Rum Pie 282
Sweet Potato Pie 282
Pumpkin Chiffon Pie 283
Strawberry Pie 283
Graham Cracker Pie Crust 284
Fresh Strawberry Pie 284
Traditional Pie Crust 284

Brownies, Cookies & Candy

Apricot Balls 285
Crystallized Apricots 285
Blond Brownies 285
Bourbon Balls #1 286
Bourbon Balls #2 286
Butterscotch Brownies 286
Brownies #1 287
Brownies #2 287
Brownies #3 288
Wafer Brownies 288
Brownies #4 289
Easy Cheese Cake Squares 289
Chocolate Dips 290
Chocolate Mint Desserts 290
Cinnamon Crisps 291
Christmas Cookies 291
Chocolate Covered Cherries 291
Chocolate Cookies 292
Crazy Crunch 292
Cream Cheese Cookies 293
Coconut Cookies 293
Crescent Cookies 294
Divinity Pecan Roll Candy 294
Divinity 295

Fudge #1 295
Fudge #2 295
Fudge Squares 296
Sour Cream Fudge 296
Chocolate Fudge 297
Milk Chocolate Fudge 297
Goldie's Cookies 297
Mrs. Rhymes Lemon Squares 298
Gingerbread Boys 298
Gooey 299
Heavenly Hash Candy 299
Aunt Ruth's Icebox Cookies 299
Katy's Cornettes 300
Kisses 300
Lemon Puffs 300
Candy Coated Chocolate
    Color Cookies 301
Magic Marshmallow Crescent Puffs 301
Dark Chocolate Coconut Cookies 302
Panocha 302
Peanut Butter Crunch 302
Oatmeal Cookies 303
Candied Orange Peel 303
Orange Balls 303

Brownies, Cookies & Candy continued

Peanut Butter Cookies 304
Pecan Bars 304
Pecan Puffs 304
Pecan Cookies 305
Pecan Brittle 305
Pecan Pralines 305
Pralines #1 306
Pralines #2 306
Pralines #3 306
Praline Strips 307

Pink Icebergs 307
Ranger Cookies 308
Somemores 308
Spice Drop Cookies 308
Sea Foam 309
Snickerdoodles 309
Sugar Cookies #1 310
Sugar Cookies #2 310
Sugar Cookies #3 310

Desserts

Apple Crisp 311
Apple Dumplings 311
Apple-Pecan Dessert 312
Apple Torte #1 312
Apple Torte #2 312
Apple Torte #3 313
Banana Split Dessert 313
Banana Pudding 314
Butterscotch Torte 314
Creamy Banana Pudding 315
Cherry Cobbler 315
Cherry Crunch Dessert 315
Blueberry Torte 316
Boiled Custard 316
Cherries Jubilee 317
Choc-O-Date Dessert 317
Date-Nut Roll 317
Baked Custard 318
Chocolate Dessert 318
Chocolate Mousse 319
Chocolate Macaroon Mold 319
Coffee Jelly 320
Christmas Gelatin Dessert 320
Floating Island 321

Curried Fruit Bake 321
Fruit Whip 321
Sherried Hot Fruit Casserole 322
Almond or Pecan Icebox Cake 322
Grape Dessert 323
Icebox Cake 323
Lemon Bisque 324
Lemon Fluff 324
Lemon Pudding 324
Lemon Snow 325
Peach Cobbler 325
Lemon and Strawberry Surprise 326
Dried Peach Custard 326
Pear Crisp 327
Pineapple Crisp 327
Pineapple Delight 327
Grated Potato Pudding 328
Strawberry Cool 328
Strawberry Dessert 328
Tipsy Squire 329
Trinity Dessert 329
Strawberry Parfaits 329
Fresh Raspberry Mousse 330

Frozen Desserts

Fudge Sundae Pie 330
Banana Ice Cream 331
Frozen Toasted Almond Ball
    with Hot Fudge 331
Cheese Tortoni 331
Biscuit Tortoni #1 332
Biscuit Tortoni #2 332
Cranberry Sherbet 332
Grasshopper Pie 333
Heavenly Hash 333

Skinny Ice Cream 333
Ice Cream Pie Spectacular 334
Susie's Ice Cream 334
Ice Cream Dessert 335
Mix for Bought Ice Cream 335
Orange Sherbet 335
Persian Velvet 336
Raspberry Jazz 337
Vanilla Ice Cream 337

1-2-3-4 Cake

1	cup butter	2	heaping teaspoons baking
2	cups sugar		powder
4	eggs	1	cup cold water
3	cups flour		

Cream butter and sugar together. Add 4 beaten egg yolks. Add flour sifted with baking powder and water alternately. After beating, fold in 4 stiffly beaten egg whites. Bake either in loaf or 2 layers. Ice as desired.

Mrs. Nettie Keller

Amalgamation Cake

Cake

1	cup butter	3	teaspoons baking powder
2	cups sugar	1	teaspoon vanilla extract
3½	cups flour, sifted twice	6	egg whites, beaten stiff
½	teaspoon salt		

Cream butter and sugar. Blend egg whites and flour into butter mixture. Bake in layers at 350 degrees.

Filling

2	cups sugar	1	cup coconut
6	egg yolks	1	cup pecans
1	cup butter	1	cup cherries
1	teaspoon vanilla	1	cup raisins

Add sugar to egg yolks and butter. Cook over low heat until butter melts. Stir constantly. Cook to complete boil. Cool. Then add remaining ingredients. Fill between layers. Ice.

Mrs. Nettie Keller

Angel Cake

⅔	cup granulated sugar	1	dozen extra large egg whites
1½	cups powdered sugar	½	teaspoon salt
¾	cup sifted pastry flour	1¼	teaspoons vanilla
¼	cup cocoa	1⅓	teaspoons cream of tartar

Beat egg whites with wire whip to a foam. Add salt and cream of tartar, then beat egg whites until they stand in peaks. Add all granulated sugar at one time and beat in. Sifted pastry flour, powdered sugar and cocoa together. Add this to mixture all at one time folding in gently. Add vanilla; stir gently. Pour into ungreased tube cake pan. Cut through several times with spatula to get rid of any air bubbles. Bake at 275 degrees for 30 minutes. Increase the heat to 325 degrees and bake for another 45 minutes. Turn upside down on cake rack to cool.

Icing

1	cup whipping cream that has turned sour (do not use commercial sour cream)	1	cup sugar
		2½	cups ground pecans meats
		1	teaspoon vanilla

Boil sour cream, sugar and nuts until a soft ball has formed. Remove from heat; add vanilla. Spread on cake.

Mrs. George Nichols

Apple Walnut Cake

4	cups apples, coarsely chopped	2	cups sifted flour
2	cups sugar	2	teaspoons soda
2	eggs, beaten slightly	2	teaspoons cinnamon
½	cup vegetable oil	1	teaspoon salt
2	teaspoons vanilla	1	cup chopped walnuts

Mix apples and sugar together and set aside. Mix eggs, oil and vanilla and set aside. Sift dry ingredients together. Add alternately to egg mixture with apples and sugar. Stir in walnuts. Bake in 13x9x2-inch greased and floured pan at 350 degrees for 1 hour. Let get cold in pan before taking out.

Mrs. E.G. Barham

Apple Cake

1	cup oil	2	eggs
2	cups sugar	1	teaspoon salt
2½	cups plain flour	1	teaspoon soda
2½	cups diced tart apples	2	teaspoons baking powder
1	teaspoon vanilla	1	teaspoon cinnamon
¾	cup pecans	½	teaspoon nutmeg

Cover apples with sugar. Let stand for 20 minutes. Sift together flour, salt, soda, baking powder, cinnamon and nutmeg. Add flour mixture, oil, eggs, vanilla and pecans to apples. Mixture will be thick. Spread in a greased oblong dish. Bake at 325 degrees about 1 hour.

Sour Cream Topping

1	cup sugar	½	teaspoon soda
½	cup sour cream		

Combine above ingredients in saucepan. Cook over medium heat, stirring constantly, until mixture comes to a boil. Remove from heat. Prick warm cake with fork. Pour hot topping over cake, sprinkle with ¼ cup pecans.

Mrs. Bucky Anderson

Apricot Cake

1	package white cake mix	⅔	cup vegetable oil
1	package lemon jello	4	eggs
⅔	cup apricot nectar		

Mix cake mix and jello in mixer. Add apricot nectar and oil. Add eggs, one at a time and beat well. Bake 1 hour at 300 degrees in tube pan.

Glaze

1	cup 4x sugar	⅓	cup lemon juice
			(or part apricot nectar)

Mix in bowl and put on hot cake.

Mrs. Jack Sullivan

Apple Spice Cake

3	cups plain flour	1¼	cups cooking oil
2	cups sugar	3	eggs
1	teaspoon baking soda	1	teaspoon vanilla
1	teaspoon salt	3	medium-sized apples, cubed
1	teaspoon cinnamon	1	cup nuts, finely chopped
1	teaspoon allspice		

Place flour, sugar, soda, salt and spices in mixing bowl Add oil and blend well. Add eggs, one at a time, beating after each addition. Add vanilla, cubed apples and nuts. Stir. Place in cold oven and turn heat to 275 degrees for 10 minutes. Then turn to 350 degrees and bake for 1 hour. Remove from oven and let cool before taking out of pan. This cake is best baked in a Bundt pan.

Filling

1	cup light brown sugar	¼	cup evaporated milk or
1	stick butter		cream

Mix and cook for 2 minutes and let cool. Spread on cake.

Mrs. J. Fred Anderson

Brown Sugar Pound Cake

1½	cups butter	½	teaspoon salt
1	pound light brown sugar	1	cup milk
1	cup white sugar	1	teaspoon vanilla
5	large eggs	1	cup nuts
3	cups flour		

Cream butter and sugars, adding eggs, one at a time, beating well after each addition. Sift dry ingredients together and add to above mixture, alternately with milk. Add vanilla and nuts. Bake in tube pan for 1 hour at 350 degrees.

Mrs. Doug Jones

Butter Pecan Cake

2	cups chopped pecans
1½	cups butter
3	cups sifted all-purpose flour
2	teaspoons baking powder
½	teaspoon salt

2	cups sugar
4	unbeaten eggs
1	cup milk
2	teaspoons vanilla

Toast pecans in ¼ cup butter at 350 degrees for 20 to 25 minutes, stirring frequently. Sift flour with baking powder and salt. Cream 1 cup butter, gradually add sugar, creaming well. Blend in eggs, one at a time and beat well after each addition. Add dry ingredients alternately with milk, beginning and ending with dry ingredients. Blend well after each addition. Stir in vanilla and 1⅓ cups pecans. Put into 3 (8- or 9-inch) round layer pans. Bake at 350 degrees for 25 or 30 minutes; cool. Spread frosting between and on top of layers.

Butter Pecan Frosting

¼	cup butter
1	pound sifted powdered sugar

1	teaspoon vanilla
4-6	tablespoons evaporated milk or cream

Cream butter. Add powdered sugar. Add vanilla and milk or cream until of spreading consistency. Stir in remaining toasted pecans.

Mrs. Joyce Mixson

Butter Sponge Cake

1	dozen egg yolks
2	cups sugar
1	cup scalded milk
1	teaspoon vanilla

2¼	cups cake flour
2	teaspoons baking powder
¼	cup melted butter

Beat egg yolks and sugar until light and fluffy; add milk and vanilla. Add sifted flour and baking powder. Fold in butter. Bake in 2 (9-inch) layer pans that have been lined with waxed paper. Bake in 350 degrees oven for 30 minutes or until done. Cool. Split into 4 layers. Ice with Buttermilk Icing.

Mrs. George Nichols

Carrot Cake #1

2	cups flour	2	cups sugar
2	teaspoons baking powder	4	eggs
1½	teaspoons soda	2	cups grated carrots
1	teaspoon salt	1	small can crushed
2	teaspoons cinnamon		pineapple
1½	cups cooking oil	¾	cup chopped nuts, optional

Sift first 5 ingredients together and set aside. Mix oil, sugar, and eggs, beating after each addition. Add to first ingredients. Mix well. Add carrots, pineapple and nuts. Grease and flour 2 (13x9x2½-inch) pans or 4 round cake pans. Bake 30 to 35 minutes at 325 degrees. Cool.

Icing

1	(8-ounce) package cream cheese	2	teaspoons vanilla
		1	cup chopped pecans
1	stick margarine	1	cup coconut
1	box confectioners' sugar		

Mix first 4 ingredients. Add pecans and coconut. Spread on cake.

Mrs. Horace Aycock

Butter Peanut Cake

1	cup peanut oil	2½	cups plain flour
2	cups sugar	1	cup sweet milk
4	eggs	1	tablespoon butter extract
½	cup self-rising flour		

Cream peanut oil, sugar and eggs. Beat 10 minutes. Add flour, milk and extract. Mix thoroughly. Bake in 4 layers at 350 degrees.

Frosting

1	stick butter	1	cup chopped, roasted peanuts
1	(8-ounce) package cream cheese		
1	box confectioners' sugar	1	tablespoon butter extract

Cream together butter, cream cheese, and confectioners' sugar. Add peanuts and butter extract. Spread on cake.

Mrs. W.B. Sullivan

Carrot Cake #2

1	teaspoon salt	3	cups carrots, grated
2	cups plain cake flour	4	eggs
2	cups sugar	2	teaspoons cinnamon
2	teaspoons soda	1¼	cups vegetable oil

Sift cake flour, and combine all dry ingredients. Mix evenly. Add oil and eggs alternately; mix together. Then add carrots. May use mixer, but not necessary. Pour into 3 cake pans, and bake 30 to 40 minutes at 350 degrees.

Icing

½	stick butter	1	box confectioners' sugar
1	(8-ounce) package cream cheese, room temperature	2	teaspoons vanilla
		1	cup pecans

Blend butter and cheese. Add sugar and blend together. Add vanilla. Then add pecans and cream together.

Marolyn Bearden

Chocolate Layer Cake

½	cup butter (not margarine)	1¾	cups cake flour
1	cup sugar	2½	teaspoons baking powder
2	eggs	1	teaspoon vanilla
½	cup milk		

Cream butter an sugar. Add eggs, one at a time; add milk, baking powder and flour alternately. Add vanilla. Bake in layers at 375 degrees for about 30 minutes.

Icing

2	cups sugar	1	stick butter
½	cup cocoa	1	teaspoon vanilla
⅔	cup milk		

Sift sugar and cocoa together. Add milk. Cook over medium heat until comes to a boil. Cook for 4 minutes or until forms soft ball. Add butter and vanilla. Beat until of spreading consistency.

Mrs. Bill Keller

Cheese Cake #1

4	(3-ounce) packages cream cheese
2	eggs, well beaten
½	cup sugar
1	teaspoon vanilla
	Dash nutmeg (optional)
18	graham crackers, crushed

¾	cup butter, melted
¼	cup sugar
1	package sour cream
4	tablespoons sugar
1	teaspoon vanilla
	Chopped pistachios

Mix cream cheese, eggs, sugar, and vanilla. May add a dash of nutmeg. Mix crackers, butter, and sugar to make crust. Line pan with crust mixture. Save a few crumbs to sprinkle on top. Pour cream cheese mixture onto crust. Bake 20 minutes at 350 degrees. Cool. Mix sour cream, sugar, and vanilla. Pour on top and bake at 350 degrees for 6 minutes. Top with crackers and pistachios.

Mrs. Bill Lester

Cheese Cake #2

2	cups sweet oat cracker crumbs
½	cup granulated sugar
1½	teaspoons cinnamon
½	cup melted butter
4	eggs
1	cup granulated sugar
1½	tablespoons lemon juice

⅛	teaspoon salt
1	cup light cream
3	cups cottage cheese
¼	cup flour
2	teaspoons grated lemon rind
¼	cup chopped pecans

Combine crumbs with next 3 ingredients. Reserve ¾ cup. With spoon press rest to bottom and sides of 9-inch springform pan. Beat eggs with 1 cup sugar. Add next 5 ingredients; beat until blended. Stain through sieve. Stir in lemon rind. Pour into large springform pan and sprinkle on reserved crumbs then nuts. Bake for 1 hour at 350 degrees. Turn off heat, open oven door. Let cake cool in oven for 1 hour. Chill and then remove from pan.

Mrs. Richard Beckmann

Chocolate Cheese Cake

2	cups flour	½	cup buttermilk
2	cups sugar	2	eggs
¼	teaspoon salt	1	teaspoon vanilla
2	sticks butter	1	teaspoon cinnamon
4	tablespoons cocoa	1	teaspoon soda
⅞	cup water		

Sift flour, sugar, and salt together. Bring to boil the butter, cocoa and water and pour over the flour mixture. Add remaining ingredients. Pour into greased and floured 16x11-inch pan. Bake 20 minutes at 400 degrees.

Frosting

1	stick butter	1	box powdered sugar
4	tablespoons cocoa	1	teaspoon vanilla
6	tablespoons milk	1	cup chopped nuts

Five minutes before cake is done; bring to a boil butter, cocoa and milk. Remove from heat and add powdered sugar, vanilla and chopped nuts. Mix and pour over cake immediately upon taking from oven.

Mrs. Jack Sullivan

Company Cake

1	small angel food cake	½	cup hot water
2	envelopes plain gelatin	2	packages instant lemon
½	cup cold water		pudding mix
½	pound marshmallows	3	cups cold milk

Tear angel food cake into pieces, and put in a mixing bowl. Soften gelatin in cold water. Over low heat, dissolve marshmallows, cut into cubes in hot water, add gelatin and dissolve. Remove from heat. Prepare lemon pudding mix with cold milk and pour over angel cake. Let set and fold the gelatin mixture into cake-pudding mixture. Turn into an 8x8x2-inch glass dish that has been lined with wax paper. Refrigerate at least 40 minutes before serving. Cake may be removed from pan to a serving plate. Top with whipped cream or whipped topping.

Mrs. D.L. Burns

Chocolate Pound Cake

1½	cups butter	½	teaspoon baking powder
3	cups sugar	4	teaspoons cocoa
5	eggs	1	cup milk
3	cups flour	1	teaspoon vanilla
½	teaspoon salt		

Cream butter and sugar. Add eggs, one at a time. Beat 1 minute after each egg. Sift flour, salt, baking powder, and cocoa together. Alternate flour mixture with milk. Add vanilla. Pour into greased tube pan and cook at 325 degrees for 1 hour and 20 minutes or bake as a 3 layer cake. This also makes a delicious yellow cake by omitting the cocoa.

Chocolate Cream Frosting

2½	cups cream	4	tablespoons sifted cocoa
3	cups sugar	3	tablespoons butter

Mix sugar, cocoa and cream. In a sauce pan, cook on moderate heat until it forms a soft ball. Cool and add butter. Beat until right consistency to spread.

Mrs. Jack Sullivan

Cranberry Confection Cupcakes

¾	cup flour	3½	cups chopped pecans
½	teaspoon baking powder	2	eggs
½	teaspoon salt	1	teaspoon lemon extract
2	cups fresh cranberries	¾	cup sugar
1	(8-ounce) package pitted, chopped dates		

Sift flour, baking powder and salt together. Combine cranberries, dates, and pecans with flour. Toss together until each piece of fruit is evenly coated. Beat eggs, extract, and sugar together until light and fluffy. Pour over fruit flour mixture. Mix thoroughly to coat fruit and nuts with egg mixture. Preheat oven to 300 degrees. Line muffin tins with paper liners. Pack fruit mixture tightly until ⅔ full. Bake 45 to 50 minutes or until cake tests done. Cool in pan for 15 minutes. Store in refrigerator or freeze.

Mrs. Jack Sullivan

Coconut Cake ~ Old Recipe

2½ cups cake flour, sift before measuring
2½ teaspoons baking powder
1   teaspoon salt
1⅔ cups sugar

½   cup butter
1   cup milk
½   cup egg yolks
2   teaspoons vanilla

Sift first 4 ingredients together in large bowl or mixer. Add butter and ¾ cup milk. Beat 2 minutes, scrape sides of bowl. Add egg yolks, ¼ cup milk, and vanilla. Beat 1 minute or until well mixed. Pour into 2 buttered and floured 9-inch cake pans. Bake 20 minutes in 350 degrees oven. Cool and frost.

Frosting

2   cups sugar
1   cup water
     Pinch of salt
½   cup egg whites

2   tablespoons sugar
1   teaspoon vanilla
1   large coconut, coarsely grated

Cook sugar, water, and salt over high heat to make syrup. Stir mix until sugar is dissolved. Do not stir after mix reaches boiling point. Cover pan for 30 seconds to wash sugar crystals from sided of pan. Beat egg whites stiff with 2 tablespoons sugar and gradually pour syrup over them beating constantly. Add vanilla. Spread frosting between layers. Sprinkle generously with coconut. Frost top and sides of cake. Sprinkle with coconut.

Crunch Cake

1½ cups shortening
2¼ cups sugar
1   cup eggs (about 4)
3   cups flour

1   teaspoon baking powder
¾   cup water
1   teaspoon vanilla extract
1   teaspoon lemon extract

Cream shortening and sugar. Add eggs. Sift flour with baking powder. Add water and flour mixture alternately. Add extracts. Bake 1 hour at 350 degrees in tube pan.

Mrs. David Steinberg

Cupcakes

⅓	cup butter	½	teaspoon cinnamon
1	(15-ounce) jar unsweetened applesauce	½	teaspoon nutmeg
		1	cup seedless raisins
¾	cup sugar		Orange juice
2	cups flour		Light wine
1	teaspoon salt	2	teaspoons soda
½	teaspoon cloves	1	tablespoon cold water

Melt butter over low heat with applesauce and sugar; cool. Sift flour, salt, cloves, cinnamon, and nutmeg, together. Soak raisins in a small amount of orange juice or light wine for 20 minutes. Combine applesauce mixture, flour mixture, and raisins. Dissolve soda in the tablespoon of cold water, and fold in gently. Bake in small muffin tins in a 350 degrees oven until done.

Mrs. C. C. Varnedoe

Date Cake

1	cup oil	1	teaspoon allspice
3	eggs	1	teaspoon baking soda
1½	cups sugar	1	cup buttermilk
2	cups sifted flour	1	cup chopped pecans
1	teaspoon salt	1	cup chopped dates
1	teaspoon nutmeg	1	teaspoon vanilla
1	teaspoon cinnamon		

Combine oil and eggs, beating until smooth and creamy. Sift together dry ingredients adding alternately with buttermilk to egg mixture. Mix until smooth. Stir in pecans, dates, and vanilla. Grease and flour a 13x9x2-inch pan. Bake 55 to 60 minutes at 300 degrees or until done. Cool in pan. Spread with ½ recipe for Buttermilk Icing.

Makes 24 squares

Mrs. George Nichols

Dark Fruit Cake

1	pound butter	1	pound citron, diced
1	pound flour	2	pounds raisin, seeded and diced
2½	teaspoons nutmeg		
½	teaspoon cloves	3	pounds dates, diced
2	teaspoons mace	1	pound crystallized pineapple, diced
2	tablespoons cinnamon		
2	tablespoons allspice	1	pound crystallized cherries, diced
1	tablespoon vanilla		
1	cup dark brown sugar	½	pound orange and lemon peel, mixed and diced
1	cup white sugar		
10	eggs	2	pounds shelled pecan meats, diced
¾	cup syrup		
1	teaspoon soda dissolved in little water	¾	cup whiskey

Mix butter, flour (sifted with nutmeg, cloves, mace, cinnamon, and allspice), vanilla, brown sugar, white sugar, and eggs. Add syrup with soda. Add fruit and mix well. Add whiskey. Put in bread pans and bake at 225 degrees for 2 to 2½ hours or until brown.

Mrs. Alex Little

Date Nut Loaf

1	cup flour	4	cups chopped nuts
	Dash salt	1	cup sugar
2	teaspoons baking powder	4	eggs, separate yolks and whites
1	pound dates, chopped and floured		
		1	teaspoon vanilla

Combine flour, salt, baking powder, dates, and nuts. Cream sugar and egg yolks and add to other ingredients. Add vanilla. Beat egg whites and fold in. Bake at 325 degrees for 1 hour in loaf pan.

Mrs. Chandler Blanton

Devil's Food Cake

1	cup sugar	2	cups sifted flour
1	cup cocoa	1	teaspoon soda dissolved in
1	cup milk		1 teaspoon water
1	stick butter	½	cup milk
1	cup sugar	1	teaspoon vanilla
3	eggs		

Mix sugar, cocoa, and milk to make custard. Cook until thick and set aside to cool. Cream butter and sugar. Add eggs, flour, soda dissolved in water, milk, and vanilla. Add custard to this. Bake in 2 round 9-inch cake pans at 350 degrees for 30 minutes. Frost with white or chocolate frosting.

Mrs. Grady Durden

French Coffee Cake

½	pound butter	1	teaspoon baking soda
1	cup sugar		Vanilla
4	eggs	½	cup brown sugar
3	cups flour	½	cup white sugar
4	teaspoons baking powder	1	cup chopped nuts
1	cup sour cream		Cinnamon

Cream butter and sugar. Add eggs, one at a time beating well after each. Add flour sifted with baking powder alternating with sour cream and baking soda. Add vanilla. Pour half of batter into 10-inch greased tube pan. Mix brown and white sugar, nuts and cinnamon. Sprinkle batter in pan with ¾ of sugar and nut mixture. Cover with remainder of batter and sprinkle rest of sugar and nut mixture over top. Bake at 325 degrees for 55 minutes.

Mrs. Alex Culbreth

Dutch Cocoa Cream Cake

1½ cups cake flour
1¼ cups sugar
3   teaspoons baking powder
1   teaspoon salt

¼   cup cocoa
½   cup shortening
1   teaspoon vanilla
⅔   cup evaporated milk

Preheat oven to 350 degrees. Sift first 5 ingredients together. Add shortening, vanilla, and milk. Beat 2 minutes. Bake in 2 layers, about 8x1¼-inch pans at 350 degrees for about 30 minutes. Cool. With sharp knife, split to make 4 thin layers.

Filling
1½ cups chilled whipping
     cream
1   teaspoon vanilla

4   tablespoons confectioners'
     sugar
     Vanilla
     Confectioners' sugar

Whip first 3 ingredients in chilled mixing bowl until very stiff. Beat in vanilla and confectioners' sugar to create desired flavor. Spread between layers.

Milk Chocolate Icing
4   tablespoons butter
6   tablespoons cocoa
5   tablespoons hot milk

2   cups confectioners' sugar
¼   teaspoon salt
1   teaspoon vanilla

Melt butter and cocoa over hot water. Pour hot milk into confectioners' sugar and salt. Stir until dissolved. Stir in vanilla and the hot cocoa mixture. Mixture will be thin. Beat until thick enough to spread. Frost top and sides.

Mrs. Fred Dodson

Fruit Cake #1

½	pound cherries	1	cup flour
½	pound pineapple	½	pound sugar
½	pound white raisins	½	pound butter
¼	pound orange peel	6	eggs
¼	pound lemon peel	1	cup flour
½	pound citron	1	teaspoon baking powder
1	quart chopped pecans	1	teaspoon salt
2	cans extra moist coconut or fresh coconut	1	teaspoon vanilla

Prepare fruit night before with 1 cup of flour. Cream sugar and butter until smooth. Add eggs, one at a time. Add 1 cup flour with baking powder and salt. Add vanilla. Bake at 200 degrees for 5½ hours in tube pan.

Mrs. John Howell

Fruit Cake #2

1	pound cherries	5	eggs
1	pound pineapple	2	teaspoons vanilla
1	pound white raisins	1	teaspoon nutmeg
4	cups nuts	1	teaspoon cinnamon
2	cups flour	1	orange rind, grated
2	sticks butter	1	lemon rind, grated
1	cup sugar		

Chop fruit and nuts; dredge with part of the flour. Mix butter, sugar, eggs, remaining flour, fruit, nuts, vanilla, seasonings and rinds in this order. Bake at 300 degrees for 2 hours or longer. Makes 1 large tube cake or 3 loaf cakes.

Mrs. Walton Carter

🎋 *Fruit Cake #3*

1 pound pineapple, diced	2 quarts pecans, chopped
1 pound cherries, diced	2 cans sweetened condensed
1 pound coconut	milk
1 box white raisins	

Mix together, and bake at 250 degrees for 2 hours or until good and brown.

Susan Mackey

Japanese Fruit Cake

2 cups sugar	1 teaspoon cinnamon
1 cup butter	1 teaspoon allspice
4 eggs	½ teaspoon cloves
3¼ cups flour, saving ¼ cup to dredge raisins	¼ teaspoon mace
	¼ pound raisins, finely
2 teaspoons baking powder	chopped and dredged in
1 scant cup milk	remaining ¼ cup flour
1 teaspoon vanilla	

Cream sugar and butter. Add eggs, one at a time. Sift flour and baking powder. Alternately add, flour and milk to egg mixture. Add vanilla. Divide batter into two parts. Into part one add spices and raisins to make spice layers. Part two will make white layers. Bake part one into 2 layers. Bake part two into 2 layers.

Filling

Juice of 2 lemons	2 cups sugar
Grated rind of 1 lemon	1 cup boiling water
Grated rind of 1 orange	2 tablespoons cornstarch
1 good sized coconut, grated (or 2 packages frozen coconut)	

Put all together into saucepan except cornstarch. When mixture begins to boil, add the cornstarch dissolved in ½ cup cold water. Continue to cook, stirring constantly until mixture drops in a lump from spoon. Cool. Spread filling between layers. Alternate layers, starting with spice layer and ending with white on top. Top with filling.

Seventeen-Pound Fruit Cake

½	pound butter	1	pound candied cherries
1	pound powdered sugar	1	small bottle lemon extract
12	eggs	1	small bottle vanilla extract
1	pound box cake flour	1	pound candied orange peel
1	teaspoon salt	1	pound candied lemon peel
1	teaspoon baking soda	1	pound candied pineapple
2	pounds dark or white raisins	1	cup blackberry wine
3	pounds pecans		All the liquid from large can of sliced pineapple
1	pound citron		

Sift together flour, salt and baking powder. Dredge fruit thoroughly with this mixture. Cream butter and sugar. Add 12 beaten egg yolks. Whip egg whites stiff and fold into cream mixture. Stir in prepared fruit and blend thoroughly. Stir in pineapple liquid. Bake at 200 degrees in any size pan or pans you desire. Sprinkle wine over cake while it is still hot.

Mrs. Carol Sherwood

Franklin Nut Cake

1	pound butter	2	cups nuts
2	cups sugar	4	cups flour
6	eggs, beaten	1	teaspoon baking powder
½	pound cherries	¼	teaspoon salt
½	pound pineapple	2	teaspoons vanilla

Cream butter and sugar. Add eggs. Dredge mixed fruit and nuts well in 1 cup of flour. Add 3 cups flour, baking powder, and salt to butter mixture and mix well. Then add nuts and fruit. Add vanilla. Pour into greased tube pan. Bake at 250 degrees for 2½ to 3 hours.

Mrs. Virginia Noel

Top of Stove Fruit Cake

1	cup soft butter	1	cup self-rising flour
1	cup sugar	1	pound cherries, diced
4	eggs	1	pound pineapple, diced
2	teaspoons vanilla	1½	quarts pecans, chopped

Cream butter and sugar; add eggs, one at a time and beat well after each. Add vanilla. Put cup of flour over nuts and fruit. Pour batter mixture over fruit and nuts and cook over medium heat in a heavy pot on top of stove, stirring for 15 to 20 minutes. Then pack down well in lined cupcake pan and bake for 25 minutes at 300 degrees. Refrigerate.

Mrs. Ray M. Fite

White Fruit Cake

½	pound butter	1	teaspoon vanilla extract
2	cups sugar	1	pound white raisins
6	eggs	4	cups pecans
4	cups flour	1	pound pineapple, diced
1	scant cup pineapple juice	½	pound citron
1	teaspoon lemon juice	1	pound cherries

Cream butter and sugar well. Add eggs, one at a time. Add flour and juice alternately, start with flour and end with flour (reserving 1 cup flour for fruit). Add vanilla, then fruit that has been dredged in 1 cup of flour. Bake at 225 degrees in 3 (4½x9-inch) loaf pans. Wrap in waxed paper while hot.

Mrs. L.O. Smith

Fudge Cake or Pie

½	cup butter	½	cup all-purpose flour
1	cup sugar	1	teaspoon vanilla
2	egg yolks	2	egg whites
2	ounces chocolate	⅛	teaspoon salt

Cream butter and add the sugar gradually. Beat in the egg yolks. Melt the chocolate over hot water, cool slightly and beat into the sugar mixture. Sift flour before measuring and beat into the sugar mixture. Add the vanilla. Whip egg whites and salt until stiff; fold into the batter. Bake in a greased 8½-inch pie plate in a 325 degrees oven for about ½ hour.

Note: ½ cup crushed or chopped pecans may be added to the top before the pie is baked. Serve the cake topped with ice cream.

Mrs. Roger M. Budd

Jelly Roll

3	eggs	1	teaspoon baking powder
1	cup sugar	¼	teaspoon salt
⅓	cup water		Confectioners' sugar
1	teaspoon vanilla		Jelly of choice
1	cup cake flour		

Beat eggs until thick and lemon colored. Gradually beat in sugar. Blend in water and vanilla on low speed. Mix in dry ingredients that have been sifted together, on low speed. Pour into jelly roll pan, 15x10x1-inch, which has been greased and dusted with flour. Bake 12 to 15 minutes in preheated oven at 375 degrees. Turn immediately upside down on a towel, which has been sprinkled with confectioners' sugar. While cake is still hot, roll cake and towel from narrow end. Cool on rack. Unroll cake, remove towel, spread with jelly and roll again.

Mrs. Fred Dodson

Tunnel of Fudge Cake

1½	cups soft butter	1	package double Dutch
6	eggs		fudge buttercream frosting
1½	cups sugar		mix
2	cups plain flour	2	cups chopped walnuts

Cream butter in large mixer bowl. Add eggs, one at a time, beating well after each. Gradually add sugar; continue creaming at high speed until light and fluffy. By hand, stir in flour, frosting mix and walnuts until well blended. Pour batter into greased Bundt pan or 10-inch tube pan. Bake at 350 degrees for 60 to 65 minutes. Cool 2 hours. Remove from pan. Cool completely before serving.

Mrs. Jack Sullivan

Jam Cake

1	cup butter	1	cup cold water
2	cups sugar	1	cup nuts
4	eggs	1	cup raisins
3	cups flour	1	cup coconut
2	heaping teaspoons baking powder	1	cup strawberry or blackberry jam

Cream butter and sugar together. Add 4 beaten egg yolks. Reserve ½ cup of flour and then add remaining flour, sifted with baking powder, and water alternately. After beating, fold in 4 stiffly beaten egg whites. Bake either in loaf or 2 layers. Ice as desired. Then mix cake as usual. Grind nuts, raisins, and coconut together. Add jam and reserved flour to nut and raisin mixture. Then add this mixture to cake mixture. Bake in 3 layers for large cake or 4 layers for 2 smaller cakes.

Filling

3	cups sugar	½	fresh coconut, grated (may use canned)
1	cup milk		
1	cup ground raisins	½	stick butter
2	cups ground nuts		

Boil sugar and milk until a soft ball forms in cold water. Then add raisins, nuts, coconut and butter. Continue cooking until well blended. Put between layers and on top and sides of cake.

Mrs. Nettie Keller

German Chocolate Cake

1	(12-ounce) package sweet cooking chocolate or German chocolate	4	egg yolks, unbeaten
		1	teaspoon vanilla
½	cup boiling water	2½	cups sifted cake flour
1	cup butter, margarine or shortening	1	teaspoon baking soda
		½	teaspoon salt
2	cups sugar	1	cup buttermilk
		4	egg whites, stiffly beaten

Melt chocolate in boiling water. Cool. Cream butter and sugar until light and fluffy. Add egg yolks, one at a time, beating after each. Add vanilla and melted chocolate and mix until blended. Sift flour with soda and salt. Add sifted dry ingredients alternately with buttermilk, beating after each addition until batter is smooth. Fold in stiffly beaten egg whites. Pour batter into 3 (8- or 9-inch) layer pans, lined on bottoms with paper. Bake at 350 degrees for 35 to 40 minutes. Cool. Frost top between layers with Coconut-Pecan Frosting.

Coconut-Pecan Frosting

1	cup evaporated milk or half-and-half	1	teaspoon vanilla
		1	(7-ounce) can tender-thin flaked coconut
1	cup sugar		
3	egg yolks	1	cup chopped pecans
¼	pound margarine		

Combine evaporated or milk half-and-half, sugar, egg yolks, margarine and vanilla in a saucepan. Cook over medium heat 12 minutes, stirring constantly, until mixture thickens. Add coconut and pecans. Beat until cool and of spreading consistency. Makes enough to cover tops of 3 (9-inch) layers. Do not frost sides of cakes.

Mrs. Jack Sullivan

Lane Cake

1 cup butter	1 cup milk
2 cups sugar	1 tablespoons vanilla
3¼ cups flour	8 eggs whites, reserve yolks
2 teaspoons baking powder	for filling

Cream butter with sugar. Sift together flour and baking powder. Add to first mixture alternately with milk and vanilla. Blend well. Fold in stiffly beaten egg whites. Bake in 3 (8-inch) layers at 375 degrees for 25 to 30 minutes. Cool.

Filling

½ cup butter	1 cup raisins
1 cup sugar	1 cup pecans
1 tablespoon cornstarch	1 cup coconut
8 egg yolks	2 jiggers bourbon

Cream butter, sugar and cornstarch. Add egg yolks. Cook over hot water 15 to 20 minutes, or until thick. Add other ingredients. Cool Spread between layers of cake.

Frosting

2½ cups granulated sugar	⅔ cup water
⅛ teaspoon salt	2 egg whites, beaten
⅓ cup dark corn syrup	1 teaspoon vanilla

Combine sugar, salt, water, and syrup in sauce pan. Cook on stovetop. When syrup reaches boiling point, pour 3 tablespoonfuls into egg whites. Continue beating until stiff. Cook remaining syrup to 240 degrees on candy thermometer. Gradually pour over egg whites, beating until frosting begins to lose its gloss. Add vanilla. Spread on sides and top of cake.

Mrs. Richard Beckmann

Lemon Cheese Cake #1

½	cup butter	2	teaspoons baking powder
1½	cups sugar	1	cup milk
2	cups flour		Pinch of salt
2	heaping teaspoons cornstarch	1	teaspoon vanilla
		3	egg whites, beaten stiff

Cream butter and sugar. Sift flour, cornstarch, baking powder and add to sugar mixture, alternately with milk. Add salt and vanilla and fold in egg whites. Cook in 2 round cake pans at 350 degrees for 25 or 30 minutes.

Filling

3	egg yolks	1	tablespoon cornstarch
1	cup sugar		Pinch of salt
2	lemons, grated rind and juice	1	cup boiling water
1	tablespoon flour	1	tablespoon butter

Cook above ingredients in double boiler until thick. Remove from heat and beat until stiff.

Mrs. H. Briggs Smith

Lemon Cheese Cake #2

2	sticks butter	1	cup ice water
1¾	cups sugar	1	teaspoon vanilla
3	cups plain flour		Pinch of salt
4	teaspoons baking powder	8	egg whites, beaten stiff

Cream butter and sugar. Add other ingredients, folding in egg whites last. This makes 3 large layers. Bake at 350 degrees.

Filling

8	egg yolks		Rind of 1 lemon
1½	cups sugar		Pinch of salt
	Juice from 2 lemons	1	apple, grated

Cream yolks and sugar. Add remaining ingredients. Place in double boiler and cook until thick enough to spread. Fill cake.

Mrs. Chandler Blanton

Marble Cake

2	sticks butter	2	cups self-rising flour
1½	cups sugar	1	teaspoon vanilla
4	eggs, separated	1	(5½-ounce) can chocolate
½	cup milk		syrup

Cream butter and sugar. Add egg yolks and milk. Add flour. Add vanilla. Fold in stiffly beaten egg whites. Pour ¾ of mixture into greased and floured tube pan. Add chocolate to other ¼ mixture. Spoon on top of mixture in pan. Cut in with knife. Bake 1 hour and 15 minutes at 300 degrees.

Mrs. Diane M. Smith

Oatmeal Cake

1¼	cups boiling water	2	eggs, beaten
1	cup instant oats	1⅓	cups plain sifted flour
1	stick butter	1	teaspoon soda
1	cup brown sugar	1	teaspoon cinnamon
1	cup plain sugar		

Pour boiling water over oats and set aside. Mix remaining ingredients together. Combine the two mixtures and pour into a 9x12-inch pan and bake 30 minutes at 350 degrees.

Icing

1	stick butter, melted	1	cup pecans
¾	cup coconut	1	teaspoon vanilla
¼	cup canned milk	¾	cup plain sugar

Mix above ingredients and spread over baked cake. Place under broiler until icing is bubbly.

Mrs. Jack Rudolph

Mayonnaise Cake

1	cup sugar	4	tablespoons cocoa
1	cup mayonnaise		Pinch of salt
2	cups flour	1	cup cold water
2	teaspoons baking soda	1	teaspoon vanilla

Cream sugar and mayonnaise together. Mix all dry ingredients and sift together. Combine both mixtures and water and then beat until very smooth. Add vanilla. Bake in loaf pans at 350 degrees for 30 minutes or more.

Mrs. Richard Beckmann

Orange Cake

1	cup butter or margarine	5	eggs
2	cups sugar	3	cups cake flour
½	teaspoon vanilla	1	tablespoon baking powder
2	tablespoons grated orange rind		Pinch of salt
		¾	cup milk

Butter and flour a 10-inch tube pan. Cream butter and sugar until light and fluffy. Add vanilla and orange rind. Add eggs, one at a time, beating well after each addition. Sift together twice the cake flour, baking powder and salt. Add to the cream mixture a little at a time, alternately with the milk, ending up with flour, beating well after each addition. Spoon into prepared tube pan. Bake in a 350 degree oven for about 1 hour or until top of cake springs back when touched. Cool pan on wire cake rack for 2 minutes.

Glaze

¼	cup butter or margarine	⅔	cup sugar
⅓	cup orange juice		

Heat ingredients for glaze in a saucepan until sugar is dissolved. Pour evenly over cake in pan while cake is still hot. Allow the cake to cool thoroughly in pan before removing.

Serves 14 to 16

Mrs. Joyce Mixson

Orange Coconut Cake

¾ cup butter
2 cups sugar
1½ teaspoons grated orange rind
2 egg yolks
3 cups flour

4½ teaspoons baking powder
¼ teaspoon salt
½ cup orange juice
¾ cup water
½ cup coconut
4 egg whites, beaten stiff

Cream butter and sugar, then blend in orange rind and egg yolks. Sift flour, baking powder and salt together. Add to first mixture alternately with orange juice and water. Beat just enough to make batter smooth. Blend in coconut and egg whites. Bake in 3 (9-inch) pans, about 30 minutes at 350 degrees. Ice with any white icing or good plain.

Will keep for days and is really better after several days.

Mrs. O.C. Carruthers

Orange Layer Cake

½ cup butter
1½ cups sugar
2 eggs
Grated rind of 1 orange
2¼ cups flour

2 teaspoons baking powder
¼ teaspoon soda
½ cup orange juice
¼ cup milk

Cream butter and sugar. Add orange rind. Beat in eggs. Sift dry ingredients and then add to butter mixture alternating with orange juice and milk. Bake in layers.

Filling
3 tablespoons flour
½ cup orange juice
½ cup butter

½ cup sugar
½ cup chopped nuts
2 cups powdered sugar

Cook flour and juice together until thick paste. Blend butter and sugar and add to paste. Beat until fluffy. Add nuts and sugar. Frost cake layers.

Mrs. Bill Keller

Orange Slice Cake

3½	cups sifted all-purpose flour	1	(3¾-ounce) can flaked
½	teaspoon salt		coconut
1	pound orange slice candy,	1	cup butter
	cut up	2	cups sugar
1	(8-ounce) package pitted	4	eggs
	dates, chopped	1	teaspoon baking soda
2	cups pecans or walnuts,	½	cup buttermilk
	chopped		

Preheat oven to 300 degrees. Sift flour and salt together. Combine candy, dates, nuts, and coconut. Mix well. Add ½ cup flour mixture candy, fruit and nuts. Cream butter. Add sugar gradually and beat light. Add eggs, one at a time, beating well after each. Combine soda and buttermilk; mix well. Add alternately with remaining flour to egg mixture. Add floured candy to mixture. Mix well and spoon into greased 10-inch tube pan. Bake 1 hour and 45 minutes or until done. Remove from oven.

Glaze (optional)

1	cup orange juice	2	cups confectioners' sugar

Combine orange juice and sugar and mix until blended and pour over hot cake. Cool. Let stand in refrigerator overnight before removing from pan.

Mrs. Ray M. Fite

Pineapple Chiffon Cake, Quickie

1	orange chiffon cake, slice in	1	can crushed pineapple
	3 layers	1	package vanilla pudding

Cook pineapple and vanilla pudding 1 or 2 minutes. Bring to a boil. Cool. Fold in 1½ small containers of whipping cream, whipped. Put between layers and on top and sides. Refrigerate overnight.

Mrs. Bill Lester

Pecan Whiskey Cake

3	cups sifted flour	1	cup plus 2 tablespoons
2	teaspoons baking powder		100 proof bourbon
2	teaspoons nutmeg	3½	cups pecan halves, coarsely
1	cup butter or margarine		chopped
2	cups sugar	1½	cups seedless raisins
6	eggs, separated	½	cup diced candied fruit

Sift together flour, baking powder and nutmeg. Cream butter and sugar; thoroughly beat in egg yolks, one at a time. Beat in sifted dry ingredients alternately with 1 cup bourbon; batter should be smooth. Stir in pecans, raisins and candied fruit. Beat egg whites until stiff: fold in. Turn into a 10-inch tube pan. Line with greased brown paper. Bake at 250 degrees for about 4 hours or until wire cake tester inserted in center comes out clean. Place a shallow pan of water on top oven shelf for first 2½ hours of baking. Cool cake in pan on wire rack for 30 minutes. Turn cake out. Remove paper and finish cooling. Dribble top of cake with 2 tablespoons bourbon; wrap tightly and store overnight in airtight container. Refrigerate to slice easily.

Mrs. William M. Gabard

Pumpkin Cake

4	eggs	1	cup vegetable oil
2	cups sugar	3	ounces cream cheese,
2	cups flour		softened
1	teaspoon baking powder	1	teaspoon vanilla
2	teaspoons baking soda	¾	stick margarine
½	teaspoon salt	1	tablespoon cream
2	teaspoons cinnamon	1¾	cups powdered sugar
2	cups canned pumpkin		

Beat eggs and sugar. Sift dry ingredients. Add pumpkin and oil. Then add sifted dry ingredients. Put in greased oblong pan. Bake at 350 degrees for 45 minutes. Cool. Mix cream cheese, vanilla, margarine, cream and powdered sugar to make frosting. Frost cake.

Dean Brooks

Pineapple Upside Down Cake

Filling

¾ cup sifted brown sugar

1 (20-ounce) can crushed pineapple, drained

Sprinkle brown sugar evenly into oblong pan. Spoon crushed pineapple over brown sugar.

Cake

1 stick margarine
1 cup sugar
1¾ cups flour
½ teaspoon salt
1⅔ teaspoons baking powder

2 eggs
¾ cup milk (or ⅜ cup milk and ⅜ cup pineapple juice)
1 teaspoon vanilla

Cream margarine and sugar. Sift dry ingredients together. Add eggs, one at a time; beating after each. Add sifted dry ingredients alternately with milk, beating after each addition. Add vanilla. Pour over pineapple. Bake at 350 degrees for 25 to 30 minutes. Serve upside down with whipped cream.

Mrs. William R. Davis

Pound Cake

1 cup butter
½ cup shortening
3 cups sugar
6 eggs
3 cups cake flour

½ teaspoon baking powder
¼ teaspoon salt
1 cup milk
1 teaspoon extract of choice

Cream butter, shortening and sugar. Add eggs, one at a time and beat well. Combine flour, baking powder and salt. Sift. Add half of flour and milk, beat well, and then add remaining flour and milk. Add extract. Line tube pan with brown or waxed paper. Pour mixture into pan and bake at 350 degrees for 1 hour.

Mrs. Maude Willis

Mrs. Hensley's Delicious Pound Cake

1	cup butter (½ pound)	1	teaspoon mace
½	cup shortening		Dash of salt
2¾	cups sugar	1	cup milk
5	eggs, add one at a time	1	tablespoon almond extract
3	cups cake flour		Dash of yellow food coloring

Mix all ingredients together in order, and put in a greased tube pan. Bake at 350 degrees for 1 hour and 10 or 15 minutes. Do not open oven while cooking.

Susan Mackey

Hershey Pound Cake

2	sticks butter	1	cup buttermilk
2	cups sugar	2	teaspoons vanilla
4	whole eggs	8	Hershey bars, melted over
2½	cups sifted flour		hot water
¼	teaspoon soda dissolved in buttermilk	1	cup chopped pecans

Mix in order. Pour into greased and floured tube pan. Bake at 325 degrees for 1½ hours.

Mrs. Bill Keller

Whipping Cream Pound Cake

2	sticks butter, room temperature	6	large eggs
		½	pint whipping cream
3	cups sugar	3	cups flour

Blend butter and sugar gradually until well creamed. Add eggs, one at a time. Add whipping cream and flour alternately to egg and butter mixture. Bake at 300 degrees in greased and floured tube pan about 1½ hours.

Mrs. John B. Lasintger

🍃 *Peach Brandy Pound Cake*

3	cups sugar	1	cup sour cream
1	cup butter	½	teaspoon lemon extract
6	eggs	1	teaspoon orange extract
3	cups all-purpose flour	¼	teaspoon almond extract
¼	teaspoon baking soda	2	teaspoons rum
	Pinch of salt	½	cup peach brandy

Combine sugar and butter; cream until light and fluffy. Add eggs, one at a time, mixing well after each addition. Combine dry ingredients. Add to creamed mixture alternately with sour cream, beating after each addition. Stir in remaining ingredients. Pour batter into a well-greased and floured 10-inch Bundt or tube pan. Bake at 325 degrees for 1 hour and 20 minutes, or until cake tests done. Cool 10 minutes in pan. Remove.

Ingrid Carroll

Red Cake

½	cup butter	1	teaspoon salt
1½	cups sugar	1	teaspoon vanilla
2	eggs	1	teaspoon soda
2	tablespoons cocoa	1	cup buttermilk
2	ounces red food coloring	1	tablespoon vinegar
2¼	cups plain flour		

Cream butter and sugar. Add eggs, one at a time. Make a paste with cocoa and food coloring. Add to butter mixture. Add flour and salt alternately with buttermilk. Add vanilla, soda and vinegar. Blend. Bake in 2 greased and floured 8-inch pans at 350 degrees for 30 minutes.

Frosting

3	tablespoons flour	½	cup plus 2 tablespoons butter
1	cup milk	2	tablespoons shortening
1	cup sugar	1	teaspoon vanilla

Cook flour and milk over low heat until thick. Cool. Cream sugar, butter, shortening, and vanilla until fluffy. Add to milk mixture and beat until mixture is like whipped cream. Spread on layers.

Mrs. Richard Beckmann

Sour Cream Pound Cake

2	sticks butter	3	cups cake flour
3	cups sugar	¼	teaspoon soda
6	eggs	¼	teaspoon salt
1	teaspoon almond extract	½	pint sour cream

Beat butter slightly. Add part of sugar and mix smooth. Add remaining sugar and beat until very smooth and fluffy. Add eggs, one at a time, beating well after each addition. Stir in extract. Add dry ingredients alternately with sour cream. Bake at 325 degrees in greased and floured Bundt or tube pan for 30 minutes. Reduce heat to 300 degrees and cook 45 to 50 minutes or until cake is done. Cool cake 5 minutes before taking out of pan.

Mrs. E.G. Barham

Sour Cream Nut Cake

1	cup sweet whipped butter	¼	teaspoon soda
3	cups sugar	1	cup sour cream
5	eggs	½	teaspoon vanilla extract
3	cups plain flour (reserve some for dusting nuts)	½	teaspoon lemon extract
		1	quart chopped pecans

Cream butter and sugar, adding eggs, one at a time. Mix flour and soda and add alternately with sour cream to butter mixture. Add extracts and pecans. Bake at 325 degrees in greased and floured tube pan for 1½ hours. Remove from pan. While cake is still hot pour glaze over top.

Glaze

⅔	cup sugar	⅓	cup orange juice
¼	cup melted butter		

Combine above ingredients. Mix to dissolve sugar.

Mrs. George Cross

261

Shortcake

8	egg whites	1	cup sugar
1	teaspoon baking powder		

Beat whites until foamy, then add baking powder, beat stiff. Add sugar very slowly and beat until eggs stand in peaks. Bake in 2 layers in well greased cake tins. Bake about 1 hour at 200 degrees. Serve with strawberries or soft fresh peaches. Garnish with whipped cream.

Mrs. B.G. Lastinger

Sweet Potato Cake

4	eggs, separated	1½	cups grated sweet potatoes
1½	cups oil	½	cup chopped nuts
2	cups sugar	1	teaspoon cinnamon
2	cups sifted cake flour	1	teaspoon nutmeg
3	tablespoons baking powder	1	teaspoon vanilla
¼	teaspoon salt	4	tablespoons hot water

Beat egg whites and place aside. Cream oil and sugar until fluffy, add egg yolks, flour, baking powder, salt, sweet potatoes, nuts, cinnamon, nutmeg, vanilla and water. Fold in egg whites. Bake in 350 degrees oven for 25 to 30 minutes, in greased layer pans.

Filling

1	cup evaporated milk	¼	pound margarine
1	cup sugar	1	cup coconut
3	egg yolks	1	teaspoon vanilla

Place milk, sugar, egg yolks and margarine in a double boiler and cook for 10 minutes. Remove from heat and add coconut and vanilla. When cool spread on cake layers.

Mrs. Jack Rudolph

Strawberry-Pecan Cake

1	box white cake mix	1	cup frozen strawberries
1	small box strawberry jello	1	cup coconut
¾	cup vegetable oil	1	cup pecans or walnuts,
¾	cup milk		chopped
4	eggs		

Mix cake mix and jello together dry. Add other ingredients. Bake in 3 layers at 350 degrees for 30 to 45 minutes.

Icing

1	stick margarine	½	cup strawberries, drained
1	box confectioners' sugar	½	cup pecans or walnuts
½	cup coconut		

Cream margarine and sugar, adding other ingredients. Then spread on cake.

Sue Dennard

Strawberry Cake

1	box white cake mix	½	cup warm water
1	regular box strawberry jello	4	eggs
1	scant cup vegetable oil	½	cup frozen strawberries

In a mixing bowl, mix together the cake mix and jello. Blend in oil, water and eggs, adding eggs one at a time and stirring after each addition. Next, stir in berries. Grease 3 layer cake pan and pour in batter. Bake in a 350 degrees oven for 25 to 30 minutes. Cool and frost with Strawberry Frosting.

Strawberry Frosting

1	box confectioners' sugar	½	cup strawberries
1	stick butter or margarine		

Blend all ingredients together smoothly.

Mrs. Wright Bazemore

Sour Cream Chocolate Cake

½ cup cocoa	½ teaspoon salt
¾ cup boiling water	½ cup sour cream
½ cup butter	½ teaspoon baking soda
2 cups sugar	1 teaspoon vanilla
2 cups sifted cake flour	3 egg whites

Mix cocoa in boiling water and stir until smooth. Cool. Cream butter and sugar together until fluffy. Add cocoa mix to creamed mixture. Sift flour, salt and soda together. Add dry ingredients alternately with cream to first mixture. Add vanilla. Fold in stiffly beaten egg whites. Grease and flour 2 (9-inch) layer pans. Bake at 350 degrees for 30 minutes. Frost with fudge icing.

Mrs. Laurence Alvarez

White Chocolate Cake

¼ pound white chocolate	2½ cups cake flour
½ cup boiling water	1 teaspoon baking powder
1 cup butter	1 cup buttermilk
2 cups sugar	1 cup flaked coconut
4 eggs	1 cup finely chopped nuts
1 teaspoon vanilla	

Melt chocolate in boiling water and let cool. Cream butter and sugar. Beat in eggs one at a time. Add chocolate and vanilla. Add flour, sifted with powder, alternately with buttermilk. Stir in coconut and nuts. Bake in 3 layers at 350 degrees for 20 to 25 minutes.

Icing

½ cup water	4 egg whites
¼ cup white corn syrup	1 teaspoon vanilla
3 cups sugar	1 cup powdered sugar
½ teaspoon cream of tartar	

In saucepan, cook water, syrup, and sugar together until syrup spins first thread stage. Beat egg whites with cream of tartar until very stiff. Pour hot syrup into egg whites. Add vanilla and powdered sugar. Spread on layers.

Regular seven minute icing will not hold on this cake.

Mrs. Jim Tunison

Caramel Frosting #1

½	cup sugar	1	cup milk
2½	cups sugar	1	stick margarine

Brown ½ cup of sugar over low heat. Bring to boil, 2½ cups of sugar, milk and margarine. Add the browned sugar and stir constantly until well mixed and cook until a soft ball forms when dropped into cold water.

Mrs. Nettie Keller

Caramel Frosting #2

12	tablespoons (or ¾ cup) brown sugar	6	tablespoons top milk
6	tablespoons melted butter	1	cup powdered sugar
		½	teaspoon vanilla

Add brown sugar to melted butter and top milk. Let boil for 1 minute. Remove from heat and cool slightly. Add powdered sugar and vanilla. If too thick to spread, add more milk or cream until right consistency. This requires no beating.

Mrs. Bill Keller

Fudge Icing

3	squares unsweetened baking chocolate	1	cup water
		3	tablespoons white corn syrup
3	cups sugar	6	tablespoons butter
½	scant teaspoon salt	1½	teaspoons vanilla

Break chocolate into small pieces. Add sugar, salt, water and corn syrup. Cook slowly until it 234 degrees with occasional stirring. Remove from heat. Add butter and let cool to 120 degrees. Add vanilla and beat until it loses its glossy appearance.

Mrs. Lawrence Alvarez

White Frosting

2   egg whites
10 marshmallows

1   cup white corn syrup

Beat all together in an electric mixture. Frost cake.

Mrs. Jack Sullivan

Buttermilk Icing

2   cups sugar
2   cups buttermilk
1   teaspoon baking soda

1   teaspoon vanilla extract
1   cup butter

Combine all ingredients in a pan and cook over medium heat to a soft ball stage, stirring constantly. Remove from heat and cool for 5 minutes. Beat until it starts to thicken and of spreading consistency.

Mrs. George Nichols

Chocolate Frosting

2   cups white sugar
½   cup light brown sugar
2   squares chocolate

1   tablespoon white corn syrup
1   scant cup sweet milk
¾   stick butter

Cook all except butter until the soft ball stage. Remove from heat and add butter. Whipped topping until creamy. Add top cream if hardens.

Mrs. Jack Sullivan

White Icing

1   cup sugar
¼   teaspoon salt
½   teaspoon cream of tartar

2   egg whites
3   tablespoons water
1   teaspoon vanilla

Place first 5 ingredients in double boiler. Beat 3 minutes. Remove from heat. Add vanilla and beat 1 or 1½ minutes.

Mrs. Chandler Blanton

Milk Chocolate Icing

6	tablespoons cocoa	2	cups confectioners' sugar
4	tablespoons shortening	¼	teaspoon salt
5	tablespoons scalding hot milk	1	teaspoon vanilla

Place cocoa and shortening in double boiler until shortening melts. Pour hot milk over confectioners' sugar and salt. Stir to dissolve completely. Add hot cocoa mixture. Add vanilla. The mixture will be very thin while hot. It is not necessary to beat until cool.

Mrs. Robert Hornbuckle

Burnt Sugar Caramel Filling

3	cups sugar	1¼	sticks creamery butter
¾	cup sweet milk	1	teaspoon vanilla
¼	teaspoon baking soda		

Combine 2½ cups sugar and milk in which the soda has been dissolved. In a large saucepan. Start heating this slowly. Place remaining ½ cup sugar in a skillet and brown it until it starts to smoke. At this exact time add ⅓ cup boiling water and let it cook until it is very syrupy. Pour into the milk and sugar that you have been heating. Cook on medium heat for 8 to 10 minutes, or until it forms a soft ball in cold water. Remove from heat and add butter and vanilla. Cool until it is spreading consistency.

Mrs. Robert S. Adair, Jr.

Lemon Cheese Filling

4	egg yolks	2	tablespoons cornstarch
½	stick butter		Juice and rind of 2 lemons
1½	cups sugar		

Put all together: cook in double boiler until thick; let cool before spreading between layers of cake.

Mrs. Bill Keller

Chocolate Sauce

2	squares bitter chocolate	½	cup evaporated milk
2	tablespoons margarine	1	teaspoon vanilla
⅔	cup sugar	¼	cup sherry or brandy

Melt chocolate and margarine. Add sugar and milk. Simmer over low heat until sauce thickens. Add vanilla and sherry or brandy.

Mrs. Michael Kaiser

Chocolate Sauce For Ice Cream

½	cup white corn syrup	2½	squares bitter chocolate
1	cup sugar	1	teaspoon vanilla
1	cup water	1	cup evaporated milk

Cook syrup, sugar, and water together until it will form a soft ball in cold water. Remove from heat. Add chocolate and vanilla. Add evaporated milk. Stir until thick. Serve warm.

Mrs. Joyce Mixson

Chocolate Sauce for Hot Fudge Cake

1	stick butter or margarine	2	cups confectioners' sugar,
1	cup chocolate chips		sifted
1¼	cups evaporated milk		

Combine. Cook over low heat about 8 minutes. Pour over devils food cake that has a cube of vanilla ice cream between 2 pieces of cake.

Peggy Gayle

Deep Dish Apple Pie

10-12 tart cooking apples, sliced (or about 8 cups sliced apples)	**1 stick butter or margarine**
½ cup sugar	**1 cup sifted flour**
2 tablespoons lemon juice	**½ cup brown sugar, firmly packed**

Pare apples and cut into small pieces into bowl; stir in sugar and lemon juice to coat fruit well. Spoon into buttered 9-inch shallow baking dish. Combine flour and brown sugar in the same bowl; cut in butter or margarine with pastry blender or 2 knives; sprinkle over apples; pat down. Bake at 350 degrees for about 45 minutes, or until juice bubbles around edge and topping is golden brown.

Serve warm with cream, ice cream or snappy cheese.

Mrs. S.G. Bullington

Apple Pie "Henri"

1 can apple pie filling	**½ package applesauce spice cake mix**
¼ cup rum	
1 stick butter	

Pour in apple pie filling in a buttered 1- or 1½-quart casserole dish. Sprinkle rum over this. Take applesauce spice cake mix and sprinkle dry over apples. Melt butter and dribble over this, be sure top is wet. Bake 45 minutes at 350 degrees.

Serves 6 or 8

Good hot, room temperature, or cold with whipped cream or ice cream on top.

Mrs. Howard Dasher, Sr.

Blackberry Pie #1

1 quart blackberries, washed	1½ cups sugar
Unbaked pie pastry, top	2 tablespoons flour
and bottom	½ stick butter

Put blackberries in unbaked pie shell; cover with sugar and flour, dab with butter. Cover with crust. Slit top. Bake at 425 degrees for 1 hour.

Mrs. Wright Bazemore

Blackberry Pie #2

1½ cups sugar 3 tablespoons butter
1 quart blackberries, washed

Mix sugar blackberries and butter and then cover with water. Let come to a boil and turn off. Make pie crust for 2 layers and cut in strips. Alternate in deep dish between blackberries and pie crust ending with crust. Bake at 375 degrees for 45 minutes.

Mrs. George Varn

Black Bottom Pie

2½ cups scaled milk
5 beaten egg yolks
1 heaping cup sugar
2 tablespoons cornstarch
1 teaspoon vanilla
2 (6-ounce) packages
chocolate chips

1 heaping tablespoon gelatin
dissolved in ¼ cup cold
water
5 egg whites
1 teaspoon vanilla

Add scaled milk to beaten egg yolks. Then stir in combined ½ heaping cup sugar and cornstarch. Cook until a custard. Add 1 teaspoon vanilla. Then melt chocolate chips in double boiler. Add enough custard to make the consistency of pie. Add gelatin to remaining custard while hot. Add egg whites to remaining ½ cup sugar and beat. Add this to custard after it cools, add vanilla and put chocolate custard in crust as soon as it is made so it can set.

Mrs. Clarence Paine

Caramel Banana Pie

1   **can condensed milk**
2   **tablespoons hot water**
1   **baked pie shell**

1   **banana, sliced**
    Whipped cream

Place can of condensed milk into a pan of water. Heat. When water comes to a boil, cover and let simmer for 3 hours. Let cool. Open can and put milk into mixing bowl and add hot water. Stir very well. Put mixture into cool pie shell and refrigerate. When ready to serve put bananas and whipped cream on top.

May cook several cans of condensed milk at one time and keep in refrigerator for several weeks.

Mrs. Charles E. Davis

Sour Cherry Pie

Filling

⅓   **cup lemon juice**
1   **can condensed milk**
½   **cup whipping cream, whipped**

1   **teaspoon vanilla**
½   **teaspoon almond extract**

Stir together until thickened.

Topping

1   **can sour pitted cherries**
1   **tablespoon cornstarch**
½   **teaspoon almond extract**

    Pie pastry
¼   **cup slivered almonds**

Drain liquid from cherries. Add cornstarch and cook over medium heat until thickened and clear. Add extract. Sprinkle almonds on pastry before baking. Add filling, then topping. Bake.

Mrs. Walton Carter

Chess Pie

1	stick butter	1	teaspoon vanilla extract
2	eggs	1	teaspoon lemon extract
1	cup sugar		Unbaked pie pastry
1	tablespoon cornmeal		

Brown butter slightly. Beat eggs; add sugar slowly. Add cornmeal and extracts. Pour into unbaked pastry and then bake at 300 degrees for 45 minutes. The top should be crusty and the center transparent.

Dr. William M. Gabard

Lemon Chess Pie

4	whole eggs	¼	cup fresh orange juice
1½	cups sugar	¼	teaspoon salt
¾	stick butter	1	teaspoon flour
	Juice and rind of 2 lemons		Unbaked pie pasty
3	teaspoons plain cornmeal		

Beat eggs, sugar, and butter together well. Add all other ingredients, beating well. Pour into pastry and bake at 400 degrees about 10 minutes, or until pie is set. Reduce heat to 325 degrees and bake until brown and pie shakes a little in the middle (about 30 minutes).

Mrs. Grady Durden

Southern Chess Pie

1	cup brown sugar	1	teaspoon vanilla extract
½	cup regular sugar	½	cup melted butter
1	tablespoon flour	1	cup pecans
2	eggs		Unbaked pie shell
2	tablespoons milk		

Preheat oven to 375 degrees. Mix sugars and flour. Beat in eggs, milk, vanilla and butter. Add nuts. Pour in unbaked pie shell and bake at 350 degrees for 50 minutes or until done.

Mrs. Diane M. Smith

Chocolate Pie

4	tablespoons flour	5	eggs
2	cups sugar	3	tablespoons butter
2	cups milk		Baked pie crust
¼	cup cocoa		Meringue

Cook ingredients in a saucepan, stirring constantly. Remove from heat when thickened. Pour into crust. Put meringue on top and brown at 350 degrees.

Mrs. Robert Hornbuckle

French Silk Chocolate Pie

½	cup butter	2	large eggs
¾	cup granulated sugar	1	cup pecans, chopped
1	ounce unsweetened chocolate, melted	1	(9-inch) baked pie shell
1	teaspoon vanilla	1	cup whipping cream, whipped

Cream butter. Add sugar gradually and beat until light and fluffy. Add melted chocolate and vanilla. Add eggs one at a time. Beat 3 minutes between additions of eggs. Fold in pecans. Pour in crust and chill. Top with whipped cream. Refrigerate.

Carol Barker

Chocolate Almond Pie

5	almond chocolate bars	Graham cracker crumb
18	large marshmallows	crust, baked and chilled in
½	cup milk	refrigerator
½	pint whipped cream	

Melt chocolate bars and marshmallows with milk in top of double boiler. Chill in refrigerator. When cold, fold in whipped cream. Pour in pie crust. Chill in refrigerator for 3 or 4 hours.

German Chocolate Pie

1½ teaspoons flour	1 large can evaporated milk
2½ cups sugar	1 teaspoon vanilla
1 teaspoon cornstarch	Pinch of salt
2 eggs	1 cup coconut
1 stick margarine, melted	2 unbaked (9-inch) pie crusts
2 ounces bittersweet chocolate, melted (2 squares)	1 cup pecans, chopped

Mix sugar, flour, and cornstarch. Add eggs, mixing well. Then add melted margarine and chocolate. Continue mixing. Add milk, vanilla, and salt. Sprinkle coconut over bottom of 2 unbaked deep-dish pie crusts. Sprinkle pecans over coconut. Pour chocolate mixture into shells, and bake about 50 minutes in 350 degree oven.

Cindy Fann

Coconut Cream Pie

1 envelope gelatin	⅔ cup sugar
2 tablespoons cold water	1 cup coconut, grated or flaked
3 eggs	1 teaspoon vanilla
1½ cups milk	
Pinch of salt	

Soak gelatin in water. Separate eggs; beat yolks slightly in double boiler. Blend in milk and ⅓ cup sugar. Add salt. Cook over low heat or in top of double boiler until custard thickens and coats spoon. Remove from heat; add gelatin and stir until dissolved. Cool. Beat egg whites stiff, gradually adding remaining ⅓ cup sugar. Fold into custard mixture into which vanilla has been added. Add coconut and fill baked pie shell. Place in refrigerator to set. Top with ½ pint of whipping cream, stiffly whipped.

One cup of mashed bananas may be added to pie instead of coconut, if you prefer banana cream pie.

Mrs. Roger M. Budd

Cream Cheese Pie

Crust

1½ cups graham cracker crumbs

¼ pound melted butter
¼ cup powdered sugar

Mix and press in pie pan

Filling

3 small cakes cream cheese
½ cup sugar
2 eggs, beaten

1 whole lemon, juice and grated rind

Soften cheese and beat smooth. Add individually the sugar, eggs and lemon. Beat well after each addition. Put in crust and bake at 350 degrees for 25 to 30 minutes. Cool.

Topping

1 cup thick sour cream
2 tablespoons sugar

1 teaspoon vanilla

Mix sour cream, sugar, and vanilla. Spread on top of cream cheese mixture. Return to oven for 5 minutes. Chill.

Mrs. Bill Keller and Mrs. John O'Neal

Japanese Fruit Pies

4 eggs
2 sticks butter or margarine, melted
2 cups sugar
1 cup raisins

1 cup coconut
1 cup pecans, chopped
2 tablespoons vinegar
2 (9-inch) unbaked pie shells

Mix all ingredients together with spoon and wire whisk. Pour mixture into pie shells. Bake at 325 degrees for 40 minutes.

Karen Girardin

Graham Cracker Pie

1	cup graham cracker crumbs	½	cup chopped nuts
½	cup sugar	2	eggs
1	teaspoon baking powder	2	tablespoons milk

Mix crumbs, sugar, baking powder and nuts. Then add eggs, then milk. Bake at 350 degrees for 20 minutes in a greased pan. Turn out and cover with whipped cream.

Mrs. Dave Wainer

Different Lemon Pie

3	large eggs	⅓	cup lemon juice
1¼	cups sugar	3	tablespoons water
2	tablespoons flour	1	(8-inch) uncooked pastry for double crust pie
2	tablespoons butter or margarine, melted and cooled		

Beat eggs until foamy and thick. Add sugar and flour, stir until smooth, then butter, lemon juice and water. Mix well. Pour into pastry shell. Place top crust over filling. Seal edges and flute. Bake at 400 degrees for 35 minutes. Cool before cutting.

Mrs. Earl Taylor

Old-Fashioned Lemon Pie

1	cup sugar		Juice of 1½ lemons
2	tablespoons butter, melted	1	unbaked pie shell
3	eggs, beaten		

Mix together and put in unbaked pie shell. Bake at 300 to 325 degrees oven about 1 hour, until top is brown.

Mrs. Frank Strickland

Lemon Luscious Pie

1	cup sugar	½	teaspoon lemon extract
4	tablespoons cornstarch	1	cup milk
⅓	cup butter	4	unbeaten egg yolks
2	tablespoons lemon rind, grated	1	cup sour cream
¼	cup lemon juice	1	baked (10-inch) pie shell
			Meringue or whipped cream

Combine sugar and cornstarch in saucepan. Add butter, lemon rind, juice, extract, milk, and egg yolks. Cook over medium heat, stirring constantly until thick. Cool. Fold in sour cream. Spoon into baked pie shell. Chill at least 2 hours. Top with either meringue or whipped cream.

Serves 8

Sue Cox

Lime Meringue Pie

7	tablespoons cornstarch	½	cup lime juice
1	tablespoon flour	1	tablespoon butter
1¾	cups sugar	¼	teaspoon salt
2	cups boiling water	1	baked pie shell
4	egg yolks, beaten		Meringue or whipped cream
2	teaspoons grated lime rind		

Sift cornstarch, flour and sugar. Blend in boiling water until smooth. Cook in double boiler, stirring constantly until clear and thickened. Add yolks slowly. Cover and cook 5 minutes. Add rind, lime juice, butter and salt. Pour into baked pie shell. Cover with meringue or whipped topping.

Mrs. Roger M. Budd

Key Lime Pie

1 can condensed milk	4 egg whites
4 egg yolks	6 tablespoons sugar
½ cup lime juice and pulp	1 graham cracker crust
Sugar to taste	

Combine milk, yolks, lime juice and pulp, and a little sugar. Beat 1 egg white until stiff. Fold into lime mixture. Pour mixture into crust. Beat other 3 whites and 6 tablespoons sugar to make meringue. Top pie with meringue. Bake at 350 degrees until whites are golden. Cool and chill.

Serves 6 to 8

Macaroon Pie

1 cup sugar	3 egg whites
1 cup nuts	1 teaspoon almond extract
12 dates, finely cut	1 unbaked pie shell
12 square soda crackers, finely crushed	

Mix all ingredients except egg whites and extract. Add stiffly beaten egg whites and extract. Pour mixture in pie shell. Bake at 350 degrees for 20 minutes.

Mrs. Loyce Turner

Pecan Pie ~ Silver Springs Coffee Shop

⅛ pound butter	1 cup white corn syrup
1 cup granulated sugar	1 cup chopped pecan meats
¼ teaspoon salt	Unbaked pasty shell
2 eggs, well beaten	

Cream butter and sugar; add salt, eggs, syrup, and chopped nutmeats, mix well. Bake in uncooked pasty shell for 1 hour at 350 degrees.

Mrs. Howard Dasher, Sr.

Open Sesame Pie

Crust
2-4 tablespoons sesame seeds

Ingredients for single pie crust

Toast seeds at 450 degrees for 2 minutes, until golden brown, watch closely. Cool. Make pie crust, adding toasted seeds. Bake. Cool.

Date Chiffon Filling

1 **cup milk**	1 **cup pitted dates, cut into**
2 **egg yolks**	**small pieces**
¼ **cup sugar**	¾ **cup whipping cream, beaten**
¼ **teaspoon salt**	**very thick**
1 **tablespoon gelatin, softened**	2 **egg whites**
with ¼ cup cold water	2 **tablespoons sugar**
1 **teaspoon vanilla extract**	**Sprinkle of nutmeg**
	(optional)

Beat milk, yolks, ¼ cup sugar, and salt together in double boiler until well-blended. Cook over hot water, stirring constantly until mixture coats spoon. Add softened gelatin. Chill until partially set. Stir occasionally. Stir in vanilla and dates. Fold in whipping cream. Beat egg whites until slight mounds form. Add 2 tablespoons sugar, gradually, beating well until stiff peaks form. Fold gently but thoroughly into date mixture. Spoon into cooled pie crust. Chill until firm. Sprinkle with nutmeg if you choose.

For stronger date flavor, add dates to custard mixture while it is still hot.

Mrs. Clarence Paine

Blue Ribbon Peach Pie

6-8	ripe peaches	3	tablespoons cornstarch
½	cup firmly packed brown sugar	½	cup orange juice
½	cup sugar	2	tablespoons butter
¼	teaspoon salt	2	pie pastries

Peel and slice peaches. Combine sugars, salt, and cornstarch in a saucepan. Blend in orange juice, stirring until smooth. Cook over medium heat until thickened, stirring constantly. Remove from heat and add butter. Pour hot mixture over sliced peaches and cool. Prepare pastry and line 10-inch pan. Make lattice strips. Spoon peach mixture into unbaked crust and top with lattice strips. Bake at 375 degrees for 40 or 50 minutes. As mixture cooks and comes to a boil it will not appear very thick. Mixture will thicken during baking.

Mrs. Ralph Murphine

Down South Pecan Pie

½	cup butter or margarine	1	teaspoon vanilla extract
½	cup granulated sugar	2	cups pecan meats
¾	white corn syrup	1	(9-inch) unbaked pie pastry
¼	cup maple syrup		Ice cream or whipped
3	eggs, slightly beaten		cream to top

Preheat oven to 350 degrees. Cream butter well and then add sugar slowly, creaming until light. Slowly stir in syrups, eggs, vanilla, and 1 cup nutmeats. Pour into pastry. Top with remaining nuts. Bake at 350 degrees for about 55 minutes. Cool. Top with ice cream or whipped cream.

Mrs. C.E. Davis

Sour Cream Pecan Pie

1	cup broken pecans	1	cup sour cream
1	(9-inch) pastry shell	2	eggs, beaten
1	teaspoon flour	1	cup sugar
¼	teaspoon cinnamon	½	teaspoon grated lemon rind
¼	teaspoon cloves		Whipped cream

Preheat oven to 450 degrees. Sprinkle nuts into pie shell. Mix flour, spices and sour cream. Add eggs, sugar and lemon rind. Pour into shell over nuts. Place in oven and immediately reduce heat to 325 degrees. Bake 40 minute until firm. Serve hot or cold with whipped cream.

Mrs. Richard Beckmann

Praline Pie

⅓	cup brown sugar, firmly packed	2¾	cups milk
⅓	cup margarine	1	small container of whipped topping
½	cup pecans, finely chopped	1	tablespoon pecans, finely chopped
1	(9-inch) pie shell		
1	(5-ounce) package regular vanilla pudding		

Heat brown sugar, margarine, and ½ cup pecans in saucepan until margarine is melted and well blended. Spread in bottom of baked pie shell. Bake at 450 degrees for 5 minutes; then cool. Prepare pudding mix with milk. Cook as directed. When done, remove 1 cup of pudding; and place in a separate container. Cover both and chill. When completely chilled, pour largest amount of pudding into pie shell. Fold 1 cup pudding into whipped topping, and pour on top of pie. Garnish with 1 tablespoon pecans. Refrigerate uncovered overnight or at least 8 hours.

Ingrid Carroll

Southern Pecan Pie

1 cup chopped pecans	¼ cup milk
¼ stick butter	1 cup cane syrup
3 eggs	1 teaspoon vanilla extract
1 cup sugar	Unbaked pie shell

Toast nuts and butter slightly. Beat eggs thoroughly. Add sugar, milk, syrup, and vanilla. Mix well. Sprinkle buttered nuts in unbaked pie shell; pour mixture over nuts into shell. Bake at 325 degrees for 30 minutes or until set. Do not over bake.

Mrs. Robert B. Anderson, Jr.

Patton House Rum Pie

¼ ounce plain gelatin	⅓ cup light rum
¼ cup cold water	1 cup heavy whipping cream, whipped
1¼ cups milk	
3 egg yolks, slightly beaten	2 graham cracker pie shells
⅔ cup sugar	Whipped cream or
Pinch salt	chocolate chips to top

Soften gelatin in water for 5 minutes. Pour milk into egg yolks gradually. Cook slowly until creamy and coats spoon. Add sugar and salt. Remove from heat. Stir in gelatin and cool. Blend in rum. Chill until partially set. Fold in whipped cream. Pour into graham cracker pie shells. Chill until firm. Serve topped with whipped cream or chocolate chips.

Mrs. Bill Keller

Sweet Potato Pie

1 cup mashed sweet potatoes	1 scant cup sweet milk
¾ cup butter	1 teaspoon lemon juice
1 cup sugar	1 unbaked pie shell
1 egg	

Combine ingredients and spoon into unbaked pie shell. Bake at 325 degrees for 1 hour.

Mrs. Frank Strickland

Pumpkin Chiffon Pie

1½ cups cooked pumpkin	1 tablespoon unflavored gelatin
¾ cup brown sugar, firmly packed	¼ cup cold water
½ cup milk	3 egg whites
3 egg yolks, beaten	¼ cup granulated sugar
½ teaspoon salt	1 (9-inch) baked pie shell
1 teaspoon cinnamon	Whipped cream
½ teaspoon nutmeg	

Combine pumpkin, brown sugar, milk, beaten egg yolks, salt and spices in top of double boiler. Cook over boiling water. Stir every 10 minutes. Soften gelatin in cold water and dissolve in hot pumpkin mixture. Pour into medium-size bowl. Chill just until beginning to set. Beat egg whites until foamy; add granulated sugar 1 tablespoon at a time. Beat well after each addition until meringue forms soft peaks. Fold into pumpkin mixture. Pour into baked pie shell. Chill until firm enough to cut. Garnish with a ring of whipped cream.

Mrs. S.G. Bullington

Strawberry Pie

Crust

2 cups flour	⅓ cup milk
⅔ cup vegetable oil	1 teaspoon salt

Mix and bake at 325 degrees for 30 minutes or until light brown.

Filling

3 baskets fresh strawberries	2 heaping tablespoons flour
1 cup sugar	Whipped cream

Take 1½ baskets of strawberries and cut them into halves. Put into cooled shell. Slice the berries in the remaining 1½ baskets. Mix sliced berries with sugar and flour. Cook in saucepan until thick and clear. Pour over berries in shell. Top with whipped cream.

Mrs. Stanley Bishop

Fresh Strawberry Pie

1½	cups sugar	4	tablespoons strawberry jello
½	cup water		Red food coloring
¼	cup cornstarch	1	baked pie shell
¾	cup water	1	quart whole fresh
⅛	teaspoon salt		strawberries
1	tablespoon lemon juice		Whipped topping

Boil sugar and ½ cup water until clear. Mix with cornstarch and ¾ cup water. Add salt, lemon juice and jello. Bring to a boil and add a few drops red food coloring. Cool. Then pour small amount in cool pie shell. Fill with berries and drip rest of glaze over berries. Refrigerate. Cover with whipped topping when ready to serve.

Mrs. Chandler Blanton

Traditional Pie Crust

1	heaping cup flour	⅓	cup shortening
¾	teaspoon salt	3½	tablespoons ice water

Sift flour and salt together. Mix shortening and blend until pea-size. Add water. Press into pie pan. Bake at 400 degrees for 15 to 20 minutes.

Mrs. Bill Lester

Graham Cracker Pie Crust

16	graham crackers, rolled finely	¼	cup softened butter or margarine
¼	cup sugar		

Mix crumbs and sugar. Blend in butter well. Press firmly into pie pan. Bake at 375 degrees until lightly browned.

Mrs. Bill Keller

Apricot Balls

1	pound dried apricots	2	cups sugar
1	whole orange		Coconut or chopped nuts

Grind together apricots and orange. Add sugar and mix thoroughly. Cook until sugar is dissolved. Let cool. Make in balls and roll in coconut or chopped nuts. Chill.

Mrs. Bill Keller

Crystallized Apricots

1	package dried apricots	Pecan halves
1	cup sugar	Loose granulated sugar
¾	cup water	

Put above 3 ingredients in pan together. Let come to a boil and boil 6 minutes, no longer. Lift out apricots with wire egg beater and place on waxed paper. Take one at a time and place ½ pecan on top of each apricot. Dip each side into granulated sugar. Place on more waxed paper until cool.

These keep well stored in a tin.

Mrs. Maxwell Oliver

Blond Brownies

1	stick butter	1	teaspoon baking powder
1	cup light brown sugar	¼	teaspoon salt
1	egg	1	cup coarsely chopped
1	cup flour		nutmeats

Cream butter and sugar. Add egg then flour, baking powder and salt. Mix thoroughly. Add nuts. Bake in 350 degrees oven for 20 to 30 minutes.

Mrs. Frank Strickland

Bourbon Balls #1

30	vanilla wafers, crushed	2	tablespoons white corn syrup
1	cup powdered sugar	1	cup chopped pecans
4	tablespoons liquor		Loose powdered sugar

Mix wafers and sugar. Add liquor, syrup and pecans. Make into balls and roll in powdered sugar. Store in sealed jar for 10 days or longer.

Mrs. Bill Keller

Bourbon Balls #2

1	stick butter, melted	½	block paraffin
1	box 4x powdered sugar	1	package semi-sweet
¼	cup bourbon		chocolate bits
2	cups pecans, chopped		

Mix butter, sugar, bourbon, and nuts together and roll into small balls. Place on waxed paper. Dip each in paraffin and chocolate melted together.

Mrs. Wayne Ellerbee

Butterscotch Brownies

4	eggs, separated	1	teaspoon baking powder
½	cup white sugar		Pinch of salt
2	sticks butter, melted	1	teaspoon vanilla
1	box dark brown sugar	2	cups nuts
2	cups flour		Loose powdered sugar

Beat egg whites until stiff. Add white sugar and beat until well mixed. Set aside. Melt butter, add brown sugar, and then egg yolks: beat well. Add dry ingredients, and vanilla. Add egg white mixture. Fold in nuts. Bake at 325 degrees for 25 minutes. While warm, cut into squares and roll in powdered sugar.

Mrs. Chandler Blanton

Brownies #1

1½	sticks butter	½	teaspoon salt
3½	squares unsweetened chocolate	1	teaspoon vanilla
		2	cups cut up nuts
4	eggs	1	cup flour
2	cups sugar		

Melt chocolate and butter in top of a double boiler over warm (not hot) water. Allow to cool. Beat eggs slightly, gradually adding sugar, salt and vanilla. Add cooled chocolate butter mixture. Sift flour over nuts, mix thoroughly and add to batter. Stir only enough to combine ingredients. Pour into a buttered 8x12x2-inch pan. Bake 35 minutes at 325 degrees.

Miss Gnann Alvarez

Brownies #2

¾	cup sifted cake flour	1	cup sugar
½	teaspoon baking powder	2	eggs, beaten
¼	teaspoon salt	½	cup nuts
⅓	cup butter	1	teaspoon vanilla
1	square unsweetened chocolate	9	marshmallows

Sift dry ingredients together. Melt butter and chocolate over hot water. Add sugar gradually to eggs. Add chocolate mix and blend. Add flour mixture, nuts and vanilla; mix well. Bake in 8x8x2-inch pan lined with 2 sheets of waxed paper. Let the paper be large enough to stick up over the sides of the pan so you can lift brownies out of the pan by holding the paper. Bake at 350 degrees or less for 25 minutes or until done. Place marshmallows on top and bake about 5 minutes more. Do not let marshmallows melt; just puff up. Spread Chocolate Icing over top as soon as you take brownies out of the oven.

Chocolate Icing

1	block chocolate	¼	teaspoon salt
¼	stick butter	1	teaspoon vanilla
½	box confectioners' sugar	4	tablespoons evaporated milk

Melt chocolate and butter. Mix sugar with salt, vanilla and evaporated milk. Add chocolate mixture and mix well. If too stiff, add more milk. Let cool and cut.

Mrs. W. C. Posey

Brownies #3

½	cup butter	⅔	cup flour
1	cup sugar	2	squares bitter chocolate, melted
2	eggs		
1	teaspoon vanilla	1	cup nuts
¼	teaspoon salt		

Cream butter. Add sugar to creamed butter. Mix eggs and add vanilla. Stir in salt and flour. Add chocolate and nuts. Bake in greased brownie tin, 25 minutes at 325 degrees.

Icing

1	cup sugar	⅓	cup milk
⅛	teaspoon salt	2	tablespoons butter
1	square bitter chocolate	1	teaspoon vanilla

Boil sugar, salt, chocolate, milk, and butter together for 1 minute. Take from stove and add vanilla. Beat until thick enough to spread on brownies. Cut into squares. This makes a chewy brownie.

Mrs. Diane M. Smith

Wafer Brownies

2	squares unsweetened chocolate	¼	teaspoon salt
½	cup butter	2	eggs, beaten
1	cup sugar	1	teaspoon vanilla
½	cup sifted flour	½	cup chopped nuts

Melt in the top of a double boiler, chocolate and butter. Add sugar, flour and salt. Beat well, and then beat in eggs and vanilla. Add chopped nuts. Spread very thin in a greased shallow 10x14-inch baking pan. Bake in a 400 degree oven for 10 minutes. Cut into bars while warm.

Mrs. Doyle Johnson

Brownies #4

1	cup butter	1	cup pastry flour
2	cups sugar	¼	teaspoon salt
4	eggs	1	teaspoon vanilla
4	squares unsweetened chocolate, melted	1-2	cups broken nuts

Cream butter and sugar well. Add eggs, one at a time and beat well after each addition. Add melted chocolate that has cooled slightly. Beat well. Add flour that has been sifted and measured. Add salt and vanilla, and then nuts. Spread evenly in 2 shallow, square or rectangular pans that have been greased and floured. Bake 20 to 25 minutes at 350 degrees.

Frosting

2	heaping tablespoons cocoa	3	tablespoons cream (more if needed)
2	tablespoons butter		
2	cups confectioners' sugar	1	teaspoon vanilla

Beat together until creamy. Spread on brownies.

Mrs. J. Fred Anderson

Easy Cheese Cake Squares

1	box yellow cake mix	2	eggs
1	stick butter, melted	1	(8-ounce) package cream cheese, softened
1	egg		
1	cup pecans, chopped	1	teaspoon vanilla
1	box 4x powdered sugar		

Combine first 4 ingredients and mix well. Press in large glass dish. Mix next 4 ingredients to make topping. Pour on top of first mixture. Bake at 325 degrees for 40 minutes, or until light brown on top. The middle should be soft. Cut into small squares.

Jean Bynum

Chocolate Dips

2	packages 4x powdered sugar	1	teaspoon salt
1	stick butter	1	teaspoon vanilla
1	cup sweetened condensed milk	2	cups finely chopped pecans

Cream sugar and butter. Add milk, salt and vanilla and then cream well with hands. Add nuts and mix well. Refrigerate overnight and roll into small balls next day. Dip into Chocolate Coating.

Chocolate Coating

1	(4-ounce) package German sweet chocolate	¼	box paraffin wax

Melt together.

Mrs. A.R. Pitts

Chocolate Mint Desserts

1	small package brownie mix	½	cup margarine
2	cups 10x powdered sugar	½	cup chocolate bits
2	tablespoons crème de menthe	6	tablespoons margarine

Mix the brownie mix according to directions, and spread in a 9x13-inch pan. Bake at 350 degrees for 15 minutes. Cool slightly. Beat together the sugar, crème de menthe, and margarine. Spread it like icing on mix, and chill thoroughly. In a double boiler, melt the chocolate bits and margarine, and spread it on top of the other 2 layers. Refrigerate until set, then cut into 2-inch squares and freeze.

Serves 36

Karen Coogan

Cinnamon Crisps

1½	sticks butter		Pinch of salt
2	cups sugar	2	teaspoons cinnamon
1	egg	1	cup finely chopped pecans
2	cups flour		

Cream butter and sugar. Add egg and beat well. Mix flour, salt and cinnamon and add to butter mixture. Knead and spread thinly in a very shallow greased aluminum pan, about 15x10-inches. Press pecans on top. Bake at 250 degrees. Remove from oven when light brown. Cut cookies into small squares while still warm.

Chocolate Covered Cherries

½	cup sweetened condensed milk	½	box paraffin
1	box confectioners' sugar Maraschino cherries	1	large package semi-sweet chocolate bits

Mix milk and sugar together. Keep some powdered sugar on finger tips so you can wrap each cherry in the milk-sugar mixture. Dip cherries. Place on waxed paper. Then dip each cherry in paraffin and chocolate bits that have been melted together. Place on waxed paper to dry.

Mrs. Wayne Ellerbee

Christmas Cookies

1	cup butter	½	cup milk
1	cup brown sugar	¾	pound golden raisins
3	well beaten eggs	6	slices pineapple, diced
3	cups flour	2	cups dates, chopped
1	teaspoon baking soda	2	cups cherries, chopped
1	teaspoon cinnamon	3½	cups pecans, chopped

Cream butter and sugar. Add eggs, flour, soda, cinnamon and milk. Add remaining ingredients. Bake on greased cookie sheet at 300 degrees for 20 to 30 minutes.

Mrs. Roy McTier by Mrs. John T. McTier

Chocolate Cookies

1	cup light brown sugar	1	scant cup chopped nuts
1½	cups flour, sifted before measuring	½	cup melted or creamed butter
½	teaspoon soda	¼	cup sweet milk
1	egg	1	teaspoon vanilla
2	squares melted chocolate		

Mix as for any cake. Drop from teaspoon and bake in 400 degrees oven on a greased cookie sheet.

Icing

1½	cups powdered sugar, sifted	1	square melted chocolate
1	egg yolk	1	teaspoon vanilla
3	tablespoons cream		

Mix in double boiler. Stir until well blended. Spread on cookies while hot.

Mrs. Maxwell Oliver

Crazy Crunch

2	quarts popped corn	1⅓	cups sugar
1⅓	cups pecans	1	cup margarine
⅔	cup almonds	1	teaspoon vanilla
½	cup white corn syrup		

Mix popped corn and nuts on a cookie sheet. Combine syrup, sugar and margarine in a 1½-quart saucepan. Bring to a boil over medium heat, stirring constantly. Continue boiling, stirring occasionally, 10 to 15 minutes or until mixture turns a light caramel color. Remove from heat. Stir in vanilla. Pour over popped corn and nuts, mix to coat well. Spread out to dry. Break apart and store in tightly covered container.

2 pounds

Mrs. Jack Sullivan

Coconut Cookies

Cookie Crust

½   **cup brown sugar**   1   **cup flour**
1   **stick butter**

Mix together and spread on large cookie sheet and bake 25 minutes at 350 degrees.

Coconut Layer

1   **cup brown sugar**   2   **tablespoons flour**
2   **eggs**   ½   **teaspoon salt**
1   **teaspoon vanilla**   1½   **cups canned coconut**
½   **teaspoon baking powder**   1   **cup chopped pecans**

Mix and spread on crust. Bake for 20 minutes at 350 degrees. Cut into cookies.

Mrs. Avalon Griffin

Cream Cheese Cookies

1   **cup butter, softened**   2½   **cups all-purpose flour**
1   **(3-ounce) package cream**   1   **teaspoon vanilla extract**
    cheese, softened   **Candied cherries or pecan**
1   **cup sugar**   **halves**
1   **egg yolk**

Cream butter and cream cheese; slowly add sugar, beating until fluffy. Beat in egg yolk. Add flour and vanilla; mix well. Chill dough 1 hour. Shape dough into 1-inch balls. Place on greased cookie sheet. Gently press fruit into each cookie. Bake at 325 degrees for about 12 to 15 minutes.

Ann Dasher

Crescent Cookies

3   sticks butter
4   cups plain flour
2   teaspoons ice water
2   teaspoons vanilla

14 tablespoons powdered sugar
2   cups nuts, finely chopped
    Loose powdered sugar

Cream all ingredients except nuts. Fold nuts in after beating. Place on cookie sheet and bake at 350 degrees until light brown. Roll in powdered sugar. These may be made about the size of a marble or larger.

Mrs. Ed Garvin

Divinity Pecan Roll Candy

3   cups sugar
¾   cup water
¾   cup white corn syrup
3   large egg whites
⅛   teaspoon salt
1   teaspoon vanilla

3   cups chopped pecans, separated
1   cup candied cherries, cut in halves
4   slices candied pineapple, cut in chunks

Place sugar, water, and syrup in a pot and stir over low heat until dissolved. Cover when starts to boil and cook until 290 degrees. Take egg whites and salt and beat until stiff. When syrup reaches 270 degrees, pour a small amount over egg whites, continue beating, while syrup cooks, and repeat. When syrup reaches 290 degrees, remove immediately and pour over egg whites. Mix in mixer and rapidly add vanilla. Beat until mixture ready to handle. Spoon in 1 cup nuts, cherries and pineapple chunks. Makes about 4 rolls, about 1½ or 2 inches in diameter. On wax paper and with wet hands, work fast and roll entire mixture and shape in 2 cups chopped pecans. Repeat until all pecans are used. Wrap in waxed paper or tin foil. Store and slice as desired.

Candy will not dry and will keep for several weeks.

Mrs. O.C. Carruthers

Divinity

2	cups sugar	2	egg whites, beaten
½	cup white corn syrup	1	teaspoon vanilla
	Pinch of salt	1	cup nuts
½	cup water		

Combine sugar, syrup, salt and water and boil to 240 degrees. Pour ⅓ mixture slowly into beaten egg whites beating constantly. Cook remaining mixture to 265 degrees Pour slowly into egg mixture and beat until it holds its shape. Add vanilla and nuts. Drop by teaspoonfuls onto buttered marble slab or waxed paper. Can be doubled.

Mrs. Laurence Alvarez

Fudge #1

4	tablespoons white corn syrup	¾	cup milk
		3	tablespoons butter
2	cups sugar	1	teaspoon vanilla
6	tablespoons cocoa	1	cup pecans

Cook syrup, sugar, cocoa and milk over slow heat until sugar is dissolved. Continue to cook very, very slowly to 238 degrees. Do not stir except to keep from burning. Remove from fire and without stirring, add butter. Cool until thick. Add vanilla and beat. Add pecans and pour into buttered platter.

Can double.

Mrs. Laurence Alvarez

Fudge #2

2½	ounces chocolate	2	tablespoons white corn syrup
2	cups sugar	2	tablespoons butter
¼	teaspoon salt	1	teaspoon vanilla
⅔	cup milk	1	cup nutmeats

In a heavy saucepan, melt chocolate, sugar and salt slowly in milk and syrup. Allow to cook to soft ball stage. Remove from heat. Add butter and vanilla and cool to lukewarm. Beat vigorously until fudge becomes thick and loses its gloss. Add nutmeats. Spread in pan or roll in long roll and slice.

Mrs. George L. Shelton, Jr.

Fudge Squares

1	cake baking chocolate	¾	cup flour
	(or 4 tablespoons cocoa)	¼	teaspoon salt
1	stick butter, melted	1½	cups pecans, finely chopped
3	eggs	1	teaspoon vanilla
1⅓	cups sugar		

Melt chocolate with a little water. Add melted butter. Beat eggs in a bowl and add sugar, gradually. Be sure to beat this well, then add flour, which has been sifted twice with salt. Mix all together with chocolate and butter. Beat several minutes more, then add pecans and vanilla. Bake at 300 degrees for about 50 minutes. Wait until cool to cut.

Mrs. Howard Dasher

Sour Cream Fudge

2	cups sugar	2	tablespoons butter
1	cup sour cream	1	tablespoon vanilla
2	tablespoons light corn	½	cup candied cherries
	syrup	½	cup chopped nuts
½	teaspoon salt		

Combine sugar, sour cream, corn syrup, and salt in buttered heavy 2-quart saucepan. Cook over low heat, stirring constantly until sugar is dissolved. Turn heat to medium, and cook until mixture boils. Continue cooking, stirring occasionally until it reaches the soft ball stage (239-240 on candy thermometer). Remove from heat. Add butter and vanilla. Cool to lukewarm (110) while stirring. Beat until candy is creamy and has lost gloss. Add candied cherries and nuts. Pour into buttered 8-inch square pan. Cut into squares when hardened.

Makes 36 pieces

Susan Hogan

Chocolate Fudge

1   large can evaporated milk
4½ cups sugar
12 chocolate bars
2   (6-ounce) packages semi-
    sweet chocolate bits

1   (8-ounce) jar marshmallow
    cream
1½ teaspoons salt
1   teaspoon vanilla
2   cups nuts, chopped

Bring milk and sugar to a boil and cook over medium heat 4½ minutes. Break up candy bars in a large bowl. Add chocolate bits, marshmallow cream and salt. Pour hot milk and sugar mixture over and stir until all chocolate is dissolved. Add vanilla and nuts. Pour into a large buttered pan. Cool. Cut.

Mrs. Jack Sullivan

Milk Chocolate Fudge

2   cups sugar
½   cup white corn syrup
2   tablespoons cocoa
½   cup canned milk

½   stick butter
1   teaspoon vanilla
    Chopped nuts

Cook all ingredients excluding the butter until a firm ball is formed in cold water. Remove from heat. Drop butter on top and do not stir. Set in cold water to cool. When very cool add vanilla and beat. Add nuts. When it loses its gloss pour into buttered pan.

Mrs. Jack Sullivan

Goldie's Cookies

2   eggs
2   sticks butter
¾   cup brown sugar
½   cup granulated sugar

2   heaping cups flour
1   teaspoon vanilla
1½ cups nuts, chopped

Beat eggs and butter. Add sugars and beat. Add flour and beat. Add vanilla and nuts and mix well. Place dough, 1 teaspoonful at a time on greased cookie sheet. Bake at 350 degrees for 20 minutes.

Mrs. Jack Rudolph

Gingerbread Boys

2	cups sifted all-purpose flour	1½	teaspoons cinnamon
½	teaspoon salt	½	teaspoon nutmeg
½	teaspoon baking soda	½	cup vegetable shortening
½	teaspoon baking powder	½	cup sugar
1	teaspoon ginger	½	cup molasses
1	teaspoon cloves	1	egg, separated

On waxed paper sift flour, salt, soda, baking powder, ginger, cloves, cinnamon and nutmeg. In a bowl, cream shortening with sugar and molasses until light and fluffy. Beat in egg yolk and then flour mixture. Start heating oven to 350 degrees. On a lightly floured board, roll out dough ¼-inch thick. Then, using floured gingerbread boy cuter, cut out cookies. Place on ungreased cookie sheets, and then bake 8 to 10 minutes. Cool on wire racks. Decorate.

Mrs. J. L. Dowling, Jr.

Mrs. Rhymes Lemon Squares

1	cup butter, room temperature and cut in pats	2	cups all-purpose flour, fork-stirred
½	cup granulated sugar		Confectioners' sugar

Cream butter and sugar; beat in flour. Spread in ungreased jelly-roll pan. Bake at 350 degrees for about 15 minutes until crust edges are brown. Remove and leave oven at 350 degrees.

Filling

5	tablespoons all-purpose flour	4	extra large eggs
1	teaspoon baking powder	¼	teaspoon lemon rind, grated
2	cups granulated sugar	½	cup lemon juice

Stir together flour, baking powder, and sugar. In medium bowl and at medium speed, slightly beat eggs. Add flour mixture, and beat until blended. Add lemon rind and lemon juice; beat until blended. Pour filling over hot crust. Bake about 20 minutes until set. Sprinkle with confectioners' sugar. Cut when cool.

Shirlee Carroll

Gooey

5	large eggs, whole	⅔	cup flour
2½	cups sugar	3	tablespoons cocoa
1	cup butter	1¼	cups pecans
2	teaspoons vanilla		

Beat eggs; add sugar, and let beat 10 minutes. Add butter, vanilla, flour, and cocoa that have been sifted together. Take from beaters, and add nuts. Put in buttered 12x14-inch baking pan and bake 1 hour at 300 degrees. Place in pan of water while it is baking. Cut in squares, and serve with scoop of ice cream on top.

Serves 12

Julie Budd

Heavenly Hash Candy

1	pound milk chocolate	12	large marshmallows
1	cup chopped nuts		

Put milk chocolate in top of double boiler over hot water. Stir until melted. Pour half into tray lined with waxed paper. Cover this with chopped nuts and marshmallows that have been diced. Pour remaining chocolate over this. When cool, break into pieces.

Mrs. Jack Sullivan

Aunt Ruth's Icebox Cookies

¼	pound butter	2	cups flour
1	cup brown sugar	½	teaspoon baking soda
½	cup white sugar	½	teaspoon vanilla
1	egg	1	cup nuts, if desired

Cream butter and sugars. Add egg. Sift dry ingredients. Add vanilla and nuts. Shape dough into roll, wrap in foil and refrigerate overnight or freeze. These cookies may be sliced and baked immediately after taking from freezer. When ready to bake, slice thin and bake at 350 degrees until light brown. Watch closely to avoid burning.

Mrs. Henry Brice

Katy's Cornettes

1	quart condensed milk	1	teaspoon salt
2	tablespoons sugar	1	pint white cornmeal
6	ounces butter		

Combine first 4 ingredients in saucepan. Bring to a boil. On low heat, gradually add cornmeal, stirring constantly until mixture is a thin mush. Put some of mixture in pastry tube bag with a number 4 pastry tube, ¾-inch diameter. Squeeze into silver dollar sized mounds on a well-greased cookie sheet. Chill in refrigerator. Bake at 450 degrees for 12 minutes or until slightly brown. Serve hot.

Mrs. Joyce Mixon

Kisses

3	egg whites	1	teaspoon vanilla
1	cup sugar	2	cups chopped nuts
	Pinch of salt		

Beat egg whites until fluffy. Add sugar 1 teaspoon at a time and heat for 30 minutes. Add vanilla and nuts. Drop by spoonfuls on pan lined with waxed paper and bake 15 to 20 minutes at 250 degrees. Do not brown.

Mrs. Rudolph Howell

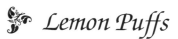 # Lemon Puffs

| 1 | package yellow cake mix | Juice of 2 lemons |
| | Juice of 1 orange | 1½ boxes 4x powdered sugar |

Make cake mix as directed on box. Grease at least 3 miniature muffin tins. Fill pans ½ full. Bake at 325 degrees for 10 to 12 minutes. Stir together juices and sugar in a large mixing bowl to make glaze. Take muffins from oven. Dip muffins in glaze and coat on all sides. Drain on waxed paper.

Makes 108 puffs

Sue Addington

Candy Coated Chocolate Color Cookies

½ cup shortening
½ cup brown sugar
¼ cup granulated sugar
½ teaspoon vanilla
¼ teaspoon water
1 egg

1 cup plus 2 tablespoons sifted all-purpose flour
½ teaspoon soda
½ teaspoon salt
¾ cup plain candy coated chocolate candies

Blend shortening and sugars. Beat in vanilla, water and egg. Sift remaining dry ingredients together and add to the sugar and egg mixture. Mix well. Stir in candies. Drop from teaspoon onto ungreased cookie sheet. Bake at 375 degrees for 10 to 12 minutes or until golden brown. Makes about 3 dozen 2½-inch cookies. For additional color, press extra candies into cookies before baking. Some candies crack slightly in baking, adding texture and interest to the cookies.

Magic Marshmallow Crescent Puffs

¼ cup sugar
1 teaspoon cinnamon
2 (8-ounce) cans refrigerated quick crescent dinner rolls

16 large marshmallows
¼ cup butter or margarine, melted
¼ cup chopped nuts

Combine sugar and cinnamon. Separate crescent dough into 15 triangles. Dip a marshmallow in melted butter, then in sugar-cinnamon mixture. Place marshmallows on wide end of triangle. Fold corners over marshmallow and roll toward point, completely covering marshmallow and squeezing edges of dough to seal. Dip point side in butter and place buttered side down in greased deep muffin pans. Repeat with remaining marshmallows. Place pan on a cookie sheet during baking. Bake at 375 degrees for 10 to 15 minutes or until golden brown. Immediately remove from pans and drizzle with icing. Sprinkle with nuts. Serve warm.

Icing

½ cup powdered sugar
2-3 teaspoons milk

½ teaspoon vanilla

Combine ingredients. Blend until smooth.

Makes 16 rolls

Mrs. Jack Sullivan

Dark Chocolate Coconut Cookies

½	cup shortening	½	teaspoon salt
½	cup brown sugar	½	teaspoon baking soda
¼	cup white sugar	½	cup chopped nuts
1	teaspoon vanilla	2	packages dark chocolate
1	egg, well beaten		and coconut candy bars,
1	cup plus 2 tablespoons		finely chopped
	sifted flour		

Cream shortening, add sugars, vanilla and egg. Combine flour, salt, and soda and add to first mixture. Stir in nuts. Blend in candy bars. Drop from teaspoon on greased pan. Bake at 375 degrees 12 to 14 minutes.

Mrs. Nettie Keller

Panocha

2½	cups brown sugar	¾	cup milk
	Dash of salt	1	teaspoon vanilla
1	tablespoon light corn syrup	½	cup broken nuts
1	tablespoon butter		

Combine sugar, corn syrup, butter and milk over moderate heat. Cool to 238 degrees, stirring until sugar dissolves, or to soft ball stage. Cool at room temperature without stirring until lukewarm or around 110 degrees. Add vanilla, beat until holds shape. Add nuts. Quickly spread in buttered pan.

Peanut Butter Crunch

1	cup sugar	1	(12-ounce) jar crunchy
1	cup corn syrup		peanut butter
		6	cups corn flakes

Combine sugar and syrup in 3½-quart saucepan and bring to a boil. Remove from heat. Stir in peanut butter. Add corn flakes and stir until all are coated with syrup mixture. Drop by teaspoonfuls on waxed paper.

Mrs. Quinton Lawson

Oatmeal Cookies

2	cups unsifted flour	1	cup sugar
½	teaspoon salt	2	eggs
¾	teaspoon baking soda	2	cups rolled quick oats
1	teaspoon cinnamon	2	cups chopped nuts or 1 cup
1	teaspoon nutmeg		nuts and 1 cup raisins
¾	cup butter		

Sift first 5 ingredients together. Cream butter and sugar. Add eggs. Add remaining ingredients and mix well. Drop on greased cookie sheet and bake for 15 or 20 minutes at 350 degrees.

Mrs. C.C. Varnedoe

Candied Orange Peel

Peelings from 4 medium oranges   2   cups granulated sugar

Quarter orange peel, cover with cold water and simmer until tender. Drain, reserve 1 cup liquid. Remove inner white portion and cut peel in ¼-inch strips. Combine sugar and reserved liquid. Cook to 238 degrees on candy thermometer, stirring until sugar dissolves. Add peel and simmer 10 minutes. Drain well in strainer. Roll peel in granulated sugar.

Mrs. Richard Beckmann

Orange Balls

1	box powdered sugar	1	cup nuts
1	stick butter, room temperature	1	(6-ounce) can orange juice concentrate, thawed
1	box vanilla wafers, crushed		Coconut

Mix sugar and butter with pastry blender. Add wafers, nuts, and concentrate. Make into small balls. Roll in coconut. May be frozen

Linda Miller

Peanut Butter Cookies

½ cup peanut butter
½ cup shortening
½ cup brown sugar
½ cup granulated sugar
1 egg, beaten

1¼ cups sifted flour
½ teaspoon baking soda
¼ teaspoon salt
2 teaspoons vanilla

Cream peanut butter and shortening together. Add sugars gradually, then egg and vanilla. Beat until fluffy. Sift flour, soda and salt together and work into peanut butter mixture. Add vanilla. Form into balls, about sized of a walnut. Place on a cookie sheet, about 2 inches apart, and press down with wet fork to make a crisscross. Bake in 350 degrees oven until light brown.

Mrs. Bill Keller

Pecan Bars

4 eggs
1 package dark brown sugar
1½ cups flour
1½ teaspoons baking powder

½ teaspoon salt
2 cups chopped nuts
1 teaspoon vanilla

Cook eggs and dark brown sugar in a double boiler for 20 minutes. Cool. Add flour, baking powder, salt, nuts and vanilla. Pour in 15½x10½-inch cookie pan and bake at 275 degrees for 45 minutes. Cut in bars while still warm.

Mrs. James Hanahan

Pecan Puffs

½ cup butter
2 tablespoons granulated sugar
2 cups cake flour sifted

1 cup finely chopped pecans
1 teaspoon vanilla
Confectioners' sugar

Cream butter and sugar well. Add flour, pecans and vanilla. Mix well. Using enough dough at the time to make 1-inch balls, work with hands until well blended. Butter must be worked in thoroughly. Roll between palms into balls. Place on greased cookie sheet. Bake 35 to 40 minutes at 300 degrees. Roll in confectioners' sugar immediately.

Mrs. J.E. Tudor, Jr.

Pecan Cookies

1	cup butter, softened	1	teaspoon vanilla
½	cup sugar	1	tablespoon water
2	cups all-purpose flour, sifted	2	cups pecans, ground in blender
½	teaspoon salt		Pecan halves

Cream butter and sugar until fluffy and smooth. Sift together flour and salt; blend into butter mixture with vanilla, water, and ground pecans. Mix well; cover and chill until dough is firm. Shape into ¾-inch balls. Place them on ungreased cookie sheet; and press pecan half on top. Bake at 325 degrees for 20 minutes.

Makes 7 dozen

Jane Crick

Pecan Brittle

2	cups nuts	¼	cup hot water
¾	cup white corn syrup	2	teaspoons baking soda
2	cups white sugar	3	tablespoons butter

Place nuts, syrup, sugar and water in pan and cook until very brown. Add soda and butter. Pour up in 2 pans in strips and spread out.

Mrs. Jack Sullivan

Pecan Pralines

2	cups white sugar	½	cup sweet milk
1	cup brown sugar	3	cups pecans
1	tablespoon butter		

Combine first 4 ingredients and bring to a boil. Add pecans, and cook 4 minutes. Remove from heat and drop on waxed paper.

Russell Lawrence

Pralines #1

1	box brown sugar	1	cup chopped pecans
⅔	cup light cream	3	tablespoons butter
	(or half-and-half)	1	teaspoon vanilla

Cook brown sugar and cream 5 minutes, then add pecans. Cook to soft boil. Add butter and vanilla. Stir and drop on waxed paper.

Mrs. A.R. Pitts

Pralines #2

2	cups light brown sugar		Pinch of salt
¾	cup milk	2	cups nuts
½	teaspoon soda	1	teaspoon vanilla

Cook until soft ball forms in cold water. Spoon onto waxed paper. Cool.

Mrs. John T. McTier

Pralines #3

4	cups granulated sugar	1	teaspoon vanilla
2	cups milk	4	cups pecans, chopped
½	teaspoon baking soda		

In a thick large pot combine sugar, milk and soda. Bring to a boil and then lower heat to medium high or medium. Cook candy, stirring occasionally with a wooden spoon until it forms a soft ball. Remove from heat and stir in vanilla and pecans. Spoon onto brown paper and remove Pralines after they have hardened.

Mrs. Frank J. Eldridge, Jr.

Praline Strips

24	whole graham crackers	1	cup brown sugar, packed
1	cup butter	1	cup chopped pecans

Arrange graham crackers in ungreased 13x9x1-inch pan. Place butter and sugar in saucepan and heat to boiling on high: reduce heat to low and cook for 2 minutes more. Stir in pecans. Spoon and spread over crackers. Bake at 400 degrees for 5 minutes. Cut each cracker in half while warm.

Mrs. Jack Sullivan

Pink Icebergs

½	cup butter	1	egg yolk
½	cup plus 2 tablespoons sugar	1	cup sifted flour
		½	teaspoon baking powder

Cream butter, sugar and egg yolk until light and fluffy. Add sifted flour and baking powder; beat until blended. Turn out on waxed paper and press into ball. Roll in a floured pastry cloth, about ¼-inch thick. Cut into rounds, about ¾-inch in diameter, or use a small fancy cutter. Bake on ungreased cookie sheet at 350 degrees for about 10 minutes, or until delicately browned. Cool.

Toppings

1	cup ground pecans or walnuts	3	tablespoons raspberry jam

Mix nuts and jam. Place a small mound of mixture on each cookie.

Icing

1½	tablespoons lemon juice	**Red food coloring**	
2	cups sifted confectioners' sugar		

Mix lemon juice and enough confectioners' sugar to make spreading consistency. Tint it delicate pink with food coloring. Dribble icing on each cookie.

Mrs. Florence Buchwald

Ranger Cookies

1	cup shortening (or ½ cup shortening and ½ cup butter)	½	teaspoon salt
		1	teaspoon soda
		1	tablespoon vanilla
1	cup white sugar	1	cup coconut flakes
1	cup dark brown sugar	1	cup quick oatmeal
2	eggs	1	cup puffed rice cereal
2	cups flour		

Mix together to make a stiff batter. Drop by teaspoonfuls onto cookie sheet. Bake at 350 degrees until light brown.

Mrs. Walton Carter

Somemores

⅓	(1½-ounce) milk chocolate bar	2	graham crackers
		1	large marshmallow

For Outdoor Cooking: Place chocolate on 1 cracker. Toast marshmallow; place on chocolate and press down gently with other cracker.

For Indoor Cooking: Line cookie sheet with crackers. Place ⅓ chocolate bar and 1 marshmallow on each. Broil in oven until marshmallow is delicately browned. Remove from oven and gently press cracker over each marshmallow. Serve immediately.

Mrs. William R. Davis

Spice Drop Cookies

1	cup butter	½	teaspoon cloves
1¾	cups brown sugar	1	cup nutmeats
3	eggs	1	pound raisins
½	teaspoon cinnamon	1½	teaspoons baking soda
½	teaspoon nutmeg	3	cups flour

Cream butter and sugar; add eggs, well beaten. Add spices, nuts and raisins, well floured. Add soda dissolved in dessert spoon in warm water, and flour. Batter will be very stiff. Take up in teaspoon and drop on buttered tin. Bake at 375 degrees until a pretty brown.

Mrs. Diane M. Smith

Sea Foam

1½	cups light brown sugar	¼	teaspoon salt
½	cup granulated sugar	2	egg whites
½	cup hot water	1	teaspoon vanilla
¼	cup light corn syrup	½	cup broken pecans

In a heavy 1½-quart saucepan with buttered sides, combine sugars, water, corn syrup and salt. Cook, stirring constantly, until sugar dissolves and mixture comes to boil. Cook to 250 degrees on candy thermometer without stirring. Remove from heat. Beat egg whites until stiff. Pour hot syrup in a thin stream over beaten whites, beating constantly. Add vanilla. Continue beating until mixture forms soft peaks and begins to lose its gloss. Stir in nuts. Drop by rounded teaspoonfuls onto waxed paper.

Mrs. H.M. Davis

Snickerdoodles

2	sticks butter	2	teaspoons cream of tartar
1½	cups sugar	1	teaspoon baking soda
2	eggs	¼	teaspoon salt
2¾	cups sifted flour		

Cream butter and sugar; add eggs, beat thoroughly. Add sifted dry ingredients and mix well. Form into 1-inch balls.

Rolling Mixture

2	tablespoons sugar	2	teaspoons cinnamon

Roll in a mixture of sugar and cinnamon. Place 2 inches apart on ungreased cookie sheet. Bake at 400 degrees for 8 to 10 minutes.

Mrs. Michael Kaiser

Sugar Cookies #1

3	sticks butter	1	teaspoon vanilla
1	cup sugar	4	cups flour
2	egg yolks		

Cream butter and sugar. Add eggs and vanilla. Add flour gradually. Roll out in small lumps and press into shape of round cookie. Bake at 375 degrees for about 12 minutes.

Mrs. E.G. Barham

Sugar Cookies #2

3	cups flour	1	cup sugar
2	teaspoons baking powder	1½	teaspoons grated lemon rind
¼	teaspoon salt		
½	teaspoon nutmeg	2	beaten eggs
½	cup shortening	1	tablespoon cream

Sift flour, baking powder, salt and nutmeg. Cream shortening and sugar until light. Add lemon rind, eggs and cream; beat. Add flour gradually. Place in refrigerator overnight before rolling out. Cut with cookie cutters.

Mrs. Loyce Turner

Sugar Cookies #3

1½	cups sifted confectioners' sugar	½	teaspoon almond extract (optional)
1	cup butter	2½	cups flour
1	egg	1	teaspoon baking soda
1	teaspoon vanilla extract	1	teaspoon cream of tartar

Heat oven to 375 degrees. Mix sugar, butter, egg and extracts thoroughly. Stir dry ingredients; blend into butter mixture in 2 steps, working in the 1st addition with hands until dough holds together. Divide dough in half and roll ³⁄₁₆-inch thick on a floured surface. Cut with a cookie cutter. Bake 7 to 8 minutes or until light golden brown. Cool. Frost and decorate.

Makes 1 dozen

Mrs. J.L. Dowling Jr.

Apple Crisp

¼	cup brown sugar	1	(30-ounce) can apples
¾	tablespoon cornstarch		(or 4 cups)
½	teaspoon cinnamon	½	teaspoon lemon juice
			Pecans, finely chopped

Lightly grease 11-inch pie plate. Add brown sugar mixed with cornstarch and cinnamon to apples. Dot with butter then add juice. Sprinkle pecans over apples.

Topping

1	cup white sugar	½	teaspoon salt
1	cup all-purpose flour	1	egg
1	teaspoon baking powder		

Sift first 4 ingredients in bowl. In another bowl, beat egg and combine with flour mixture, spoon over apples. Bake 35 minutes at 375 degrees.

Apple Dumplings

2	apples, pared and diced		Butter pats
	Biscuit dough or canned	2	cups sugar
	biscuits	1	stick butter
1	teaspoon sugar per	1	cup milk
	dumpling	½	cup cream

Use biscuit dough or canned biscuits, roll into flat circles the size of saucers. Fill centers with apples, sugar and a pat of butter. Roll up and place in pan to bake until brown. Remove from oven and make a sauce of 2 cups sugar, 1 stick of butter, milk, and cream. Cook sauce until fairly thick. Pour over dumplings, place in oven for a few minutes until bubbly.

Mrs. Nettie Keller

Apple-Pecan Dessert

2	eggs		Pinch of salt
1½	cups sugar	4	tablespoons butter
12	tablespoons flour	1	cup tart apples, finely
2½	teaspoons baking powder		chopped
1	teaspoon vanilla	1	cup broken pecans

Beat eggs until thick. Add sugar, flour, baking powder, vanilla, salt, and butter. Beat in apples and pecans. Pour into greased 8x8x2-inch pan. Bake at 350 degrees for 30 minutes.

Serves 6

Mrs. Arthur McLane

Apple Torte #1

4	eggs	3	cups chopped, peeled tart
3	cups sugar		apples
8	tablespoons flour	2	cups chopped pecans
5	teaspoons baking powder	2	teaspoons vanilla
½	teaspoon salt		

Beat eggs until frothy. Add in order the other ingredients. Pour into 2 well-buttered pans (8x12-inches). These will puff up, so be sure pans are large enough. Bake at 325 degrees for about 45 minutes or until crusty and brown. To serve, scoop up with pancake turner, cover with whipped cream or ice cream and a sprinkling of nuts.

Serves 16

Mrs. Henry Brice

Apple Torte #2

1	egg	1¼	teaspoons baking powder
¾	cup sugar	½	cup chopped nuts
2	tablespoons flour	½	chopped apples
⅛	teaspoon salt		

Beat egg thoroughly; add sugar and beat well. Sift flour, salt and baking powder. Add to egg mixture and mix well. Fold in nuts and apples. Bake in buttered pie tin for 35 minutes at 325 degrees. Serve hot or cold, with whipped cream or ice cream.

Apple Torte #3

1	stick butter	1	cup sweetened condensed milk
1	cup sugar		
9	apples, sliced	1	cup pecans (optional)
4	eggs	1	box sweet oat crackers, rolled into crumbs

Combine butter, sugar, and apples and then simmer until glossy. Beat eggs, add milk and nuts to apple mixture, and then add eggs. Line bottom of buttered pan with cracker crumbs. Save some crumbs for top. Pour the apple mixture on the crumbs and top with reserved crumbs. Bake at 325 degrees for 45 minutes.

Mrs. Doug Jones

Banana Split Dessert

2	cups graham cracker crumbs	1	(20-ounce) can pineapple, drained
1	stick margarine		
	Bananas	½	pint whipped cream or 1 large carton whipped topping
2	cups 4x powdered sugar		
2	eggs		
1	teaspoon vanilla		Chocolate syrup
2	sticks margarine		Maraschino cherries
			Chopped nuts

Work cracker crumbs and 1 stick margarine together with hands, and line the bottom of lasagna pan. Cover crumb mixture with sliced bananas. Combine powdered sugar, eggs, vanilla, and 2 sticks margarine. Beat until well mixed. It will be stiff. Spread mixture over bananas. Spread drained pineapple over creamed mixture, and cover with whipped cream. Drizzle chocolate syrup over top, and decorate with cherries and chopped nuts. Chill.

Dee Broadfoot

Banana Pudding

2	cups milk	3	egg, separated
2	tablespoons flour		Vanilla wafers
½	cup sugar		Sliced bananas
½	teaspoon vanilla extract	6	tablespoons sugar

Mix milk and flour together. Add ½ cup sugar and mix. Add vanilla and egg yolks. Mix. Cook until thickens, stirring often. In casserole dish, place 1 layer of vanilla wafers, a layer of cooked pudding, and a layer of sliced banana. Continue layering, ending with bananas on top. Make a meringue of the 3 egg whites, beating with 6 tablespoons sugar until stiff. Put meringue on top and bake until brown at 325 degrees.

Mrs. Jack Rudolph

Butterscotch Torte

3	egg whites, beaten stiff	20	butter crackers, rolled into crumbs
1	cup sugar		
½	cup chopped pecans	1	teaspoon vanilla
1	teaspoon baking powder		

Mix egg whites with sugar. Combine remaining ingredients and pour into greased pan. Cook at 350 degrees for 30 minutes. Served with ice cream and top with the sauce.

Sauce

⅓	cup white corn syrup		Pinch of salt
⅝	cup light brown sugar	1⅓	cups evaporated milk or heavy cream
2	tablespoons butter		

Boil first 4 ingredients to the consistency of heavy syrup. Cool and add evaporated milk or cream.

Sauce may be served hot or cold.

Mrs. Roger M. Budd

Creamy Banana Pudding

2	small boxes vanilla instant pudding	1	(9-ounce) carton whipped topping
3	cups whole milk		Bananas
1	can sweetened condensed milk		Vanilla wafers

Mix instant pudding and whole milk together. Pour in condensed milk and stir. Add Whipped topping. Layer this with bananas and vanilla wafers.

Serves 12

Jeaneane Grimsley

Cherry Cobbler

1	can cherries	1½	cups sugar
½	cup water	½	cup milk
6	tablespoons butter	1	cup flour

Mix cherries, water, 3 tablespoons butter, and 1 cup sugar. Pour into casserole dish. To make topping, cream ½ cup sugar with 3 tablespoons butter. Add ½ cup milk. Sift in 1 cup flour. Mix. Drop topping by spoonfuls on top of cherries. Bake at 400 degrees until golden brown on top.

Cherry Crunch Dessert

1	(1 pound, 15-ounce) can cherry pie filling	½	sugar
1	cup instant oats	½	cup brown sugar, firmly packed
½	cup all-purpose flour, unsifted	½	cup butter or margarine

Preheat oven to 350 degrees. Grease 8-inch baking pan. Pour pie filling into prepared pan. Mix oats, flour, and sugars. Cut in butter with pastry blender (or 2 knives) until mixture resembles course crumbs. Spoon crumb mixture on top. Bake for 40 to 45 minutes. Serve warm. May top with sweetened whipped cream or ice cream.

Dawn Rodgers

Blueberry Torte

Crust

⅓ box graham cracker crumbs

1 stick butter, melted
½ cup sugar

Combine and press in 8x13-inch pan.

First Layer

1 (8-ounce) package cream cheese, softened

½ cup sugar

Beat until soft and spread over crumbs. May need to add a little milk.

Second Layer

1 cup chopped nuts

Spread nuts over cheese.

Third Layer

1 cup whipping cream
1 cup sugar

2 teaspoons vanilla

Beat and spread over nuts.

Fourth Layer

1 blueberry or cherry pie filling

Spread pie filling over cream. Chill overnight.

Mrs. Hoke Smith

Boiled Custard

1 quart sweet milk
4 eggs
½-1 cup sugar

¾ teaspoon vanilla extract or other extract

Heat milk in top of double boiler. Do not boil. Beat eggs together until light. Add sugar, mix well, then pour a small portion of the hot milk into egg mixture to warm and thin. Pour mixture slowly into hot milk, cook, stirring constantly until coats spoon. Add extract and chill before serving.

Mrs. Bill Keller

🌿 Cherries Jubilee

1	cup black Bing cherry juice	1	tablespoon butter
1	tablespoon cornstarch	2	tablespoons fermented
¼	cup sugar		black cherry juice
½	cup black Bing cherries	2	tablespoons brandy

Bring juice to a boil. Mix cornstarch, sugar, and a little of the juice; add to the boiling mixture. Boil 1 minute. Add cherries. Remove from heat. Add butter, fermented black cherry juice, and brandy. Serve hot over vanilla ice cream.

Serves 6

If you wish to ignite it, pour good cognac over and light.

June Purvis

Choc-O-Date Dessert

12	cream-filled chocolate cookies, crushed	½	teaspoon salt
1	(18-ounce) package pitted dates, diced	2	cups miniature marshmallows (or 16 large marshmallows, diced)
¾	cup water	½	cup chopped walnuts
		½	teaspoon vanilla

Save ¼ cup cookie crumbs. Spread remainder in 10x6x1½-inch baking dish. In saucepan combine dates, water and salt. Bring to a boil, reduce heat and simmer for 3 minutes. Remove from heat and add marshmallows. Stir until melted. Stir in nuts. Spread over dates. Sprinkle reserved crumbs on top. Refrigerate overnight and cut in squares to serve.

Mrs. Pete Story

🌿 *Date-Nut Roll*

2	sticks butter	1	cup pecans, chopped
1	pound pitted dates	4	cups puffed rice cereal
1	small can coconut		Loose powdered sugar

Melt butter. Add dates and cook slowly, stirring constantly, for 9 minutes. Stir in coconut, pecans, and puffed rice cereal. As soon as you can handle mixture, shape into 2 long rolls. Cool and roll in powdered sugar. Thinly slice.

Kay Coleman

Baked Custard

2	cups milk	3	eggs, beaten thoroughly
½	cup sugar	1	teaspoon vanilla

Combine ingredients. Bake in custard cups, set in pan of hot water at 350 degrees for 1 hour. Serve with Caramel Sauce.

Caramel Sauce

1	box brown sugar	2	cups cream
½	pound butter	1	teaspoon vanilla extract
2	cups milk	1	teaspoon almond extract

Mix over low heat. Add milk and cream. Cook to soft ball stage. Remove from heat. Add extracts.

Mrs. J.F. Hanahan

Chocolate Dessert

1	(9-ounce) chocolate bar	5	eggs, separated
1	package chocolate chips	1	angel food cake
¼	cup water	1	pint whipping cream
2	cups pecans, shelled and chopped	2	tablespoons sugar

Melt chocolate bar, chips, and water in double boiler Let chocolate mixture cool; add beaten egg yolks. Add nuts. Fold in egg whites that have been beaten to stiff peaks. Using tube pan, tear up angel food cake. Line bottom of cake pan with broken cake. Pour some of chocolate mixture over cake in pan. Continue until all cake and chocolate mixture is used. Chill in refrigerator at least 4 hours. 30 minutes before serving, turn out cake. Whip cream with sugar. Ice cake with cream, return to refrigerator until served. Slice.

Mrs. Avalon Griggen

Chocolate Mousse

1	(6-ounce) package semi-sweet chocolate bits	1	tablespoon rum
¼	cup strong coffee	¼	cup sugar
4	eggs, separated	1	cup heavy cream

Melt chocolate bits in coffee over hot water. Set aside to cool. Add well-beaten egg yolks, blended with rum and sugar. Beat egg whites until stiff, and whip cream. Fold into chocolate mixture. Chill 3 hours. Serve in cups. Top with dollop whipped cream.

Serves 10 to 12

Lamb Lastinger

Chocolate Macaroon Mold

2	eggs	2	squares bitter chocolate, melted
¾	cup sugar		
1¼	cups milk	1	teaspoon almond extract
	Pinch of salt	1	dozen almond macaroons
1	tablespoon gelatin		Nuts, cherries, whipped cream
¼	cup water		

Beat egg yolks; add sugar, milk and salt. Cook in double boiler until spoon coats. Add gelatin, which has been soaked in water. Add melted chocolate. Remove from heat and fold in beaten egg whites and extract. Add nuts. Pour into 8-inch mold, which has been lined with crumbled macaroons. Place in refrigerator to chill. When firm remove and serve with whipped cream and garnish with cherries.

Mrs. B. F. Dolan

Coffee Jelly

1	envelope unflavored gelatin	⅓	cup sugar (or sugar
¼	cup cold strong coffee		substitute to taste)
2	cups hot strong coffee	1	teaspoon vanilla, rum, or
			brandy extract

Soften gelatin in the cold coffee. Add hot coffee. Stir until gelatin dissolves. Add sugar and extract. Stir until sugar dissolves. Mold as desired. Chill until firm. Serve with whipped or liquid cream.

Serves 4 to 6

Use leftover coffee or make double strength instant.

Mrs. Henry Louttit

Christmas Gelatin Dessert

Cubes

1	small package lime jello	1	small package cherry jello
1	small package orange jello		

Dissolve each package of jello in 1½ cups of hot water. Congeal in old ice trays the day before.

Filling

2	packages lemon jello	3	packages whipped topping
1	cup hot water	1½	cups chopped nuts
2	cups pineapple juice		Ladyfingers

Dissolve 2 packages lemon jello in hot water plus juice. Let thicken until it is the consistency of egg whites. Then, beat for 1 minute. Stir into 3 packages of whipped topping. Dice jello cubes and fold into whipped mixture. Add nuts. Stir well but carefully. Pour into pan that has been lined on bottom and sides with ladyfingers. Let stand overnight in the refrigerator.

Mrs. Jack Sullivan

Floating Island

1	quart milk	2	whole eggs
¾	cup sugar	2	tablespoons sugar
4	eggs, separated		

Warm milk and sugar in top of double boiler. Whip egg yolks and whole eggs. Add to milk and sugar and cook 10 minutes until it thickens. Whip mixture if it starts to curdle. Cool. Beat egg whites stiff, add 2 tablespoons sugar and spoon them over top of custard. Garnish each "island" with a stemmed cherry.

Serves 6 to 8

Mrs. C.W. Warner

Curried Fruit Bake

½	cup butter or margarine	1	can chunk pineapple,
1	cup brown sugar		drained and dried
4	teaspoons curry powder	2	cups plums or prunes
1	(20-ounce) can pear halves,		Maraschino cherries,
	drained and dried		drained and dried
1	(20-ounce) can peach		
	halves, drained and dried		

In flat casserole dish, place butter or margarine, brown sugar and curry powder, and arrange fruit over it. Bake 45 minutes to 1 hour at 350 degrees.

Mrs. Fred Dodson

Fruit Whip

1	(1-pound) can applesauce	½	pint whipping cream,
2	cups stewed prunes, diced		whipped

Fold fruit into cream and serve in compotes garnished with a little cream and a cherry.

Additional sugar may be added to correct fruit to taste

Mrs. D. L. Burns

Sherried Hot Fruit Casserole

1	large can sliced pineapple	1	stick butter
1	large can peach halves	½	cup sugar
1	jar apple rings	2	tablespoons flour
1	large can pears	1	cup sherry
1	large can apricot halves		

Drain all fruits. Cut pineapple and peaches in half and arrange fruit in layers in large, medium shallow casserole dish. In double boiler, heat butter, sugar, flour and sherry over boiling water, cooking and stirring until about as thick as cream. Pour over fruit and let stand in refrigerator overnight. Bake in 350 degree oven about 20 minutes or until heated through and bubbly.

Serves 12 to 14

Mrs. Joyce Mixson

Almond or Pecan Icebox Cake

18	ladyfingers	½	pound blanched almonds or
30	macaroons		pecans, grated
1	cup butter	1	pint cream, whipped
1⅓	cups 4x powdered sugar	¼	cup 4x powdered sugar
3	whole eggs		Vanilla extract
3	eggs, separated		

Separate and place ladyfingers close together on sides of 9-inch springform pan with rounded sides. Cut off ends. Lay macaroons on bottom of pan with flat sides down. Fill spaces with ladyfinger ends. Cream butter and 1⅓ cups sugar. Add 3 eggs. Add yolks of 3 eggs. Add nuts. Fold in 3 beaten egg whites. Cover macaroons with ½ of this mixture. Place another layer of macaroons on top. Cover with remaining nut mixture. Chill 30 hours. Cover top with whipped cream and ¼ cup sugar mixed with vanilla extract.

Mrs. Joyce Mixson

Grape Dessert

½	cup sugar	½	cup water
¼	instant tapioca	½	teaspoon lemon juice
2	cups bottled grape juice		

Cook first 4 ingredients over medium heat in double boiler until mixture comes to a full boil. Stir often. Remove from stove and let cool. Add lemon juice and pour in sherbet dishes. Serve with whipped cream.

Mrs. Emma Lou Paine

Icebox Cake

1	cup powdered sugar	2	eggs
¼	pound butter	1	box vanilla wafers
1	teaspoon vanilla extract	1	cup pecans, chopped
	(or ¼ cup bourbon whiskey)	½	pint cream, whipped

Cream sugar, butter and vanilla. Add 1 egg at a time and beat until creamy. Roll vanilla wafers into crumbs and combine with nuts, reserving some to sprinkle on top. Put a layer of crumbs in well buttered 2x8x12-inch pan. Spread cream mixture over crumbs. Top with custard sauce then whipped cream and sprinkle remaining crumbs on top. Refrigerate for 24 hours.

Custard Sauce

4	beaten egg yolks	2	cups scalded milk
	Pinch of salt	1	teaspoon vanilla
¼	cup sugar		

Combine egg yolks, salt, and sugar. Gradually stir in slightly cooled milk. Cook in double boiler over hot (not boiling) water, stirring constantly. As soon as custard coats a metal spoon remove from heat. Cool at once by putting in pan of water, stirring several times. Add vanilla.

Mrs. Christy Patterson

Lemon Bisque

1¼ cups boiling water	1 large can evaporated milk,
1 package lemon jello	chilled and whipped stiff
¾ cup sugar	Graham cracker or vanilla
Juice of 2 lemons	wafer pie shell
Grated rind of 1 lemon	

Pour boiling water over jello, sugar, lemon juice and rind. Stir until dissolved. Let set until it begins to gel then add whipped milk. Pour pie shell. May be served with whipped cream and cherries in sherbet dishes.

To make Lime Bisque, use lime jello.

Mrs. Chandler Blanton

Lemon Fluff

1 (12-ounce) can evaporated milk, chilled in bowl	Juice of 2 lemons
¾ cup sugar	Vanilla wafer crumbs

Whip evaporated milk. Add sugar and lemon juice. Put vanilla wafer crumbs on bottom of small square pan. Pour whipped milk, sugar, and lemon juice mix on top of crumbs. Sprinkle more crumbs on top. Freeze and serve.

Mrs. Melville Harris

Lemon Pudding

1 cup sugar	1 tablespoon grated lemon
3 tablespoons flour	rind
Pinch of salt	1 cup milk
3 tablespoons lemon juice	2 eggs, separated

Blend sugar, flour, salt, lemon juice, rind, milk and egg yolks, mixing well. Fold in stiffly beaten egg whites. Pour into a medium-sized casserole dish and set in a pan of hot water. Bake 1 hour at 300 degrees. Top will be cake-like and bottom will be custard like.

Mrs. Bill Keller

Lemon Snow

1	enveloped unflavored gelatin	¼	teaspoon finely grated lemon peel
⅔	cup sugar	⅓	cup fresh lemon juice
1½	cups boiling water	3	egg whites

In large bowl, mix gelatin and sugar. Add boiling water and stir until gelatin is completely dissolved. Add lemon peel and juice. Chill until mixture is syrupy, about ½ hour in ice bath or in refrigerator for 1 hour. Beat egg whites until stiff. Add them to lemon mixture and beat until it begins to thicken. Pour in serving dish and chill until set.

Sauce

½	cup cold heavy cream	3	tablespoons fresh lemon juice
3	egg yolks		
¼	cup sugar	1	teaspoon finely grated lemon peel
⅓	cup butter, melted		

Beat cream until thick. Refrigerate. Beat egg yolks with beater, until thick and lemon colored, while gradually adding sugar. Beat in butter and lemon juice. Fold in lemon peel and whipped cream. Chill thoroughly. Ladle some sauce over each portion of Lemon Snow.

Mrs. Joyce Mixson

Peach Cobbler

1	cup sugar	¾	cup milk
¾	cup flour	¾	stick butter
2	teaspoons baking powder	2	sliced peaches covered in
	Pinch of salt		1 cup sugar

Combine sugar, flour, baking powder, salt and milk to make batter. Melt butter in casserole dish and pour in batter. Do not stir. Pour in peach mixture. Do not stir. Bake at 350 degrees for 1 hour.

Mrs. Clarence Paine

Lemon and Strawberry Surprise

4	**egg whites**	**¾**	**cup sugar**
¼	**teaspoon cream of tartar**		

Beat egg whites with cream of tartar until very stiff. Add sugar gradually and continue to beat until meringue is glossy and stiff. Make meringue shells and bake in a preheated 225 degree oven for 1½ hours. Cool.

Lemon Filling

4	**egg yolks**	**1½**	**cups cream, separated**
½	**cup sugar**	**2**	**tablespoons sugar**
1	**teaspoon lemon rind, finely grated**		**Whole strawberries to garnish**
6	**tablespoons lemon juice**		

Place yolks, sugar, rind, and juice in top of double boiler and cook for about 15 minutes, or until thick. Cool. Beat 1 cup cream until stiff. Fold into lemon custard. Chill custard in meringue nests. Just before serving, beat ½ cup cream with 2 tablespoons sugar. Top each shell with whipped cream and whole strawberry.

Mrs. Ed Garvin

Dried Peach Custard

Peach Filling

1	**box dried peaches**	**1**	**pie crust**
1	**cup sugar, or more (if you like it sweeter)**		

Stew peaches in just enough water to get tender. Mash fine with potato masher and add sugar. After peaches have cooled, put layer of peaches on crust.

Custard

3	**eggs**	**1**	**stick butter**
1	**cup sugar**	**1**	**cup milk**

Mix to make custard. Pour over peaches, bake in moderate oven until custard is firm.

Mrs. Nettie Keller

Pear Crisp

4	cups chopped pears	¾	cup flour
½	teaspoon salt	1	cup sugar
¼	cup water	½	cup butter

Butter a shallow pan and put pears in. Sprinkle with salt and add water. Sift flour once before measuring. Mix and sift flour and sugar together and cut in butter until crumbly. Spread over pears. Bake 45 minutes at 350 degrees.

Mrs. Conner Thomson

Pineapple Crisp

1	(20-ounce) can crushed pineapple	1½	sticks butter
1	package white or yellow cake mix	½	cup crushed nuts

Place pineapple in 9x13-inch baking dish. Spread cake mix dry over pineapple. Slice butter over mix. Sprinkle with nuts. Bake at 350 degrees for 45 minutes. Serve with whipped cream.

Serves 15

Mrs. R. C. Elliott

Pineapple Delight

1	angel food cake	1	(1 pound, 4 ounce) can crushed pineapple
1	package vanilla instant pudding mix	½	pint heavy cream, whipped

Slice cake into 3 layers with serrated knife. Combine pudding mix and pineapple, mixing only until combined. Let stand for 5 minutes. Fold in the whipped cream and spread between the layers of cake and over the outside. Additional cream may be whipped and spread over the outside layer and the top garnished with cherry halves.

Mrs. D. L. Burns

Grated Potato Pudding

4	cups raw grated sweet potatoes	1	teaspoon cinnamon
1	cup sweet milk	1	cup syrup
½	cup chopped nuts	1	cup sugar
1	cup raisins	½	cup butter
1	teaspoon allspice	½	teaspoon cloves
		3	eggs, beaten

Melt a little butter in a heavy skillet. Mix ingredients, adding eggs last. Put mixture into hot skillet and stir until heated. Put in oven. When crusty, turn under and let crust again. Serve with whipped cream.

Strawberry Cool

1	box frozen strawberries	1	pint sour cream
½	cup sugar	1	tablespoon lemon juice

Thaw berries. Add sugar and mash with fork. Fold in sour cream. Add juice. Pour in freezer tray or individual molds and freeze about 3 hours. Do not stir.

Mrs. C.E. Davis

Strawberry Dessert

1	package instant strawberry pudding mix	3	egg whites, beaten stiff but not dry
1	(10-ounce) package frozen strawberries, defrosted		

Sprinkle pudding mix over strawberries and mix until combined. Let stand for 5 minutes, gradually adding 1 tablespoon of sugar. Fold egg whites into strawberry mixture, refrigerate for at least 30 minutes. Serve with whipped cream.

Mrs. D. L. Burns

Tipsy Squire

1	round sponge cake	½	cup toasted, blanched
1	cup sherry		almonds, slivered
1	quart cold boiled custard	1	cup heavy whipping cream

In large glass bowl, break cake into small pieces. Pour sherry over cake. Fold in custard and almonds. Cover top with slightly sweetened whipped cream. Chill and serve from bowl.

Mrs. Courtland Smith

Trinity Dessert

3	cups sugar	½	orange rind grated
3	cups water	3	ripe bananas, mashed
	Juice of 3 oranges and	3	ripe peaches, mashed
	3 limes	1	cup whipped cream
½	lemon rind grated		

Cook sugar and water until thin syrup. Set off to cool. Mix juice, rinds, and fruit together. Put in refrigerator until it congeals. Stir in whipped cream. Put back in freezer in 2 loaf pans.

Mrs. J. Y. Roberts

Strawberry Parfaits

2¼	cups cold milk	1	(10-ounce) package sliced
1	package instant vanilla		frozen strawberries,
	pudding		defrosted
			Whipped topping
			Nutmeg

Measure milk into 2-quart mixing cup with pouring spout. Add pudding mix and mix well. Divide even amount in parfait glasses. Let set for 3 or 4 minutes, and then spoon strawberries over pudding. Top with whipped topping. Garnish with a dash of nutmeg. Refrigerate until well chilled, about 30 minutes.

Serves 6 to 8

Mrs. D. L. Burns

Fresh Raspberry Mousse

1	cup fresh raspberry juice and pulp	¼	teaspoon salt
1	cup sugar	½	cup hot water
1	envelope unflavored gelatin	1	tablespoon lemon juice
¼	cup cold water	1	cup whipping cream, whipped

Crush berries and add sugar. Let stand for 30 minutes or so. Soften gelatin in cold water. Add salt and hot water. Dissolve mixture over hot water. Add lemon juice. Remove mixture from heat and let cool until it begins to gel. Then whip it until very fluffy with electric beater or mixer. Add berries and fold in whipped cream. Turn into favorite shaped mold.

If using frozen berries, decrease sugar by about half.

Mrs. William H. Morris

Fudge Sundae Pie

1	cup evaporated milk		Vanilla wafers or cooked graham cracker crust
1	(6-ounce) package semi-sweet chocolate pieces	2	quarts vanilla ice cream
¼	teaspoon salt		Broken pecans
1	cup miniature marshmallows		

Put evaporated milk, chocolate pieces and salt into heavy saucepan. Stir over low heat until melted and thickened. Add marshmallows to chocolate sauce and stir until melted. Let cool. Use vanilla wafers to line 9-inch pie pan for crust or use cooked graham cracker crust. Spoon ice cream on crust, cover with chocolate sauce. Repeat. Place nuts on top and freeze.

Mrs. Arthur McLane

Frozen Toasted Almond Ball with Hot Fudge

1	quart French vanilla ice cream		2	cups chopped toasted almonds
			2	cups hot fudge sauce

Shape ice cream into balls, using an ice cream dipper or tea cup and spoon. Roll ice cream balls in almonds, coat well. Freeze until firm. Serve with Hot Fudge Sauce.

Mrs. Roger M. Budd

Banana Ice Cream

6	cups milk	½-¾	cup dry milk
4	eggs	3-4	very ripe bananas, well mashed
1½	cups sugar		
1	tablespoon vanilla		

Add each in order and mix well in ice cream freezer.

Makes ½ gallon.

Mrs. Robert Hornbuckle

Cheese Tortoni

3	egg whites	2	egg yolks, slightly beaten
¼	cup granulated sugar	2	teaspoons vanilla
2	cups heavy cream	½	cup semi-sweet chocolate pieces
¼	cup sugar		
2	tablespoons instant coffee	½	cup minced, toasted almonds

Beat egg whites until stiff. Add ¼ cup sugar gradually. Whip cream. Add ¼ cup sugar and coffee. Add egg yolks and vanilla. Fold in egg white mixture. Melt chocolate over hot boiling water. Cool. Quickly fold in chocolate and almonds. Put in large freezer tray. Freeze firm. Slice and serve. Keeps for several weeks.

Mrs. John Slater

Biscuit Tortoni #1

2	cups milk	½	pint cream, whipped
3	egg yolks	3	egg whites, whipped stiff
½	cup sugar		and dry
12	stale macaroons, finely crushed		

Pour milk in double boiler. When hot, stir in eggs yolks, beaten with sugar. Cook until it coats the spoon. Let get cold, and add macaroons, whipped cream and egg whites. Freeze in refrigerator trays without stirring.

Mrs. B.G. Lastinger

Biscuit Tortoni #2

2	eggs	2	cups whipping cream
½	cup powdered sugar	½	cup dried almond
½	teaspoon vanilla		macaroon crumbs
2	tablespoons sherry		

Beat egg yolks with sugar until thick and lemon colored. Add vanilla and sherry. Fold in egg whites beaten stiff. Add cream beaten thick but not stiff. Gently fold in macaroon crumbs. Place in cups or tray and cover top with more crumbs. Freeze.

Mrs. Bill Keller

Cranberry Sherbet

2	teaspoons gelatin	2	tablespoons lemon juice
¼	cup cold water	1	teaspoon orange rind
1	can jellied cranberry sauce	1	teaspoon lemon rind
5	tablespoons orange juice	2	egg whites

Soak gelatin in water. Combine cranberry sauce, lemon and orange juice and rind. Mix well. Add gelatin to above mixture and pour into a refrigerator tray. Chill in freezer until it thickens like soft jello. Beat egg whites stiff, but not dry and fold in above mixture. Stir every ½ hour until it sets up hard.

Mrs. Stanley Bowman (Loraine)

Grasshopper Pie

24	large marshmallows		Green food coloring
⅔	cup milk	1½	cups crushed chocolate
1	jigger crème de menthe		wafers
1	jigger crème de cacao	6	tablespoons butter
½	pint whipping cream		

Melt marshmallows in milk in the top of a double boiler over hot water. Cool and add liqueurs. Add cream, whipped stiff, and add food coloring as desired. Mix melted butter with crumbs and line a 9-inch pie plate, pressing down lightly. Add cream mixture. Place in freezer, and freeze firm. Remove from freezer about 10 minutes before serving.

Heavenly Hash

25	large marshmallows	1	cup copped pecan meats
1	pint cream	1	teaspoon vanilla
25	maraschino cherries, sliced		

Cut marshmallows in 4 pieces. Mix marshmallows with cream and let stand for an hour or more then whip. Mix in other ingredients. Serve very cold.

Mrs. Avalon Griffin

Skinny Ice Cream

10	eggs, slightly beaten	2	teaspoons vanilla
1½	quarts skim milk		Pinch of salt
2	cups sugar	1	pint fruit can be added

Make boiled custard in double boiler. When done, add 1 small carton of whipped topping. Freeze in churn.

Mrs. Walton Carter

Ice Cream Pie Spectacular

	Butter			1½	cups chopped nuts
2	egg whites		1	pint coffee ice cream
¼	teaspoon salt		1	pint vanilla ice cream
¼	cup sugar				

Generously butter a 9-inch pie plate. Beat egg whites with salt until frothy. Add sugar gradually, beating well after each addition. Continue beating until stiff peaks form and egg whites do not slide when bowl is tilted. Fold in nuts. Turn into pie pan. Spread evenly over bottom and sides of pan. Prick bottom and sides with fork. Bake at 400 degrees, 10 to 15 minutes or until light brown. Cool and chill. Spoon coffee ice cream into chilled pie shell. Top evenly with vanilla ice cream. Set in freezer until ready to serve. Serve with Raisin-Caramel Sauce.

Raisin-Caramel Sauce

3	tablespoons butter	½	cup golden raisins
1	cup firmly packed light brown sugar	1	teaspoon vanilla extract
½	cup cream or evaporated milk		Pinch of salt

Heat butter in small saucepan. Add brown sugar and over low heat, stirring constantly, until smooth, about 10 minutes. Remove from heat. Add cream very slowly, stirring until blended after each edition. Heat 1 minute longer. Stir in raisins and vanilla extract. Add a pinch of salt. Serve warm or cold.

Mrs. Lamar Williams

Susie's Ice Cream

6	eggs	1	can water (using milk can to measure)
1	cup sugar		
1	quart milk	1	pint cream
1	can evaporated milk	1	tablespoon vanilla

Cook as custard, 5 minutes, stirring constantly. Cool. Add cream and vanilla.

Mrs. Jack Sullivan

Ice Cream Dessert

¼	cup sherry	12	macaroons	
½	gallon French vanilla ice cream	½	cup maraschino cherries	
		½	cups roasted almonds	

Put in bowl and mix all together. Return to freezer and serve when refrozen.

Mrs. Clarence Paine

Mix for Bought Ice Cream

½	cup puffed rice cereal	½	cup nuts
3	tablespoons brown sugar	1	quart vanilla ice cream
2	tablespoons butter		

Mix all, except ice cream, in heavy skillet. Cook over low heat, basting very slowly and thoroughly, stirring constantly. Cool. Soften ice cream, and stir this in mixture. Refreeze.

Serves 10 to 12

Sue Dennard

Orange Sherbet

6	bottles orange drink	1	small can crushed pineapple
1	can condensed milk		

Mix all together and churn in ice cream freezer.

Mrs. Clarence Paine

Raspberry Jazz

½	gallon vanilla ice cream	3	boxes frozen raspberries
2	dozen almond macaroons		

Soften ice cream, crumble almond macaroons and mash raspberries. Fold together and freeze.

Mrs. John Lastinger

❧ *Persian Velvet*

3	(1-ounce) squares unsweetened baking chocolate	¼	teaspoon peppermint extract (or rum, vanilla, or cinnamon)
2	sticks butter	1	(5-ounce) carton whipped topping, thawed
3	eggs, well chilled	1½	cups granulated sugar
2	egg whites		

Melt and slightly cool chocolate. Cream butter and sugar until very creamy and fluffy. Add chocolate. This mixture has to be beaten until every grain of sugar is dissolved. Add 1 egg at a time, beating about 2 minutes after each addition. Then add egg whites, and beat until well-fluffed. Add extract. Fold in whipped topping, and blend well. Spoon mixture into the shell.

Shell

2	sticks butter	1	cup slivered almonds, chopped and toasted
2	cups all-purpose flour		
1	cup sugar	¼	teaspoon almond extract

Melt butter in large skillet, and stir in flour, sugar, and almonds. Cook over medium heat, stirring constantly, until golden and crumbly. Remove from heat, and stir in a scant ¼ teaspoon almond extract. Reserve about 1 cup of mixture for top. Pat remaining into buttered 9x13-inch dish, and freeze at least 3 hours. After chocolate mixture is spooned over crust, sprinkle with reserved crumbs. Wrap for freezing, and place in freezer for several hours.

Serves 10 to 12

Rosemary Brannen

❧ *Vanilla Ice Cream*

4	cartons half-and-half	2	regular cans evaporated milk
2	cups sugar	1	small bottle vanilla

Put all in ice cream freezer. Stir well and freeze. Fresh fruit may be added.

Lamb Lastinger

Jellies, Jams & Preserves

Jellies, Jams & Preserves

Blackberry Jelly 339

Fig Conserve 339

Fig Preserves 339

Mayhaw Jelly 340

Muscadine Sauce 340

Peach Marmalade 340

Peach Jelly made
    from Peach Skins 341

Pear Jam 341

Pear Honey 342

Pear Conserve 342

Pear Preserves 342

Plum Sauce 343

Tutti-Frutti Jam 343

Wine Jelly or Jello 343

Watermelon Rind Preserves 344

Blackberry Jelly

	Fresh blackberries	½	**cup lemon juice (add only**
4	**cups sugar**		**if berries are ripe)**

Boil berries with a little water added. Squeeze through cloth sack to make 2 cups juice. Add sugar to juice and bring to a boil before adding lemon juice. Cook to "jelly" on candy thermometer or test your special way. Put in sterilized jars and seal with paraffin.

Mrs. Jack Sullivan

Fig Conserve

2	**pounds fresh figs, cut in**	½	**pound raisins**
	small pieces	1½	**pounds sugar**
1	**orange, cut in small pieces**		**Juice of 1 lemon**
⅛	**teaspoon salt**	¼	**cup pecans, chopped**

Combine all of the ingredients except the nuts. Cook on stove top until thick and transparent, about 1 hour. Add nuts. Cook 5 additional minutes. Remove from stove. Pack in jars and process at simmering for 30 minutes.

Mrs. Walton Carter

Fig Preserves

4	**cups sugar**	2	**quarts fresh figs, washed**
1	**cup water**		**and stemmed**

Combine the sugar and water in a saucepan to make syrup. On stovetop, bring to a rolling boil. Began dropping a few figs at a time into the boiling syrup. Do not allow the boil to stop by adding to many figs at one time. Once all figs have been added, let boil for 2 minutes. Remove from heat and let stand in syrup until next day. Boil 20 minutes. Remove from heat and let stand until the next day again. On the third day, boil another 20 minutes. Remove from heat. Immediately pack into hot sterile jars and seal at once.

Mrs. Henry Beck

Mayhaw Jelly

Fresh Mayhaw berries   **2   cups sugar**

Boil berries with a little water. Squeeze through cloth sack to make 2 cups juice. Mix sugar with juice and bring to a boil. Cook to "jelly" on candy thermometer or test your special way. Pour into sterilized jars and seal with paraffin.

Mrs. Joe Stubbs

Muscadine Sauce

20 pounds grape hull and pulp   **1   quart vinegar**
     (Scuppernongs or   **6   tablespoons cinnamon**
     Muscadine Grapes may be   **3   tablespoons mace**
     used)   **3   tablespoons cloves**
18 pounds sugar

Use all ground spices. Wash and pop each grape. Put hulls in one boiler and pulps in another. Cook pulps, adding small amount of water. Mash through a colander to get seeds out. Cook hulls until tender. Mix hulls and pulp, sugar, vinegar, spices and mace. Cook until thickens or reaches jelly stage. Seal in sterilized jars.

Mrs. William Bassford

Peach Marmalade

2   dozen peaches, peeled and   **2   oranges; grate rind, seed**
    sliced   **and section**
1   small jar maraschino   **Sugar**
    cherries   **4   teaspoons dry fruit pectin**

Combine the peaches, cherries and oranges in a food processor. Mix. Empty the fruit mixture into a large Ditch oven. Add 1 cup sugar for every cup of fruit mixture. Add fruit pectin. Cook slowly until the mixture thickens, about 30 minutes. Seal in sterile jars.

Mrs. Frank Strickland

Peach Jelly made from Peach Skins

Fresh peaches   3½ **pounds sugar**
2   boxes powdered fruit pectin

Wash peaches thoroughly but gently. Peel. Place peelings in a stainless steel or enamel kettle and cover with water. Bring to a boil and boil 10 minutes. Drain and measure liquid. You will require 6 cups peach skin juice. Mix pectin with juice in a large kettle. Bring quickly to a boil over high heat, stirring occasionally. Add sugar all at once and bring to a full rolling boil for 1 minute, stirring constantly. The boil should be able to be stirred down. Remove from heat and skim off foam with a metal spoon. Pour at once into sterilized glasses to ½-inch from top of glass, and cover with hot paraffin. Cool on rack and when cool cover with loose fitting lids.

Mrs. D. L. Burns

Pear Jam

1   orange   **1   box powdered fruit pectin**
1   lemon   **5   cups sugar**
2   pounds of fully ripe pears

Remove the rinds from the orange and lemon. Slice rinds very thin and discard about ½ of the white portion. Chop the meat of the orange and lemon and discard seeds. Peel and core pears (measure after peeling and coring) and grind. Mix fruits and place into large saucepan. You should have at least 4½ cups of prepared fruit. Stir powdered fruit pectin into prepared fruit. Place over high heat; stir constantly until fruit comes to a high boil. Add sugar all at once and bring to a full rolling boil and boil hard for 1 minute, stirring constantly. Remove from heat and skim. Stir and skim for 5 minutes to cool slightly and prevent floating fruit. Ladle quickly into sterilized glasses and cover at once with hot paraffin.

Makes 8 to 9 medium-size jelly glasses

Mrs. D. L. Burns

Pear Honey

6	pounds under ripe pears, weigh after preparing	1	(20-ounce) can crushed pineapple
2	oranges, including rind	4½	pounds sugar
		½	pint maraschino cherries

Peel, core and cut pears in pieces. Run pears and oranges through food chopper. Add pineapple and sugar. Let stand overnight. Simmer on stove until thick. Add cut cherries just before it is done. Seal in sterile jars.

Mrs. Courtland Smith

Pear Conserve

3	pounds pears	1	orange
2	pounds sugar	1	cup nuts, chopped
1	cup water		Juice of 1 lemon
½	pound raisins		

Peel, wash, dry and grind the pears. Make syrup of the sugar and water and cook until thick. Add the pears and raisins. Add orange that has been sliced thin, quartered and seeded. Add lemon juice. Cook until clear and transparent. Add nuts 5 minutes before removing from the stove. Pack into jars and process 30 minutes on simmer.

Mrs. Walton Carter

Pear Preserves

5-6	pounds pears	5	pounds sugar

Select pears that hold their shape and have a good flavor. Wash, peel and cut pears into eighths, then core. In a large non-metallic bowl layer the pears and sugar in alternate layers, being sure that sugar is spread over fruit and the last layer, is covered with sugar and let stand at least 8 or 10 hours. Drain the juice, just by pouring it off into stewing kettle and bring to a boil. Boil gently and cook until syrup is somewhat thick. Stir fruit carefully to prevent tearing it to pieces. Fill hot dry sterilized jars ¾ full with fruit and finish filling jar to ¼-inch from top with syrup and cover with hot paraffin and seal. Cool on racks.

Mrs. D. L. Burns

Plum Sauce

1	gallon plums	1½	tablespoons cinnamon	
3	quart sugar	1	tablespoon allspice	
1	pint vinegar	1	tablespoon ground cloves	

Cover plums with sugar, add vinegar. Let stand until sugar is dissolved. Add spices and cook on top of stove, stirring constantly until it gels. Put in sterile jars and seal.

Mrs. Marshall Parks

Tutti-Frutti Jam

4	cups ground pears	1	large orange
¾	cup crushed pineapple	1	tablespoon lemon juice
1	(3-ounce) bottle maraschino cherries, chopped	1	package gelatin
		5	cups sugar

Cook pears until tender. Add pineapple, cherries, orange and lemon juice. Bring to boil, and add gelatin, then sugar. Boil for 1 minute. Put in jars and seal.

Mrs. Lane Renfroe

Wine Jelly or Jello

1	envelope plain gelatin	3	tablespoons sugar
¼	cup cold water	½	cup wine
1	cup boiling water	½	cup cold water
	Juice of 2 lemons		

Dissolve gelatin in ¼ cup cold water. Add boiling water, lemon juice, sugar, and wine and ½ cup cold water. More wine and less water may be used if a stronger mixture is desired.

Note: Good made with sherry wine. Serve with meats.

Mrs. Joe Stubbs

343

Watermelon Rind Preserves

5-6 pounds prepared rinds	**¾ cup water for each pound sugar**
1 pound sugar for each pound rind	**2 lemons, sliced very thinly**

Prepare rind as follows: Cut away all green and red portions and cut rind into cubes, 1x¾-inch. Prepare lime water soak as follows: 2 teaspoons slaked lime to each 1 quart of water. Prepare quantity sufficient to cover rind completely and soak at least 3 to 5 hours. Drain, wash thoroughly and soak in cold water 1 hour. Drain and rinse lightly. During last half hour of last soak prepare a syrup as follows: Combine sugar and water and bring to a good boil and boil on a slow boil for 5 or 10 minutes, reduce heat and when you have completed last rinse of rind, bring syrup to a full boil again and drop rind in. Boil moderately for 1 hour, stirring frequently. Add lemon slices and boil slowly for 30 minutes, or until rinds are transparent and light amber in color. The syrup should be about 224 degrees. Pack in hot jars, a bit loosely, cover with syrup, seal and process for 15 minutes at simmering. Remove to rack to cool.

Note: If syrup becomes too thick before the rind is transparent, boiling water may be added.

Mrs. D. L. Burns

Pickles
& Relishes

Pickles & Relishes

Bread and Butter Pickles 347
Pickled Bell Peppers 347
Kosher Dill Pickles 347
Artichoke Pickles 348
Cabbage Relish 348
Corn Relish 349
Cucumber Crisps 349
Dilly Beans 350
Pickled Okra 350
Orange-Cranberry Relish 350
Lime Pickles 351
Pickled Onion Rings 351

Peach Pickles 352
Pear Chutney #1 352
Pear Chutney #2 352
Pear Pickles 353
Pear Relish #1 353
Pear Relish #2 353
Summer Relish 354
Tignant Relish 354
Red Tomato Relish 355
Vienna's Garlic-
     Cucumber Pickles 355
Watermelon Rind Pickles 356

Bread and Butter Pickles

4	quarts cucumbers, sliced	4½	cups sugar	
1½	cups sliced onions	1½	teaspoons turmeric	
2	large garlic cloves	1½	teaspoons celery seed	
⅓	cup salt	2	tablespoons mustard seed	
2	quarts crushed ice	3	cups white vinegar	

Put cucumbers, onions and garlic in layers in a large pan. Add salt and mix thoroughly. Cover with crushed ice. Let stand 3 hours. Drain thoroughly and remove garlic. Combine sugar, spices and vinegar and heat just to boiling. Do not let the cucumbers boil. Add drained cucumbers and onions and heat without boiling for 5 minutes.

Mrs. M. C. McLeod

Pickled Bell Peppers

	Bell peppers	2-3	peppercorns
1	quart white vinegar	1	whole allspice
2	cups sugar		Pinch of alum
1	clove garlic		

Mix bell peppers, vinegar, and sugar and boil for a few minutes. Cut up peppers and pack tightly in jars. Pour the hot liquid over peppers. As peppers soften and settle down, more liquid may be added. To each jar add garlic, peppercorn, allspice, and alum. Let cool before sealing jars.

Mrs. A. R. Pitts

Kosher Dill Pickles

20	(4-inch) cucumbers	1	quart vinegar
⅛	teaspoon alum	1	cup salt
1	clove garlic	2	quarts water
2	heads dill		Grape leaves
1	hot red pepper		

Wash cucumbers. Let stand in cold water overnight. Pack in sterilized jars. To each quart add the above amount of alum, garlic, dill and red pepper. Combine the vinegar, salt, and water and bring to a boil. Fill jars. Place grape leaf on top of each jar and seal.

Mrs. Lane Renfroe

Artichoke Pickles

2	gallons artichokes	4	tablespoons mustard seed
½	cup vegetable oil	2	tablespoons stick cinnamon
5	cups sugar	1	tablespoon whole cloves
5	cups vinegar	1	small red pepper
2	tablespoons celery seed	1	clove garlic
2	tablespoons whole allspice	2	onions, cut in rings

Wash and scrub well the artichokes. Soak overnight in brine (½ cup salt to 1 gallon water). Make syrup of sugar, vinegar and spices tied in cheesecloth. Simmer 30 minutes. Fill jars with artichokes and 1 small red pepper, 1 garlic clove and a few onion rings to each jar. Cover with hot syrup and seal.

Mrs. Walton Carter

Cabbage Relish

1	large cabbage, shredded very finely	3	tablespoons yellow mustard seed
1	quart onions, sliced very fine	3	tablespoons celery seed
	Salt	3	tablespoons turmeric
	Vinegar	1	cup sugar
		3	tablespoons whole allspice

Pack cabbage and onions in layers in a non-metallic bowl and sprinkle each layer with salt. Use about ¾ cup salt to 1 gallon of vegetables. Let stand overnight. Drain very dry. Place in kettle. Cover with vinegar. Add mustard seed, celery seed, turmeric, and sugar to the cabbage and onion mixture. Mix well. Tie allspice in cheesecloth bag and drop in kettle and boil hard for 10 minutes. Ladle into hot sterilized jars and seal while hot.

Mrs. D. L. Burns

348

Corn Relish

12	**large ears of corn, cut from cob**
1	**cup green sweet pepper**
1	**cup red canned pimiento pepper**
1¼	**cups chopped onion**
1	**cup chopped celery**
1½	**cups sugar**

1	**quart vinegar**
	Salt and hot pepper to taste
2	**tablespoons prepared mustard**
½	**tablespoon mustard seed**
1	**tablespoon celery seed**
1	**teaspoon turmeric**

Peppers, celery and onions may be put through food chopper. Combine all ingredients and simmer for 45 minutes. Seal in sterilized pint jars.

Makes 8 pints

Mrs. William Bassford

Cucumber Crisps

8	**medium cucumbers**
2	**tablespoons salt**
	Crushed ice
6	**medium onions, thinly sliced**

1	**quart vinegar**
2	**teaspoons mustard seed**
2	**teaspoons celery seed**
2	**teaspoons turmeric**
2	**cups sugar**

Wash and cut unpeeled cucumbers in paper-thin slices. This will make about 4 quarts. Cover with salt and crushed ice. Let soak 10 or 15 minutes. Drain cucumbers. Add sliced onions and other ingredients. Bring to a boil. Immediately remove from heat. Spoon cucumbers and onions into 4-pint jars. Pour the vinegar mixture over to cover. Seal.

Mrs. Finice Barker

Dilly Beans

2	cups vinegar	¼	teaspoon hot red pepper
3	cups water	2	teaspoons dill seed
½	cup salt	2	cloves garlic, split
	Fresh string beans		

Bring vinegar, water and salt to a boil. In sterile jars arrange fresh string beans standing on end. Add red pepper, dill seed, and garlic to each jar. Add the vinegar mixture, boiling hot, to the very top of each jar. Cap jars. Allow to sit at least 1 week at room temperature.

This recipe may also be used for okra.

Mrs. Tom Smith

Pickled Okra

1	clove garlic per jar	1	quart white vinegar
1	hot pepper per jar	1	cup water
	Okra	½	cup salt
1	teaspoon dill seed per jar		

Place the garlic and hot pepper in the bottom of clean, hot pint jars. Pack firmly with clean, young okra pods from which only part of the stem has been removed. Add dill seed. After packing jars, bring vinegar, water and salt to a boil. Simmer about 5 minutes and pour while boiling hot over the okra. Seal immediately.

Makes 5 to 7 pint sized jars

Mrs. Jack Gayle

Orange-Cranberry Relish

1	can whole cranberry sauce	1	orange

Cut orange in quarters and remove seeds. Cut quarters in halves and chop in blender or run through food chopper. Stir orange into cranberry sauce. Cover and chill.

Mrs. D. L. Burns

Lime Pickles

7	pounds green cucumbers, sliced thick	1	teaspoon cloves
1½	cups lime	1	teaspoon ginger
1	gallon water	1	teaspoon allspice
4	pounds sugar	1	teaspoon celery seed
3	pints vinegar	1	teaspoon cinnamon
		1	teaspoon mace

Soak cucumbers 24 hours in a mixture of lime and water. Drain and wash in fresh lime water, made as before, 4 times, once each hour. Boil remaining ingredients. Pour over cucumbers and let stand overnight. Boil cucumber mixture slowly for 1 hour. Then put in sterile jars and seal.

Mrs. Finice Barker

Pickled Onion Rings

Peel, slice and separate into rings, 4 medium-sized onions. Pour boiling water over to cover.

Make a mixture of:

1	cup white vinegar	½	teaspoon salt
1	cup water		Pepper to taste
½	cup sugar		

Drain the boiling water from the onions, add the vinegar mixture and let marinate and chill for at least 1 hour. Before serving, drain the onions well and arrange to overlap and look attractive.

Mrs. Jerry Purvis

Peach Pickles

½	bushel ripe peaches, peeled	4	dozen whole cloves
1	quart cider vinegar	6	tablespoons broken stick
14	pounds sugar		cinnamon
2	quarts water		

Boil vinegar, sugar, water and spices tied in cheesecloth to a moderate syrup. Add half of the peaches and cook until peaches can be stuck with straw to the seed. Stir. Fill jars with peaches. Cook rest of peaches and put in jars. Continue to boil syrup until thick again. Fill jars to cover peaches and seal.

Mrs. Clarence Paine

Pear Chutney #1

¾	cup cider vinegar	2	teaspoons mustard seed
1	cup granulated sugar	½	cup candied ginger
1	cup light brown sugar	1	small onion, thinly sliced
1½	teaspoons crushed red pepper	1	cup raisins
		2	cloves garlic, crushed
2	teaspoons salt	4	cups pears, chopped

Mix vinegar and sugar. Bring to a boil. Add remaining ingredients, mixing well. Cook over low heat until thick. If desired, add 1 cup chopped pecans during last few minutes of cooking. Seal in sterilized jars.

Mrs. Henry Brice

Pear Chutney #2

1	lemon, chopped	3	ounces crystallized ginger
1	clove garlic, chopped	1½	teaspoons salt
5	cups peeled, chopped pears	¼	teaspoon red pepper
2½	cups brown sugar	2	cups cider vinegar
½	pound seedless raisins		

Cook all together until fruit is tender.

Makes 1½ quarts

Mrs. Edward Willis

Pear Pickles

1	gallon pears	2	tablespoons whole allspice
2	quarts sugar	2½	sticks cinnamon bark,
1	pint water		broken into pieces
1	quart cider vinegar		

Wash, peel and cut pears into quarters or eighths and core. Cover with water and boil 10 minutes. Combine sugar, water and vinegar in kettle. Tie spices loosely in cheesecloth sack and drop in kettle. Bring to a boil and boil about 5 minutes. Drain pears and place in large non-metallic container and pour syrup over them. Let set overnight in syrup. Next morning drain off syrup and boil until thick. Add pears and cook until easily pierced with fork. Do not stir but keep pears under the syrup. Ladle fruit into hot sterilized jars, cover with syrup and seal.

Mrs. D. L. Burns

Pear Relish #1

1	peck pears, peeled, cored and cut into quarters	2	pounds sugar
5	medium onions	1	tablespoon salt
3	red bell peppers	1	tablespoon mixed greens
3	green bell peppers	1	tablespoon turmeric
		5	cups vinegar

Run pears, onion and peppers through food chopper. Add other ingredients. Cook for 30 minutes after boiling begins. Put in jars and seal.

Mrs. M. E. Crago

Pear Relish #2

1	peck pears, chopped	3	cups sugar
6	large onions, chopped	1	tablespoon salt
6	red peppers, chopped	5	cups vinegar
6	green peppers, chopped	1	tablespoon allspice
1	bunch celery, chopped		

Mix together and let stand overnight. Put in clean jars and process 20 minutes in hot water bath at simmering.

Mrs. Tom Smith

Summer Relish

2	cups sugar	2	cups yellow corn, cut from cob
2	cups white vinegar		
1½	teaspoons salt	2	cups chopped cabbage
1½	teaspoons celery	2	cups chopped onion
½	teaspoon turmeric	2	cups chopped tomatoes
		2	cups chopped cucumber

In a large kettle, combine sugar, vinegar, salt, celery, and turmeric. Bring to a boil and add vegetables and cook 25 minutes, uncovered, stirring very often. Pack in hot sterilized jars and seal.

Makes 3 pints

Mrs. D. L. Burns

Tignant Relish

5	pounds onions	½	gallon vinegar
10	pounds cabbage (use hard heads)	1	cup sugar
		2	boxes celery seed
½	cup salt	2	boxes mustard seed

Grind onions and cabbage together. Sprinkle salt over all. Put in a porous bag, such as an old pillow case. Hang up and let drip overnight. Place vinegar, sugar, celery and mustard seed in big boiler and let come to boil. Pour over cabbage and onions. Pack in jars.

Carol Sherwood family

Red Tomato Relish

5	quarts or 14 pounds chopped tomatoes	1	cup sugar
2	cups red bell peppers	3	cups vinegar
2	cups green bell peppers	1	teaspoon cloves
1½	cups chopped onion	1	teaspoon allspice
3	tablespoons salt	1	teaspoon cinnamon

Cook together over low heat for 5 to 6 hours. Fill sterilized jars. Cap.

Mrs. Lane Renfroe

Vienna's Garlic-Cucumber Pickles

1	bushel small cucumbers	15	pounds sugar
6	tablespoons alum	3	boxes pickling spices
½	teaspoon turmeric		Fresh garlic cloves
1½	gallons and 1½ pints white vinegar		

Wash and cut cucumbers. Make brine to cover from 2 gallons of water and 2 cups of salt. Bring brine to a boil and pour over cucumbers. Let stand 3 days. Reheat brine and pour back over. Let stand 2 days. Remove cucumbers and rinse in cold water. Next, bring to a boil 2 gallons of water mixed with alum and turmeric. Pour over cucumbers. Let stand until next mourning. Remove cucumbers and rinse in cold water. Pack in sterilized jars. Turn upside down to drain while preparing the syrup. Boil vinegar, sugar and pickling spices tied in cheesecloth for 30 minutes. Put 1 garlic clove in each jar and fill with hot syrup. This is best made in a new plastic garbage can and should be kept cool during the pickling process.

Makes 25 quarts of pickles

Mrs. Walton Carter

Watermelon Rind Pickles

5-6	pounds watermelon rinds	5	pounds sugar
1	tablespoon whole cloves	3	cups white vinegar
1	tablespoon whole allspice	2-3	cups water
3	(1-inch) pieces of cinnamon bark	½	lemon, thinly sliced
1	(1-inch) piece of gingerroot or 1 tablespoon ground ginger	½	bottle red maraschino cherries, drained and cut in half

Prepare rind as for preserves. Secure cloves, allspice, cinnamon bark, and ginger in 2 or 3 thickness of cheesecloth. Combine sugar, vinegar, and water then bring to a boil. Drop bag of spices in and boil 5 or 10 minutes. Drop rind into boiling syrup, keeping a moderate boil for 1 hour. Reduce to a slower boil and add lemon and boil for 30 minutes or until rind is transparent and amber in color. During last 5 or 10 minutes add cherries.

Mrs. D. L. Burns

General Measurements Equivalents Table

1 teaspoon = ⅙ ounce

1 tablespoon = ½ ounce

4 tablespoons = 2 ounces = ¼ cup

5 tablespoons = 2⅔ ounces = ⅓ cup

8 tablespoons = 4 ounces = ½ cup

10 tablespoons = 5⅓ ounces = ⅔ cup

12 tablespoons = 6 ounces = ¾ cup

16 tablespoons = 8 ounces = 1 cup

2 cups = 16 ounces = 1 pint = 1 pound

4 cups = 32 ounces = 1 quart

4 quarts = 128 ounces = 1 gallon

Number 1 can - 8 ounces

Number 2 can - 20 ounces

Number 2½ can - 30 ounces

Number 303 can - 16 ounces

Soup can = 11¾ ounces

Food Equivalents Table

Broccoli or Cauliflower	1 pound	=	3 cups florets
Butter or Margarine	1 stick	=	½ cup
	1 pound	=	2 cups
Chicken	4 pound fryer	=	4½ cups chopped
Cream (whipping or heavy)	1 cup	=	2 cups whipped

Crumbs

Dry Bread	4 slices	=	1 cup fine
Graham Crackers	14 crackers	=	1 cup fine
Soda Crackers	28 crackers	=	1 cup fine
Cookies	21 cookies	=	1 cup fine

Lemon or Lime	1 medium grated rind or about 2 tablespoons juice	=	1-3 tablespoons

Marshmallows	¼ pound	=	16 large
	1 large	=	10 miniature

Rice

Instant	1 cup	=	2 cups cooked
Uncooked	1 cup	=	3½ cups cooked

Shelled Nuts

Almonds or Peanuts	1 pound	=	3¼ cups
Pecans or Walnuts	1 pound	=	4¼ cups

Acorn Squash 190
Almond or Pecan Icebox Cake 322
Amalgamation Cake 229
Angel Biscuit 207
Angel Cake 230

Appetizers (also see Dips and Spreads)
Bacon Crisps 20
Barbecued Meatballs 34
Beef and Mushrooms 21
Brandied Mushrooms 35
Cereal Nibbles 21
Chee Wees 25
Cheese Straws #1 26
Cheese Straws #2 26
Cheese Wheels 27
Chicken Liver Wrap-Ups 30
Chili Meat Turnovers 30
Cocktail Meatballs 34
"Crispen Island" Cheese Straws 25
Flaming Cabbage 22
Foolproof Cheese Straws 26
Glorified Onions 36
Ham and Cheese Balls 24
Honey Chicken Wings 31
Hot Bacon-Cheese Roll Ups 20
Hot Cheese Puffs 25
James' Marinated Oysters 37
Marinated Cauliflower 22
Marinated Mushrooms 35
Marinated Shrimp 39
Mushroom Appetizers 35
Olive Surprises 36
Salt-Rising Bread Cheese Straws 27
Sesame Bread Sticks 36
Shrimp Sandwich Filling 82

Apples
Apple Cake 231
Apple Crisp 311
Apple Dumplings 311
Apple Pie "Henri" 269
Apple Spice Cake 232
Apple Torte #1 312
Apple Torte #2 312
Apple Torte #3 313
Apple Walnut Cake 230
Apple-Cheese Casserole 166
Apple-Pecan Dessert 312
Cranberry Ring Mold 53

Cranberry Soufflé 176
Deep Dish Apple Pie 269
Dove or Quail 119
Scalloped Apples 166
Sherried Hot Fruit Casserole 322
Spicy Glazed Apple Ring 166
Sweet and Sour Red Cabbage 174

Apricots
Apricot Aspic 44
Apricot Balls 285
Apricot Bread 207
Apricot Cake 231
Apricot Salad 45
Crystallized Apricots 285
Frozen Fruit Salad 57
Sherried Hot Fruit Casserole 322
Arroz Con Pollo 136

Artichokes
Artichoke Hearts Salad 45
Artichoke Pickles 348
Artichoke Ramaki 167
Consommé Salad 51
French Artichokes 167
Salad Surprise for Jean 64
Savannah Seafood Casserole 122
Shrimp and Artichoke Dip 38
Spinach and Artichoke Casserole 190
Asheville Salad 45

Asparagus
Asparagus and Ham Casserole 112
Asparagus Casserole 168
Asparagus Delight 167
Asparagus Roll-Ups 81
English Pea Casserole 187
Molded Asparagus Salad 46
Tart Salad 67
Aunt Ruth's Creole Peas 187
Aunt Ruth's Icebox Cookies 299
Aunt Willie's Chicken Dish 145

Avocados
Avocado Salad Dressing 72
Grapefruit-Avocado Mold 58
Guacamole 33
Guacamole-Tomato Salad 59
Jodie's Avocado Vichyssoise 89
Mother's Avocado Salad 46

Index

B

Bacon (see Pork)

Baked Beans 169
Baked Custard 318
Baked Fish 126
Baked Hominy Bread 198
Baked Shrimp 125
Baked Squash 191
Baked Stuffed Onions 185

Bananas

Banana Bread #1 208
Banana Bread #2 208
Banana Bread #3 208
Banana Ice Cream 331
Banana Nut Muffins 209
Banana Pudding 314
Banana Split Dessert 313
Caramel Banana Pie 271
Cranberry Banana Bread 213
Creamy Banana Pudding 315
Jellied Ambrosia 44
Strawberry Jello Salad 65
Trinity Dessert 329

Barbecue Leg of Lamb 111
Barbecue Sauce 77
Barbecue Sauce for Steaks 78
Barbecued Meatballs 34
Barbecued Pork Chops 113
Barbecued Spareribs 112
Barbeque Sauce for Chicken 77

Beans and Peas

Arroz Con Pollo 136
Aunt Ruth's Creole Peas 187
Baked Beans 169
Barbequed Butter Beans 168
Bean Salad 47
Black Bean Soup 83
Brunswick Stew 135
Chicken Cashew Casserole 144
Chicken Casserole #5 141
Chili 96
Chinese Beef & Rice Casserole 95
Cold Green Beans 183
Congealed Salad #2 52
Conversation Bean Pie 170
Corn Salad 53
Deviled Peas 188
Dilly Beans 350

English Pea Casserole 187
Epicurean Peas 188
French Green Bean Casserole 183
Green Bean and Corn Casserole 180
Green Bean Casserole #1 181
Green Bean Casserole #2 181
Green Bean Casserole #3 182
Green Bean Casserole #4 182
Green Bean Casserole #5 183
Green Bean Congealed Salad
    with Cucumber Dressing 59
Green Bean Salad 60
Green Beans with Onions 184
Hamburger Casserole
    with Leftover Vegetables 96
Hamburger Pie 98
Lobster and Chicken
    Cantonese Dinner 133
Mexican Bean Rarebit 169
Mrs. Everett's Baked Beans 170
Old-Fashioned Split Pea Soup 85
Oriental Chicken Casserole 138
Oriental Salad 63
Pinto Beans 169
Plantation Casserole 114
Stay-Abed Stew 107
Three Bean Salad 47
Vegetable Casserole 196

Beef

Barbecued Meatballs 34
Beef and Mushrooms 21
Beef Burgundy 94
Beef Kabobs 94
Beef Pan Pie 95
Beef Ragoût 96
Beef Stroganoff 106
Chili 96
Chili Meat Turnovers 30
Chinese Beef & Rice Casserole 95
Cocktail Meatballs 34
Company Casserole #1 97
Company Casserole #2 97
Corned Beef for Sandwich Filling 81
Corned Beef Salad 51
Deep Dish Pizza 103
Easy Lasagna Casserole 99
Ground Beef Casserole 98
Hamburger Casserole
    with Leftover Vegetables 96

Hamburger Pie 98
Lasagna 100
Macaroni and Hamburger Casserole 99
Meat Loaf 101
Meat Pie 101
Paella 153
Peppercorn Steak 102
Picadillo Dip
   (from San Antonio Country Club) 37
Pizza-Style Meat Pie 103
Roast in Foil 104
Rolled Round Steak in Wine 104
Sauerbraten 105
Savory Pepper Steak 102
Sirloin Tip Roast or Steak 105
Skid Row Stroganoff 106
Spaghetti 107
Stay-Abed Stew 107
Swiss Steak 108
Taghiarena 108
Tamale Pie 109
Thick Beef Soup 83
Beets, Spiced 168

Beverages
Brunch Bloody Mary Mix 15
Glug 16
Hot Buttered Rum Cider 16
Hot Chocolate Mix 15
Iced Tea 19
Mrs. Clelland's Cubes 15
Party Punch 17
Punch 17
Ramos Fizz 18
Russian Tea 19
Tea Syrup 18
Tingle Bells Punch 17
Wassail Bowl 18
Wine 19

Bing Cherry (see Cherries)
Biscuit Crust for Chicken Pie 148
Biscuit Tortoni #1 332
Biscuit Tortoni #2 332
Biscuits 207
Black Bean Soup 83
Black Bottom Pie 270

Blackberries
Blackberry Jelly 339
Blackberry Pie #1 270
Blackberry Pie #2 270

Blender Cheese Soufflé 158
Blond Brownies 285
Blue Cheese Dressing 72
Blue Cheese Ring Mold 48
Blue Ribbon Peach Pie 280

Blueberries
Blueberry Jello Salad 49
Blueberry Torte 316
Boiled Custard 316
Bourbon Balls #1 286
Bourbon Balls #2 286
"Brahma" Cheese Dip 23
Brandied Mushrooms 35
Bread and Butter Pickles 347

Breads
Angel Biscuit 207
Apricot Bread 207
Banana Bread #1 208
Banana Bread #2 208
Banana Bread #3 208
Banana Nut Muffins 209
Biscuits 207
Bran Muffins 209
Caraway Sticks 210
Cheese Biscuits 210
Cinnamon Swirls 210
Corn Bread 211
Corn Fritters 212
Corn Muffins 212
Cranberry Banana Bread 213
Cranberry Bread 213
Crescent Poppy Seed Rolls 214
Date Muffins 215
Dill Bread 215
Double Braided Bread 214
Doughnuts 215
Freezer Yeast Rolls 224
Granny's Muffins 218
Herbed Cheese Bread 216
Homemade Bread 217
Hot Cakes 217
Hush Puppies #1 218
Hush Puppies #2 218
Icebox Rolls 216
Irish Soda Bread 219
Magic Muffins 219
Marge's Onion Sesame Bread 222
Mexican Corn Bread 212
No-Knead Rolls 223

Owendaw Corn Bread 211
Prune Muffins 220
Quick Yeast Rolls 222
Rye Batter's Bread 221
Rye Bread Casserole 220
Sally Lunn 223
Sesame Bread 220
Six Week Muffins 219
Sour Cream Corn Bread 211
Spoon Bread 221
Sweet Potato Biscuits 221
Virginia Spoon Bread 222
Waffles #1 224
Waffles #2 224
Yeast Rolls 223
Breakfast Casserole 158

Broccoli
Broccoli and Cauliflower 172
Broccoli and Sour Cream Casserole 172
Broccoli Casserole #1 171
Broccoli Casserole #2 171
Broccoli Casserole #3 171
Broccoli Salad 50
Chicken Devoni 148
Chicken Divine 146
Cold Broccoli Mold 49
Hot Broccoli Dip 23
Overnight Broccoli and Ham Strata 113
Broiled Peaches 188
Brown Rice 203
Brown Sugar Pound Cake 232

Brownies
Blond Brownies 285
Brownies #1 287
Brownies #2 287
Brownies #3 288
Brownies #4 289
Butterscotch Brownies 286
Wafer Brownies 288
Brunch Bloody Mary Mix 15
Brunswick Stew 135
Burnt Sugar Caramel Filling 267
Butter Peanut Cake 234
Butter Pecan Cake 233
Butter Pecan Frosting 233
Butter Sponge Cake 233
Buttermilk Icing 266
Buttermilk Salad 49
Butterscotch Brownies 286

Butterscotch Torte 314

C

Cabbage
Cabbage and Tomatoes 173
Cabbage Relish 348
Cabbage-Stir Fried 174
Flaming Cabbage 22
Jan Carter's Slaw 65
New England Boiled Dinner 111
Scalloped Cabbage 173
Summer Relish 354
Sweet and Sour Red Cabbage 174
Tignant Relish 354

Cakes
1-2-3-4 Cake 229
Amalgamation Cake 229
Angel Cake 230
Apple Cake 231
Apple Spice Cake 232
Apple Walnut Cake 230
Apricot Cake 231
Brown Sugar Pound Cake 232
Butter Peanut Cake 234
Butter Pecan Cake 233
Butter Sponge Cake 233
Carrot Cake #1 234
Carrot Cake #2 235
Cheese Cake #1 236
Cheese Cake #2 236
Chocolate Cheese Cake 237
Chocolate Layer Cake 235
Chocolate Pound Cake 238
Coconut Cake ~ Old Recipe 239
Company Cake 237
Cranberry Confection Cupcakes 238
Crunch Cake 239
Cupcakes 240
Dark Fruit Cake 241
Date Cake 240
Date Nut Loaf 241
Devil's Food Cake 242
Dutch Cocoa Cream Cake 243
Franklin Nut Cake 246
French Coffee Cake 242
Fruit Cake #1 244
Fruit Cake #2 244
Fruit Cake #3 245
Fudge Cake or Pie 248

German Chocolate Cake 250
Hershey Pound Cake 259
Jam Cake 249
Japanese Fruit Cake 245
Jelly Roll 248
Lane Cake 251
Lemon Cheese Cake #1 252
Lemon Cheese Cake #2 252
Marble Cake 253
Mayonnaise Cake 254
Mrs. Hensley's Delicious
    Pound Cake 259
Oatmeal Cake 253
Orange Cake 254
Orange Coconut Cake 255
Orange Layer Cake 255
Orange Slice Cake 256
Peach Brandy Pound Cake 260
Pecan Whiskey Cake 257
Pineapple Chiffon Cake, Quickie 256
Pineapple Upside Down Cake 258
Pound Cake 258
Pumpkin Cake 257
Red Cake 260
Seventeen-Pound Fruit Cake 246
Shortcake 262
Sour Cream Chocolate Cake 264
Sour Cream Nut Cake 261
Sour Cream Pound Cake 261
Strawberry Cake 263
Strawberry-Pecan Cake 263
Sweet Potato Cake 262
Top of Stove Fruit Cake 247
Tunnel of Fudge Cake 249
Whipping Cream Pound Cake 259
White Chocolate Cake 264
White Fruit Cake 247

Candies

Apricot Balls 285
Bourbon Balls #1 286
Bourbon Balls #2 286
Candied Orange Peel 303
Chocolate Covered Cherries 291
Chocolate Dips 290
Chocolate Fudge 297
Crazy Crunch 292
Crystallized Apricots 285
Divinity 295
Divinity Pecan Roll Candy 294

Fudge #1 295
Fudge #2 295
Fudge Squares 296
Heavenly Hash Candy 299
Kisses 300
Lemon Puffs 300
Milk Chocolate Fudge 297
Orange Balls 303
Panocha 302
Peanut Butter Crunch 302
Pecan Brittle 305
Pecan Pralines 305
Pecan Puffs 304
Praline Strips 307
Pralines #1 306
Pralines #2 306
Pralines #3 306
Sea Foam 309
Snickerdoodles 309
Sour Cream Fudge 296
Candy Coated Chocolate Color Cookies 301
Caramel Banana Pie 271
Caramel Frosting #1 265
Caramel Frosting #2 265
Caramel Sauce 318
Caraway Sticks 210

Carrots

Carrot Cake #1 234
Carrot Cake #2 235
Carrot Casserole 175
Carrot Ring 176
Frosted Orange Salad 61
Glazed Carrots 176
Homemade Vegetable Soup 88
Marinated Carrots 174
New England Boiled Dinner 111
Stay-Abed Stew 107
Vegetable Soup 88

Casseroles and Soufflés

Apple-Cheese Casserole 166
Arroz Con Pollo 136
Asparagus and Ham Casserole 112
Asparagus Casserole 168
Asparagus Delight 167
Aunt Ruth's Creole Peas 187
Baked Beans 169
Baked Hominy Bread 198
Baked Shrimp 125
Barbequed Butter Beans 168

Index

Beef Pan Pie 95
Biscuit Crust for Chicken Pie 148
Blender Cheese Soufflé 158
Breakfast Casserole 158
Broccoli and
    Sour Cream Casserole 172
Broccoli Casserole #1 171
Broccoli Casserole #2 171
Broccoli Casserole #3 171
Broccoli Casserole #4 172
Cabbage and Tomatoes 173
Carrot Casserole 175
Celery Casserole 175
Cheese Strata 159
Chicken and Almond Casserole 136
Chicken and Dressing Casserole 142
Chicken and Stuffing Bake 150
Chicken Casserole #1 139
Chicken Casserole #2 139
Chicken Casserole #3 140
Chicken Casserole #4 140
Chicken Casserole #5 141
Chicken Devoni 148
Chicken Pie 148
Chicken Soufflé 150
Chicken Tetrazzini #1 156
Chicken Tetrazzini #2 156
Chinese Beef & Rice Casserole 95
Company Casserole #1 97
Company Casserole #2 97
Conversation Bean Pie 170
Corn Soufflé 177
Crab Casserole 122
Crab Mornae 123
Crab Pie 125
Cranberry Soufflé 176
Creamed Eggs Chartres 157
Curried Fruit 177
Dearing Street Casserole 121
Deviled Crab 124
Dot's Sausage-Wild Rice
    Casserole 117
Duke's Special ~
    John Wayne's Favorite! 189
Easy Lasagna Casserole 99
Eggplant Casserole #1 178
Eggplant Casserole #2 178
Eggplant Casserole #3 178
Eggplant Casserole Patrice 180
Eggplant Soufflé #1 179

Eggplant Soufflé #2 179
English Pea Casserole 187
Epicurean Peas 188
Escalloped Tomatoes 194
French Green Bean Casserole 183
Golden Shrimp 128
Green Bean and Corn Casserole 180
Green Bean Casserole #1 181
Green Bean Casserole #2 181
Green Bean Casserole #3 182
Green Bean Casserole #4 182
Green Bean Casserole #5 183
Green Chili Pepper Rice Casserole 204
Grits Casserole #1 197
Grits Casserole #2 198
Ground Beef Casserole 98
Ham and Cheese Fondue 114
Hamburger Casserole
    with Leftover Vegetables 96
Hamburger Pie 98
Impossible Quiche 162
Lasagna 100
Macaroni and Cheese 199
Macaroni and Hamburger
    Casserole 99
Macaroni Casserole 199
Meat Pie 101
Minced Oysters 131
Mixed Vegetable Mornay 195
Mother's Rice Casserole 203
Mrs. Everett's Baked Beans 170
Mushroom Casserole 184
Mushroom Quiche 161
Onion Pie 185
Onion-Celery-Almond Casserole 186
Oriental Chicken Casserole 138
Overnight Broccoli and Ham Strata 113
Pasta Casserole Marie-Blanche 198
Pinto Beans 169
Pizza-Style Meat Pie 103
Plantation Casserole 114
Pork Chops and Dressing 117
Potato Casserole 200
Potatoes with Cheese 199
Quiche Lorraine 162
Rice Casserole 203
Rye Bread Casserole 220
Savannah Seafood Casserole 122
Scalloped Apples 166
Scalloped Cabbage 173

Scalloped Eggplant 177
Scalloped Oysters 134
Scalloped Potatoes #1 200
Scalloped Potatoes #2 200
Seafood Casserole Supreme 123
Shrimp and Cheese Casserole 127
Shrimp Casserole #1 129
Shrimp Casserole #2 129
Shrimp Delight 130
Spiced Beets 168
Spinach and Artichoke Casserole 190
Spinach Casserole 189
Spinach Soufflé 190
Squash Casserole #1 191
Squash Casserole #2 192
Squash Casserole #3 192
Squash Casserole #4 193
Squash Soufflé #1 193
Squash Soufflé #2 194
St. Paul's Rice Casserole 117
Sweet Potato Casserole #1 202
Sweet Potato Casserole #2 202
Sweet Potato Soufflé #1 201
Sweet Potato Soufflé #2 201
Tamale Pie 109
Tomato Casserole 194
Tomatoes Au Gratin 196
Two Layer Chicken Pie 149
Vegetable Casserole 196
Zucchini 197

Cauliflower
Broccoli and Cauliflower 172
Cauliflower Dip 20
Marinated Cauliflower 22
Caviar, Cream Cheese and 27

Celery
Celery Casserole 175
Onion-Celery-Almond Casserole 186
Celery Seed Dressing 73

Cereals and Grains (also see Grits or Rice)
Bran Muffins.. 209
Caraway Sticks 210
Cereal Nibbles 21
Cherry Crunch Dessert 315
Chicken Casserole #1 139
Cranberry Soufflé 176
Date-Nut Roll 317
Green Bean Casserole #3 182

Mix for Bought Ice Cream 335
Oatmeal Cake 253
Oatmeal Cookies 303
Peanut Butter Crunch 302
Ranger Cookies 308
Six Week Muffins 219
Chafing Dish Crab 31

Cheese
Apple-Cheese Casserole 166
Blender Cheese Soufflé 158
Blue Cheese Dressing 72
Blue Cheese Ring Mold 48
"Brahma" Cheese Dip 23
Cabbage and Tomatoes 173
Carrot Casserole 175
Chee Wees 25
Cheese Ball 24
Cheese Biscuits 210
Cheese Omelet 158
Cheese Roll 24
Cheese Strata 159
Cheese Straws #1 26
Cheese Straws #2 26
Cheese Tortoni 331
Cheese Wheels 27
Chicken and Kraut 145
Chicken Tetrazzini #2 156
"Crispen Island" Cheese Straws 25
Duke's Special ~
    John Wayne's Favorite! 189
Egg and Cheese Salad 57
Eggplant Casserole Patrice 180
Faucon Salad 56
Foolproof Cheese Straws 26
Golden Shrimp 128
Green Bean Casserole #4 182
Green Chili Pepper Rice Casserole 204
Ham and Cheese Balls 24
Ham and Cheese Fondue 114
Herbed Cheese Bread 216
Hot Bacon-Cheese Roll Ups 20
Hot Cheese Dip 22
Hot Cheese Puffs 25
Hot Cheese Spread 28
Hot Clam Dip #1 32
Macaroni and Cheese 199
Macaroni Casserole 199
Macaroni Salad 61
Mexican Bean Rarebit 169

Overnight Broccoli and Ham Strata 113
Plantation Casserole 114
Potato Casserole 200
Potatoes with Cheese 199
Roquefort Dressing 74
Roquefort Mound 29
Rye Bread Casserole 220
Salt-Rising Bread Cheese Straws 27
Shrimp and Cheese Casserole 127
Shrimp Casserole #1 129
Spinach Soufflé 190
Swiss Fondue 31
Taghiarena 108
Tuna Sandwich Torte 82
Cheese Cake #1 236
Cheese Cake #2 236

Cherries
Amalgamation Cake 229
Bing Cherry Congealed Salad 48
Bing Cherry Salad 47
Cherries Jubilee 317
Cherry Cobbler 315
Cherry Crunch Dessert 315
Chocolate Covered Cherries 291
Christmas Cookies 291
Dark Fruit Cake 241
Divinity Pecan Roll Candy 294
Franklin Nut Cake 246
Fruit Cake #1 244
Fruit Cake #2 244
Fruit Cake #3 245
Heavenly Hash 334
Pink Frozen Salad 62
Seventeen-Pound Fruit Cake 246
Sour Cherry Pie 271
Top of Stove Fruit Cake 247
Tutti-Frutti Jam 343
White Fruit Cake 247
White Salad 71
Chess Pie 272

Chicken (see Poultry)
Chili 96
Chili Meat Turnovers 30
Chinese Beef & Rice Casserole 95
Chinese Fried Rice 133
Chinese Skewered Shrimp 126

Chocolate
Angel Cake 230
Black Bottom Pie 270

Bourbon Balls #2 286
Brownies #1 287
Brownies #2 287
Brownies #3 288
Brownies #4 289
Candy Coated Chocolate
    Color Cookies 301
Cheese Tortoni 331
Choc-O-Date Dessert 317
Chocolate Almond Pie 273
Chocolate Cheese Cake 237
Chocolate Cookies 292
Chocolate Covered Cherries 291
Chocolate Cream Frosting 238
Chocolate Dessert 318
Chocolate Dips 290
Chocolate Frosting 266
Chocolate Fudge 297
Chocolate Icing 287
Chocolate Layer Cake 235
Chocolate Macaroon Mold 319
Chocolate Mint Desserts 290
Chocolate Mousse 319
Chocolate Pie 273
Chocolate Pound Cake 238
Chocolate Sauce 268
Chocolate Sauce for
    Hot Fudge Cake 268
Chocolate Sauce For Ice Cream 268
Dark Chocolate Coconut Cookies 302
Devil's Food Cake 242
Dutch Cocoa Cream Cake 243
French Silk Chocolate Pie 273
Frozen Toasted Almond Ball
    with Hot Fudge 331
Fudge #1 295
Fudge #2 295
Fudge Cake or Pie 248
Fudge Icing 265
Fudge Squares 296
Fudge Sundae Pie 330
German Chocolate Cake 250
German Chocolate Pie 274
Gooey 299
Grasshopper Pie 333
Heavenly Hash Candy 299
Hershey Pound Cake 259
Marble Cake 253
Mayonnaise Cake 254
Milk Chocolate Fudge 297

Milk Chocolate Icing 243, 267
Persian Velvet 336
Red Cake 260
Somemores 308
Sour Cream Chocolate Cake 264
Tunnel of Fudge Cake 249
Wafer Brownies 288
White Chocolate Cake 264
Christmas Cookies 291
Christmas Gelatin Dessert 320
Cinnamon Crisps 291
Cinnamon Swirls 210

Citron

Dark Fruit Cake 241
Fruit Cake #1 244
Seventeen-Pound Fruit Cake 246
White Fruit Cake 247
Clam Chowder 84
Cocktail Meatballs 34

Coconut

Amalgamation Cake 229
Carrot Cake #1 234
Coconut Cake ~ Old Recipe 239
Coconut Cookies 293
Coconut Cream Pie 274
Coconut-Pecan Frosting 250
Dark Chocolate Coconut Cookies 302
Date-Nut Roll 317
Five Cup Salad 56
Fruit Cake #1 244
Fruit Cake #3 245
Jam Cake 249
Japanese Fruit Cake 245
Japanese Fruit Pies 275
Lane Cake 251
Orange Coconut Cake 255
Orange Slice Cake 256
Ranger Cookies 308
Shrimp Curry 128
Strawberry-Pecan Cake 263
Sweet Potato Cake 262
Sweet Potato Casserole #2 202
White Chocolate Cake 264
Coffee Jelly 320
Cold Broccoli Mold 49
Cold Green Beans 183
Company Cake 237
Company Casserole #1 97
Company Casserole #2 97

Condiments and Sauces (also see Jellies,

Jams and Preserves or Pickles and Relishes)

Barbecue Sauce 77
Barbecue Sauce for Steaks 78
Barbeque Sauce for Chicken 77
Gravy 105
Hollandaise Sauce 78
Homemade Mayonnaise #1 76
Homemade Mayonnaise #2 76
Lemon Barbeque Sauce 154
Mushroom Sauce 146
Rémoulade Sauce 64
Ridgewood Bar-B-Q Sauce 78
Shrimp Mayonnaise 51
Sweet 'n Sour Sauce 133
Tangy Sauce for Cabbage,
Broccoli, Etc. 77
Congealed Salad #1 52
Congealed Salad #2 52
Consommé Salad 51
Conversation Bean Pie 170

Cookies and Bars

Aunt Ruth's Icebox Cookies 299
Candy Coated Chocolate
Color Cookies 301
Chocolate Cookies 292
Chocolate Mint Desserts 290
Christmas Cookies 291
Cinnamon Crisps 291
Coconut Cookies 293
Cream Cheese Cookies 293
Crescent Cookies 294
Dark Chocolate Coconut Cookies 302
Easy Cheese Cake Squares 289
Gingerbread Boys 298
Goldie's Cookies 297
Gooey 299
Katy's Cornettes 300
Magic Marshmallow
Crescent Puffs 301
Mrs. Rhymes Lemon Squares 298
Oatmeal Cookies 303
Peanut Butter Cookies 304
Pecan Bars 304
Pecan Cookies 305
Pink Icebergs 307
Ranger Cookies 308
Somemores 308
Spice Drop Cookies 308

Sugar Cookies #1 310
Sugar Cookies #2 310
Sugar Cookies #3 310
Cordon Bleu Chicken Breasts 141

Corn

Brunswick Stew 135
Corn Fritters 212
Corn Relish 349
Corn Salad 53
Corn Soufflé 177
Green Bean and Corn Casserole 180
Ground Beef Casserole 98
Homemade Vegetable Soup 88
Mexican Corn Bread 212
Plantation Casserole 114
Sour Cream Corn Bread 211
Summer Relish 354
Taghiarena 108
Tamale Pie 109
Thick Beef Soup 83
Corn Bread 211
Corn Muffins 212

Corned Beef

Corned Beef 109
Corned Beef for Sandwich Filling 81
Corned Beef Hash 110
Corned Beef Salad 51
New England Boiled Dinner 111
Court Bouillon 125

Crab (see Seafood)

Cranberry and Cranberry Sauce

Cranberry Banana Bread 213
Cranberry Bread 213
Cranberry Confection Cupcakes 238
Cranberry Mold 54
Cranberry Ring Mold 53
Cranberry Sherbet 332
Cranberry Soufflé 176
Cranberry-Raspberry Salad 52
Frozen Cranberry Salad #1 55
Frozen Cranberry Salad #2 55
Orange-Cranberry Relish 350
Raw Cranberry Salad 54
Crazy Crunch 292
Cream Cheese and Caviar 27
Cream Cheese Cookies 293
Cream Cheese Dressing 62
Cream Cheese Log 28

Cream Cheese Pickapeppa 28
Cream Cheese Pie 275
Creamed Eggs 157
Creamed Eggs Chartres 157
Creamed Stuffed Eggs 159
Creamy Baked Chicken 137
Creamy Banana Pudding 315
Crescent Cookies 294
Crescent Poppy Seed Rolls 214
"Crispen Island" Cheese Straws 25
Crunch Cake 239
Crystallized Apricots 285

Cucumbers

Bread and Butter Pickles 347
Cucumber Crisps 349
Cucumber Dressing 59
Cucumber Marinade 55
Cucumber Salad 56
Herbed Tomato Platter &
    Dutch Cucumbers 68
Kosher Dill Pickles 347
Lime Pickles 351
Sea Dream Salad 65
Summer Relish 354
Vienna's Garlic-Cucumber Pickles 355
Cupcakes 240
Curried Deviled Eggs 159
Curried Eggs 160
Curried Fruit 177
Curried Fruit Bake 321
Custard Sauce 323

D

Dark Chocolate Coconut Cookies 302
Dark Fruit Cake 241

Dates

Banana Bread #2 208
Choc-O-Date Dessert 317
Christmas Cookies 291
Cranberry Confection Cupcakes 238
Dark Fruit Cake 241
Date Cake 240
Date Muffins 215
Date Nut Loaf 241
Date-Nut Roll 317
Macaroon Pie 278
Open Sesame Pie 279
Orange Slice Cake 256
Dearing Street Casserole 121

Deep Dish Apple Pie 269
Deep Dish Pizza 103
Desserts (also see Brownies, Cakes, Candies,
Chocolate, Cookies and Bars, Frostings, Icings,
Fillings and Sauces, Frozen Desserts and Pies)
   Almond or Pecan Icebox Cake 322
   Apple Crisp 311
   Apple Dumplings 311
   Apple Torte #1 312
   Apple Torte #2 312
   Apple Torte #3 313
   Apple-Pecan Dessert 312
   Baked Custard 318
   Banana Pudding 314
   Banana Split Dessert 313
   Blueberry Torte 316
   Boiled Custard 316
   Butterscotch Torte 314
   Cherries Jubilee 317
   Cherry Cobbler 315
   Cherry Crunch Dessert 315
   Choc-O-Date Dessert 317
   Chocolate Dessert 318
   Chocolate Macaroon Mold 319
   Chocolate Mousse 319
   Christmas Gelatin Dessert 320
   Coffee Jelly 320
   Creamy Banana Pudding 315
   Curried Fruit Bake 321
   Date-Nut Roll 317
   Dried Peach Custard 326
   Floating Island 321
   Fresh Raspberry Mousse 330
   Fruit Whip 321
   Grape Dessert 323
   Grated Potato Pudding 328
   Icebox Cake 323
   Lemon and Strawberry Surprise 326
   Lemon Bisque 324
   Lemon Fluff 324
   Lemon Pudding 324
   Lemon Snow 325
   Peach Cobbler 325
   Pear Crisp 327
   Pineapple Crisp 327
   Pineapple Delight 327
   Sherried Hot Fruit Casserole 322
   Strawberry Cool 328
   Strawberry Dessert 328
   Strawberry Parfaits 329
   Tipsy Squire 329
   Trinity Dessert 329
Deviled Crab 124
Deviled Peas 188
Devil's Food Cake 242
Different Lemon Pie 276
Dill Bread 215
Dilly Beans 350

Dips and Spreads
   Bacon Sandwich Spread 81
   "Brahma" Cheese Dip 23
   Cauliflower Dip 20
   Chafing Dish Crab 31
   Cheese Ball 24
   Cheese Roll 24
   Crab Newburg Dip 32
   Cream Cheese and Caviar 27
   Cream Cheese Log 28
   Cream Cheese Pickapeppa 28
   Dip For Shrimp 38
   Dip for Vegetables 40
   Guacamole 33
   Ham and Chutney Spread 82
   Hot Broccoli Dip 23
   Hot Cheese Dip 22
   Hot Cheese Spread 28
   Hot Clam Dip #1 32
   Hot Clam Dip #2 32
   Hot Crab Spread 33
   Picadillo Dip
      (from San Antonio Country Club) 37
   Pineapple Cheese Ball 29
   Roquefort Mound 29
   Shrimp and Artichoke Dip 38
   Shrimp and Crab Mousse 40
   Shrimp Dip 38
   Shrimp Pâté 39
   Swamp Salad 40
   Swiss Fondue 31
Divinity 295
Divinity Pecan Roll Candy 294
Dot's Sausage-Wild Rice Casserole 117
Double Braided Bread 214
Doughnuts 215
Dove or Quail 119
Doves with Orange Sauce Glaze 119
Down South Pecan Pie 280
Dressing for Grapefruit Salad 74

Dried Peach Custard 326
Duke's Special ~
   John Wayne's Favorite! 189
Dutch Cocoa Cream Cake 243

E

Easy Cheese Cake Squares 289
Easy Lasagna Casserole 99

Egg Dishes
   Blender Cheese Soufflé 158
   Breakfast Casserole 158
   Cheese Omelet 158
   Cheese Strata 159
   Creamed Eggs 157
   Creamed Eggs Chartres 157
   Creamed Stuffed Eggs 159
   Curried Deviled Eggs 159
   Curried Eggs 160
   Egg and Cheese Salad 57
   Eggs Benedict ~
     Quick Version of Old Classic 161
   Eggs Continental 160
   Impossible Quiche 162
   Mushroom Quiche 161
   Quiche Lorraine 162

Eggplant
   Eggplant Casserole #1 178
   Eggplant Casserole #2 178
   Eggplant Casserole #3 178
   Eggplant Casserole Patrice 180
   Eggplant Soufflé #1 179
   Eggplant Soufflé #2 179
   Scalloped Eggplant 177
English Pea Casserole 187
Epicurean Peas 188
Escalloped Tomatoes 194

F

Faucon Salad 56

Figs
   Fig Conserve 339
   Fig Preserves 339

Fish
   Baked Fish 126
   Court Bouillon 125
   Foolproof Salmon Croquettes 134
   Poached Trout Marinier 124
   Salmon Loaf 134

Tuna Burgers 132
Tuna Garden Salad 70
Tuna Sandwich Torte 82
Five Cup Salad 56
Flaming Cabbage 22
Floating Island 321
Foolproof Cheese Straws 26
Franklin Nut Cake 246
Freezer Yeast Rolls 224
French Artichokes 167
French Coffee Cake 242
French Dressing 73
French Fried Onion Rings 186
French Green Bean Casserole 183
French Onion Soup 86
French Silk Chocolate Pie 273
Fresh Raspberry Mousse 330
Fresh Strawberry Pie 284
Frosted Orange Salad 61

Frostings, Icings, Fillings and Sauces
   Burnt Sugar Caramel Filling 267
   Butter Pecan Frosting 233
   Buttermilk Icing 266
   Caramel Frosting #1 265
   Caramel Frosting #2 265
   Caramel Sauce 318
   Chocolate Cream Frosting 238
   Chocolate Frosting 266
   Chocolate Icing 287
   Chocolate Sauce 268
   Chocolate Sauce For Ice Cream 268
   Coconut-Pecan Frosting 250
   Custard Sauce 323
   Fudge Icing 265
   Lemon Cheese Filling 267
   Milk Chocolate Icing 243, 267
   Raisin-Caramel Sauce 334
   Sour Cream Topping 231
   Strawberry Frosting 263
   White Frosting 266
   White Icing 266
Frozen Cranberry Salad #1 55
Frozen Cranberry Salad #2 55

Frozen Desserts
   Banana Ice Cream 331
   Biscuit Tortoni #1 332
   Biscuit Tortoni #2 332
   Cheese Tortoni 331

Cranberry Sherbet 332
Frozen Toasted Almond Ball
   with Hot Fudge 331
Fudge Sundae Pie 330
Grasshopper Pie 333
Heavenly Hash 334
Ice Cream Dessert 335
Ice Cream Pie Spectacular 334
Mix for Bought Ice Cream 335
Orange Sherbet 335
Persian Velvet 336
Raspberry Jazz 335
Skinny Ice Cream 334
Susie's Ice Cream 334
Vanilla Ice Cream 336
Frozen Fruit Salad 57
Frozen Toasted Almond Ball
   with Hot Fudge 331
Fruit Cake #1 244
Fruit Cake #2 244
Fruit Cake #3 245
Fruit Salad 58
Fruit Salad Dressing 73
Fruit Whip 321
Fudge #1 295
Fudge #2 295
Fudge Cake or Pie 248
Fudge Icing 265
Fudge Squares 296
Fudge Sundae Pie 330

G

Game

Dove or Quail 119
Doves with Orange Sauce Glaze 119
Quail with Mushrooms 120
Venison Pot Roast 121
Venison Steak 120
White Oak Hunting Lodge Quail 119
Wild Duck 120
German Chocolate Cake 250
German Chocolate Pie 274
Gingerbread Boys 298
Glazed Carrots 176
Glorified Onions 36
Glug 16
Golden Shrimp 128
Goldie's Cookies 297
Goldie's Turnips 196

Gooey 299
Graham Cracker Pie 276
Graham Cracker Pie Crust 284
Granny's Muffins 218

Grapefruit

Grapefruit Salad 58
Grapefruit-Avocado Mold 58

Grapes and Grape Juice

Grape Dessert 323
Wine 19
Grasshopper Pie 333
Grated Potato Pudding 328
Gravy 105

Green Beans (see Beans and Peas)

Green Chili Pepper Rice Casserole 204
Green Goddess Dressing 74

Grilling Recipes

Beef Kabobs 94
Chinese Skewered Shrimp 126
Grilled Pork Chops 115

Grits

Baked Hominy Bread 198
Grits Casserole #1 197
Grits Casserole #2 198
Owendaw Corn Bread 211
Ground Beef Casserole 98
Guacamole 33
Guacamole-Tomato Salad 59

H

Ham and Cheese Balls 24
Ham and Cheese Fondue 114
Ham and Chutney Spread 82
Hamburger Casserole
   with Leftover Vegetables 96
Hamburger Pie 98
Heavenly Hash 333
Heavenly Hash Candy 299
Herbed Cheese Bread 216
Herbed Tomato Platter
   & Dutch Cucumbers 68
Hershey Pound Cake 259
Hollandaise Sauce 78
Homemade Bread 217
Homemade Mayonnaise #1 76
Homemade Mayonnaise #2 76
Homemade Vegetable Soup 88
Honey Chicken Wings 31

Hot Bacon-Cheese Roll Ups 20
Hot Broccoli Dip 23
Hot Buttered Rum Cider 16
Hot Cakes 217
Hot Cheese Dip 22
Hot Cheese Pineapple 186
Hot Cheese Puffs 25
Hot Cheese Spread 28
Hot Chocolate Mix 15
Hot Clam Dip #1 32
Hot Clam Dip #2 32
Hot Crab Rice Salad 53
Hot Crab Spread 33
Hush Puppies #1 218
Hush Puppies #2 218

I

Ice Cream Dessert 335
Ice Cream Pie Spectacular 334
Icebox Cake 323
Icebox Rolls 216
Iced Tea 19
Impossible Quiche 162
Irish Soda Bread 219

J

Jam Cake 249
James' Marinated Oysters 37
Jan Carter's Slaw 65
Japanese Fruit Cake 245
Japanese Fruit Pies 275
Jellied Ambrosia 44

Jellies, Jams and Preserves

Blackberry Jelly 339
Fig Conserve 339
Fig Preserves 339
Mayhaw Jelly 340
Muscadine Sauce 340
Peach Jelly made
from Peach Skins 341
Peach Marmalade 340
Pear Conserve 342
Pear Honey 342
Pear Jam 341
Pear Preserves 342
Plum Sauce 343
Tutti-Frutti Jam 343
Watermelon Rind Preserves 344
Wine Jelly or Jello 343

Jelly Roll 248
Jodie's Avocado Vichyssoise 89
June's Easy Chicken 147

K

Katy's Cornettes 300
Key Lime Pie 278
Kisses 300
Kosher Dill Pickles 347
Kum Bak Dressing 75

L

Lane Cake 251
Lasagna 100
Leg of Lamb, Barbecue 111
Lemon and Strawberry Surprise 326
Lemon Barbeque Chicken 154
Lemon Barbeque Sauce 154
Lemon Bisque 324
Lemon Cheese Cake #1 252
Lemon Cheese Cake #2 252
Lemon Cheese Filling 267
Lemon Chess Pie 272
Lemon Fluff 324
Lemon Luscious Pie 277
Lemon Pudding 324
Lemon Puffs 300
Lemon Snow 325
Lemon-Caper Mayonnaise 75
Lime Meringue Pie 277
Lime Pickles 351
Lobster and Chicken
Cantonese Dinner 133

M

Macaroni and Cheese 199
Macaroni and Hamburger Casserole 99
Macaroni Casserole 199
Macaroni Salad 61
Macaroon Pie 278
Magic Marshmallow Crescent Puffs 301
Magic Muffins 219
Marble Cake 253
Marge's Onion Sesame Bread 222
Marinated Carrots 174
Marinated Cauliflower 22
Marinated Mushrooms 35
Marinated Shrimp 39
Marinated Shrimp Salad 66

Mayhaw Jelly 340
Mayonnaise Cake 254
Meat Loaf 101
Meat Pie 101
Mexican Bean Rarebit 169
Mexican Corn Bread 212
Milk Chocolate Fudge 297
Milk Chocolate Icing 243, 267
Minced Oysters 131
Mincemeat Gelatin Salad 61
Mix for Bought Ice Cream 335
Mixed Vegetable Mornay 195
Molded Asparagus Salad 46
Mother's Avocado Salad 46
Mother's Rice Casserole 203
Mrs. Clelland's Cubes 15
Mrs. Everett's Baked Beans 170
Mrs. Hensley's Delicious Pound Cake 259
Mrs. Rhymes Lemon Squares 298
Muscadine Sauce 340

Mushrooms

Beef and Mushrooms 21
Beef Ragoût 96
Beef Stroganoff 106
Brandied Mushrooms 35
Crab Casserole 122
Eggs Benedict ~
  Quick Version of Old Classic 161
Eggs Continental 160
Green Bean Casserole #4 182
Lobster and Chicken
  Cantonese Dinner 133
Marinated Mushrooms 35
Mushroom Appetizers 35
Mushroom Casserole 184
Mushroom Quiche 161
Mushroom Sauce 146
Neapolitan Pork Chops 116
Quail with Mushrooms 120
Rolled Round Steak in Wine 104
Skid Row Stroganoff 106
Spinach and Mushroom Soup 87

N

Neapolitan Pork Chops 116
New England Boiled Dinner 111
No-Knead Rolls 223

Nuts

Almond or Pecan Icebox Cake 322
Amalgamation Cake 229
Angel Cake 230
Apple Spice Cake 232
Apple Torte #1 312
Apple Walnut Cake 230
Apple-Pecan Dessert 312
Apricot Salad 45
Banana Bread #2 208
Banana Bread #3 208
Banana Nut Muffins 209
Blond Brownies 285
Blueberry Torte 316
Bourbon Balls #1 286
Bourbon Balls #2 286
Brown Sugar Pound Cake 232
Brownies #1 287
Brownies #3 288
Brownies #4 289
Butter Peanut Cake 234
Butter Pecan Cake 233
Butter Pecan Frosting 233
Butterscotch Brownies 286
Carrot Cake #1 234
Cereal Nibbles 21
Cheese Ball 24
Cheese Roll 24
Chicken and Almond Casserole 136
Chicken Cashew Casserole 144
Chicken Country Captain 144
Chicken with Pecans 147
Chocolate Almond Pie 273
Chocolate Cookies 292
Chocolate Dessert 318
Chocolate Dips 290
Chocolate Fudge 297
Christmas Cookies 291
Christmas Gelatin Dessert 320
Cinnamon Crisps 291
Coconut Cookies 293
Coconut-Pecan Frosting 250
Cranberry Confection Cupcakes 238
Cranberry Ring Mold 53
Crazy Crunch 292
Cream Cheese Log 28
Crescent Cookies 294
Dark Fruit Cake 241

Date Cake 240
Date Muffins 215
Date Nut Loaf 241
Date-Nut Roll 317
Divinity 295
Divinity Pecan Roll Candy 294
Down South Pecan Pie 280
Easy Cheese Cake Squares 289
Franklin Nut Cake 246
French Coffee Cake 242
Frosted Orange Salad 61
Frozen Cranberry Salad #2 55
Frozen Toasted Almond
    Ball with Hot Fudge 331
Fruit Cake #1 244
Fruit Cake #2 244
Fruit Cake #3 245
Fudge #1 295
Fudge #2 295
Fudge Squares 296
German Chocolate Pie 274
Goldie's Cookies 297
Gooey 299
Heavenly Hash 334
Heavenly Hash Candy 299
Ice Cream Pie Spectacular 334
Icebox Cake 323
Jam Cake 249
Japanese Fruit Pies 275
Kisses 300
Lane Cake 251
Macaroon Pie 278
Mincemeat Gelatin Salad 61
Molded Asparagus Salad 46
Oatmeal Cookies 303
Onion-Celery-Almond Casserole 186
Orange Slice Cake 256
Pear Conserve 342
Pecan Bars 304
Pecan Brittle 305
Pecan Cookies 305
Pecan Pie ~
    Silver Springs Coffee Shop 278
Pecan Pralines 305
Pecan Puffs 304
Pecan Whiskey Cake 257
Pineapple Cheese Ball 29
Pineapple-Marshmallow Salad 62
Pink Icebergs 307

Praline Pie 283
Praline Strips 307
Pralines #1 306
Pralines #2 306
Pralines #3 306
Pressed Chicken 152
Seventeen-Pound Fruit Cake 246
Sour Cream Nut Cake 261
Sour Cream Pecan Pie 281
Southern Chess Pie 272
Southern Pecan Pie 282
Spice Drop Cookies 308
Strawberry Jello Salad 65
Strawberry-Pecan Cake 263
Sweet Potato Casserole #1 202
Top of Stove Fruit Cake 247
White Chocolate Cake 264
White Fruit Cake 247

O

Oatmeal Cake 253
Oatmeal Cookies 303

Okra
Pickled Okra 350
Shrimp Gumbo 130
Turkey Gumbo 155
Old-Fashioned Lemon Pie 276
Old-Fashioned Split Pea Soup 85

Olives
Artichoke Hearts Salad 45
Chili Meat Turnovers 30
Ground Beef Casserole 98
Olive Surprises 36
Perfect Tomato Aspic 68

Onions
Baked Stuffed Onions 185
Barbecued Pork Chops 113
Brunswick Stew 135
Cabbage Relish 348
Chili 96
Cucumber Crisps 349
French Fried Onion Rings 186
French Onion Soup 86
Glorified Onions 36
Green Beans with Onions 184
New England Boiled Dinner 111
Onion Pie 185
Onion Salad 60

Onion-Celery-Almond Casserole 186
Pear Relish #1 353
Pear Relish #2 353
Pickled Onion Rings 351
Summer Relish 354
Tignant Relish 354
Open Sesame Pie 279

Oranges and Orange Juice

Candied Orange Peel 303
Five Cup Salad 56
Jellied Ambrosia 44
Orange Balls 303
Orange Cake 254
Orange Coconut Cake 255
Orange Fluff 62
Orange Layer Cake 255
Orange Sherbet 335
Orange Slice Cake 256
Orange-Cranberry Relish 350
Tea Garden Salad 66
Oriental Chicken Casserole 138
Oriental Salad 63
Overnight Broccoli and Ham Strata 113
Owendaw Corn Bread 211
Oyster Stew 86

P

Paella 153
Panocha 302
Party Bake Pork Chops 116
Party Chicken Bake 149
Party Punch 17

Pasta

Chicken Cashew Casserole 144
Chicken Casserole #5 141
Chicken Spaghetti 147
Chicken Tetrazzini #1 156
Chicken Tetrazzini #2 156
Chinese Beef & Rice Casserole 95
Company Casserole #1 97
Company Casserole #2 97
Easy Lasagna Casserole 99
Ground Beef Casserole 98
Lasagna 100
Lobster and Chicken
Cantonese Dinner 133
Macaroni and Cheese 199
Macaroni and
Hamburger Casserole 99

Macaroni Casserole 199
Macaroni Salad 61
Pasta Casserole Marie-Blanche 198
Skid Row Stroganoff 106
Spaghetti 107
Taghiarena 108
Tuna Garden Salad 70
Turkey Soup 87
Vegetable Soup 88
Patton House Rum Pie 282
Peach Brandy Pound Cake 260

Peaches

Blue Ribbon Peach Pie 280
Broiled Peaches 188
Curried Fruit 177
Curried Fruit Bake 321
Dried Peach Custard 326
Peach Cobbler 325
Peach Jelly made from Peach Skins 341
Peach Marmalade 340
Peach Pickles 352
Sherried Hot Fruit Casserole 322
Trinity Dessert 329
Peanut Butter Cookies 304
Peanut Butter Crunch 302

Pears

Congealed Salad #1 52
Curried Fruit 177
Curried Fruit Bake 321
Pear Chutney #1 352
Pear Chutney #2 352
Pear Conserve 342
Pear Crisp 327
Pear Honey 342
Pear Jam 341
Pear Pickles 353
Pear Preserves 342
Pear Relish #1 353
Pear Relish #2 353
Sherried Hot Fruit Casserole 322
Tutti-Frutti Jam 343

Pecans (see Nuts)

Peppercorn Steak 102
Perfect Tomato Aspic 68
Persian Velvet 336
Picadillo Dip
(from San Antonio Country Club) 37

Index

Pickles and Relishes

Artichoke Pickles 348
Bread and Butter Pickles 347
Cabbage Relish 348
Corn Relish 349
Cucumber Crisps 349
Dilly Beans 350
Kosher Dill Pickles 347
Lime Pickles 351
Orange-Cranberry Relish 350
Peach Pickles 352
Pear Chutney #1 352
Pear Chutney #2 352
Pear Pickles 353
Pear Relish #1 353
Pear Relish #2 353
Pickled Bell Peppers 347
Pickled Okra 350
Pickled Onion Rings 351
Red Tomato Relish 355
Summer Relish 354
Tignant Relish 354
Vienna's Garlic-Cucumber Pickles 355
Watermelon Rind Pickles 356

Pies

Apple Pie "Henri" 269
Black Bottom Pie 270
Blackberry Pie #1 270
Blackberry Pie #2 270
Blue Ribbon Peach Pie 280
Caramel Banana Pie 271
Chess Pie 272
Chocolate Almond Pie 273
Chocolate Pie 273
Coconut Cream Pie 274
Cream Cheese Pie 275
Deep Dish Apple Pie 269
Different Lemon Pie 276
Down South Pecan Pie 280
French Silk Chocolate Pie 273
Fresh Strawberry Pie 284
Fudge Cake or Pie 248
German Chocolate Pie 274
Graham Cracker Pie 276
Graham Cracker Pie Crust 284
Ice Cream Pie Spectacular 334
Japanese Fruit Pies 275
Key Lime Pie 278
Lemon Chess Pie 272

Lemon Luscious Pie 277
Lime Meringue Pie 277
Macaroon Pie 278
Old-Fashioned Lemon Pie 276
Open Sesame Pie 279
Patton House Rum Pie 282
Pecan Pie ~
    Silver Springs Coffee Shop 278
Praline Pie 283
Pumpkin Chiffon Pie 283
Sour Cherry Pie 271
Sour Cream Pecan Pie 281
Southern Chess Pie 272
Southern Pecan Pie 282
Strawberry Pie 283
Sweet Potato Pie 282
Traditional Pie Crust 284

Pineapple

Apricot Salad 45
Banana Split Dessert 313
Bing Cherry Congealed Salad 48
Bing Cherry Salad 47
Blueberry Jello Salad 49
Buttermilk Salad 49
Carrot Cake #1 234
Christmas Cookies 291
Congealed Salad #1 52
Cranberry Mold 54
Curried Fruit 177
Curried Fruit Bake 321
Dark Fruit Cake 241
Divinity Pecan Roll Candy 294
Five Cup Salad 56
Franklin Nut Cake 246
Frosted Orange Salad 61
Frozen Cranberry Salad #1 55
Fruit Cake #1 244
Fruit Cake #2 244
Fruit Cake #3 245
Hot Cheese Pineapple 186
Orange Sherbet 335
Party Punch 17
Pear Honey 342
Pineapple Cheese Ball 29
Pineapple Chiffon Cake, Quickie 256
Pineapple Crisp 327
Pineapple Delight 327
Pineapple Upside Down Cake 258
Pineapple-Marshmallow Salad 62

Pink Frozen Salad 62
Polynesian Chicken 151
Raw Cranberry Salad 54
Seventeen-Pound Fruit Cake 246
Sherried Hot Fruit Casserole 322
Strawberry Jello Salad 65
Sweet and Sour Pork 118
Sweet 'n Sour Sauce 133
Tea Garden Salad 66
Top of Stove Fruit Cake 247
Tutti-Frutti Jam 343
White Fruit Cake 247
White Salad 71
Pink Icebergs 307
Pinto Beans 169
Pizza, Deep Dish 103
Pizza-Style Meat Pie 103
Plantation Casserole 114

Plums

Curried Fruit 177
Curried Fruit Bake 321
Plum Sauce 343
Poached Trout Marinier 124
Polynesian Chicken 151

Pork

Asparagus and Ham Casserole 112
Bacon Crisps 20
Bacon Sandwich Spread 81
Barbecued Pork Chops 113
Barbecued Spareribs 112
Breakfast Casserole 158
Chicken and Pork Caribbean 155
Dot's Sausage-Wild Rice Casserole 117
Flaming Cabbage 22
Grilled Pork Chops 115
Ham and Cheese Balls 24
Ham and Cheese Fondue 114
Hot Bacon-Cheese Roll Ups 20
Impossible Quiche 162
Lasagna 100
Meat Pie 101
Neapolitan Pork Chops 116
Old-Fashioned Split Pea Soup 85
Overnight Broccoli and Ham Strata 113
Party Bake Pork Chops 116
Picadillo Dip
   (from San Antonio Country Club) 37
Plantation Casserole 114
Pork Chop Supreme 115

Pork Chops and Dressing 117
Quiche Lorraine 162
Smithfield Ham 115
St. Paul's Rice Casserole 117
Stuffed Pork Chops Calle 118
Sweet and Sour Pork 118
Tossed Club Salad 70

Potatoes

Brunswick Stew 135
Clam Chowder 84
Company Casserole #1 97
Homemade Vegetable Soup 88
New England Boiled Dinner 111
Picadillo Dip
   (from San Antonio Country Club) 37
Potato Casserole 200
Potato Salad 63
Potato Salad with Blue Cheese-
   Sour Cream Dressing 64
Potato Topper for Baked Potatoes 201
Potatoes with Cheese 199
Scalloped Potatoes #1 200
Scalloped Potatoes #2 200
Stay-Abed Stew 107
Thick Beef Soup 83
Vegetable Soup 88
Vichyssoise 89
Potatoes with Cheese 199

Poultry

Arroz Con Pollo 136
Aunt Willie's Chicken Dish 145
Biscuit Crust for Chicken Pie 148
Brunswick Stew 135
Chicken and Almond Casserole 136
Chicken and Dressing Casserole 142
Chicken and Kraut 145
Chicken and Oyster Dressing 154
Chicken and Pork Caribbean 155
Chicken and Stuffing Bake 150
Chicken Breast Sauté 138
Chicken Breast Supreme 135
Chicken Cashew Casserole 144
Chicken Casserole #1 139
Chicken Casserole #2 139
Chicken Casserole #3 140
Chicken Casserole #4 140
Chicken Casserole #5 141
Chicken Chow Mein #1 143
Chicken Chow Mein #2 143

Chicken Country Captain 144
Chicken Devoni 148
Chicken Divine 146
Chicken Liver Wrap-Ups 30
Chicken Loaf 146
Chicken Loaf and Sauce 152
Chicken 'n Cream 142
Chicken Pie 148
Chicken Royal 155
Chicken Salad 50
Chicken Soufflé 150
Chicken Spaghetti 147
Chicken Tetrazzini #1 156
Chicken Tetrazzini #2 156
Chicken with Almonds 137
Chicken with Oysters 153
Chicken with Pecans 147
Cordon Bleu Chicken Breasts 141
Creamy Baked Chicken 137
Honey Chicken Wings 31
June's Easy Chicken 147
Lemon Barbeque Chicken 154
Lobster and Chicken
    Cantonese Dinner 133
Oriental Chicken Casserole 138
Paella 153
Party Chicken Bake 149
Polynesian Chicken 151
Pressed Chicken 152
Tomato Chicken Mold 67
Tossed Club Salad 70
Turkey Gumbo 155
Turkey Soup 87
Two Layer Chicken Pie 149
Pound Cake 258
Praline Pie 281
Praline Strips 307
Pralines #1 306
Pralines #2 306
Pralines #3 306
Pressed Chicken 152

Prunes
Curried Fruit 177
Fruit Whip 321
Prune Muffins 220

Pumpkin
Pumpkin Cake 257
Pumpkin Chiffon Pie 283
Punch 17

Q
Quail with Mushrooms 120
Quiche Lorraine 162
Quick Vichyssoise 89
Quick Yeast Rolls 222

R
Raisin-Caramel Sauce 334
Ramos Fizz 18
Ranger Cookies 308

Raspberries
Cranberry-Raspberry Salad 52
Fresh Raspberry Mousse 330
Raspberry Jazz 335
Raw Cranberry Salad 54
Red Cake 260
Red Tomato Relish 355
Rémoulade Sauce 64

Rice
Arroz Con Pollo 136
Artichoke Hearts Salad 45
Beef Stroganoff 106
Brown Rice 203
Chicken and Oyster Dressing 154
Chicken Casserole #1 139
Chicken Casserole #2 139
Chicken Loaf and Sauce 152
Chicken with Almonds 137
Chinese Beef & Rice Casserole 95
Chinese Fried Rice 133
Company Casserole #1 97
Dearing Street Casserole 121
Dot's Sausage-Wild Rice Casserole 117
Green Chili Pepper Rice Casserole 204
Hot Crab Rice Salad 53
Mother's Rice Casserole 203
Paella 153
Party Bake Pork Chops 116
Party Chicken Bake 149
Rice Casserole 203
Salad Surprise for Jean 64
Seafood Casserole Supreme 123
Shrimp Casserole #1 129
Shrimp Casserole #2 129
Shrimp Fried Rice 132
Shrimp Pilau 132
St. Paul's Rice Casserole 117
Stuffed Pork Chops Calle 118

Turkey Soup 87
Ridgewood Bar-B-Q Sauce 78
Roast in Foil 104
Rolled Round Steak in Wine 104
Roquefort Dressing 74
Roquefort Mound 29
Russian Tea 19
Rye Batter's Bread 221
Rye Bread Casserole 220

S

Salad Dressings

Avocado Salad Dressing 72
Blue Cheese Dressing 72
Celery Seed Dressing 73
Crabmeat Mayonnaise Dressing 69
Cream Cheese Dressing 62
Cucumber Dressing 59
Dressing for Grapefruit Salad 74
French Dressing 73
Fruit Salad Dressing 73
Green Goddess Dressing 74
Homemade Mayonnaise #1 76
Homemade Mayonnaise #2 76
Kum Bak Dressing 75
Lemon-Caper Mayonnaise 75
Rémoulade Sauce 64
Roquefort Dressing 74
Thousand Island Dressing 75
Tomato Salad Dressing 76

Salads

Apricot Aspic 44
Apricot Salad 45
Artichoke Hearts Salad 45
Asheville Salad 45
Bean Salad 47
Bing Cherry Congealed Salad 48
Bing Cherry Salad 47
Blue Cheese Ring Mold 48
Blueberry Jello Salad 49
Broccoli Salad 50
Buttermilk Salad 49
Chicken Salad 50
Cold Broccoli Mold 49
Congealed Salad #1 52
Congealed Salad #2 52
Consommé Salad 51
Corn Salad 53
Corned Beef Salad 51

Cranberry Mold 54
Cranberry Ring Mold 53
Cranberry-Raspberry Salad 52
Cucumber Marinade 55
Cucumber Salad 56
Egg and Cheese Salad 57
Faucon Salad 56
Five Cup Salad 56
Frosted Orange Salad 61
Frozen Cranberry Salad #1 55
Frozen Cranberry Salad #2 55
Frozen Fruit Salad 57
Fruit Salad 58
Grapefruit Salad 58
Grapefruit-Avocado Mold 58
Green Bean Congealed Salad
  with Cucumber Dressing 59
Green Bean Salad 60
Guacamole-Tomato Salad 59
Herbed Tomato Platter &
  Dutch Cucumbers 68
Hot Crab Rice Salad 53
Jan Carter's Slaw 65
Jellied Ambrosia 44
Macaroni Salad 61
Marinated Shrimp Salad 66
Mincemeat Gelatin Salad 61
Molded Asparagus Salad 46
Mother's Avocado Salad 46
Onion Salad 60
Orange Fluff 62
Oriental Salad 63
Perfect Tomato Aspic 68
Pineapple-Marshmallow Salad 62
Pink Frozen Salad 62
Potato Salad 63
Potato Salad with Blue Cheese-
  Sour Cream Dressing 64
Raw Cranberry Salad 54
Salad Surprise for Jean 64
Sea Dream Salad 65
Strawberry Jello Salad 65
Tart Salad 67
Tea Garden Salad 66
Three Bean Salad 47
Tomato Aspic with Crab Mayonnaise 69
Tomato Chicken Mold 67
Tomato Soup Salad 69
Tossed Club Salad 70
Tuna Garden Salad 70

White Salad 71
Wilted Lettuce Salad 71
Sally Lunn 223
Salmon Loaf 134
Salt-Rising Bread Cheese Straws 27

Sandwiches

Asparagus Roll-Ups 81
Bacon Sandwich Spread 81
Corned Beef for Sandwich Filling 81
Ham and Chutney Spread 82
Shrimp Sandwich Filling 82
Tuna Sandwich Torte 82
Sauerbraten 105
Savannah Seafood Casserole 122
Savory Pepper Steak 102
Scalloped Apples 166
Scalloped Cabbage 173
Scalloped Eggplant 177
Scalloped Oysters 134
Scalloped Potatoes #1 200
Scalloped Potatoes #2 200
Sea Dream Salad 65
Sea Foam 309

Seafood (also see Fish)

Baked Shrimp 125
Chafing Dish Crab 31
Chicken and Oyster Dressing 154
Chicken with Oysters 153
Chinese Skewered Shrimp 126
Clam Chowder 84
Crab Casserole 122
Crabmeat and Hollandaise 123
Crabmeat Mayonnaise Dressing 69
Crab Mornae 123
Crab Newburg Dip 32
Crab Pie 125
Crab-Shrimp Bisque 84
Crab Soup #1 85
Crab Soup #2 85
Dearing Street Casserole 121
Deviled Crab 124
Dip For Shrimp 38
Golden Shrimp 128
Hot Clam Dip #1 32
Hot Clam Dip #2 32
Hot Crab Rice Salad 53
Hot Crab Spread 33
James' Marinated Oysters 37

Lobster and Chicken
    Cantonese Dinner 133
Marinated Shrimp 39
Marinated Shrimp Salad 66
Minced Oysters 131
Oriental Salad 63
Oyster Stew 86
Paella 153
Polynesian Chicken 151
Salad Surprise for Jean 64
Savannah Seafood Casserole 122
Scalloped Oysters 134
Seafood Casserole Supreme 123
Shrimp and Artichoke Dip 38
Shrimp and Cheese Casserole 127
Shrimp and Crab Mousse 40
Shrimp Casserole #1 129
Shrimp Casserole #2 129
Shrimp Creole 127
Shrimp Curry 128
Shrimp Delight 130
Shrimp Dip 38
Shrimp Fried Rice 132
Shrimp Gumbo 130
Shrimp Mayonnaise 51
Shrimp Pâté 39
Shrimp Pilau 132
Shrimp Sandwich Filling 82
Shrimp Valencia 131
Tomato Aspic
    with Crab Mayonnaise 69
Sesame Bread 220
Sesame Bread Sticks 36
Seventeen-Pound Fruit Cake 246
Sherried Hot Fruit Casserole 322
Shortcake 262
Sirloin Tip Roast or Steak 105
Six Week Muffins 219
Skid Row Stroganoff 106
Skinny Ice Cream 334
Smithfield Ham 115
Snickerdoodles 309
Somemores 308

Soups

Black Bean Soup 83
Brunswick Stew 135
Clam Chowder 84
Crab Soup #1 85
Crab Soup #2 85

Crab-Shrimp Bisque 84
French Onion Soup 86
Homemade Vegetable Soup 88
Jodie's Avocado Vichyssoise 89
Old-Fashioned Split Pea Soup 85
Oyster Stew 86
Quick Vichyssoise 89
Spinach and Mushroom Soup 87
Stay-Abed Stew 107
Thick Beef Soup 83
Turkey Soup 87
Vegetable Soup 88
Vichyssoise 89
Sour Cherry Pie 271
Sour Cream Chocolate Cake 264
Sour Cream Corn Bread 211
Sour Cream Fudge 296
Sour Cream Nut Cake 261
Sour Cream Pecan Pie 281
Sour Cream Pound Cake 261
Sour Cream Topping 231
Southern Chess Pie 272
Southern Pecan Pie 282
Spaghetti 107
Spice Drop Cookies 308
Spiced Beets 168
Spicy Glazed Apple Ring 166

Spinach

Spinach and Artichoke Casserole 190
Spinach and Mushroom Soup 87
Spinach Casserole 189
Spinach Soufflé 190
Spoon Bread 221

Squash

Acorn Squash 190
Baked Squash 191
Squash Casserole #1 191
Squash Casserole #2 192
Squash Casserole #3 192
Squash Casserole #4 193
Squash Soufflé #1 193
Squash Soufflé #2 194
Zucchini 197
St. Paul's Rice Casserole 117
Stay-Abed Stew 107

Strawberries

Fresh Strawberry Pie 284
Lemon and Strawberry Surprise 326

Strawberry Cake 263
Strawberry Cool 328
Strawberry Dessert 328
Strawberry Frosting 263
Strawberry Jello Salad 65
Strawberry Parfaits 329
Strawberry Pie 283
Strawberry-Pecan Cake 263
Stuffed Pork Chops Calle 118
Stuffed Tomatoes 195
Sugar Cookies #1 310
Sugar Cookies #2 310
Sugar Cookies #3 310
Summer Relish 354
Susie's Ice Cream 334
Swamp Salad 40
Sweet and Sour Pork 118
Sweet and Sour Red Cabbage 174
Sweet 'n Sour Sauce 133

Sweet Potatoes

Grated Potato Pudding 328
Sweet Potato Biscuits 221
Sweet Potato Cake 262
Sweet Potato Casserole #1 202
Sweet Potato Casserole #2 202
Sweet Potato Pie 282
Sweet Potato Soufflé #1 201
Sweet Potato Soufflé #2 201
Swiss Fondue 31
Swiss Steak 108

T

Taghiarena 108
Tamale Pie 109
Tangy Sauce for Cabbage, Broccoli, Etc. 77
Tart Salad 67
Tea Garden Salad 66
Tea Syrup 18
Thick Beef Soup 83
Thousand Island Dressing 75
Three Bean Salad 47
Tignant Relish 354
Tingle Bells Punch 17
Tipsy Squire 329

Tomatoes and Tomato Juice

Arroz Con Pollo 136
Brunswick Stew 135
Cabbage and Tomatoes 173

Chili 96
Escalloped Tomatoes 194
Guacamole-Tomato Salad 59
Herbed Tomato Platter &
    Dutch Cucumbers 68
Neapolitan Pork Chops 116
Red Tomato Relish 355
Shrimp Gumbo 130
Stuffed Tomatoes 195
Summer Relish 354
Taghiarena 108
Tomato Aspic with
    Crab Mayonnaise 69
Tomato Casserole 194
Tomato Chicken Mold 67
Tomato Salad Dressing 76
Tomato Soup Salad 69
Tomatoes Au Gratin 196
Top of Stove Fruit Cake 247
Tossed Club Salad 70
Traditional Pie Crust 284
Trinity Dessert 329
Tuna (see Fish)
Tunnel of Fudge Cake 249
Turkey (see Poultry)
Turnips, Goldie's 196
Tutti-Frutti Jam 343
Two Layer Chicken Pie 149

V

Vanilla Ice Cream 336
Veal Scaloppini 110
Vegetable Casserole 196
Vegetable Soup 88
Venison Pot Roast 121
Venison Steak 120
Vichyssoise 89
Vienna's Garlic-Cucumber Pickles 355
Virginia Spoon Bread 222

W

Wafer Brownies 288
Waffles #1 224
Waffles #2 224
Wassail Bowl 18
Watermelon Rind Pickles 356
Watermelon Rind Preserves 344
Whipping Cream Pound Cake 259
White Chocolate Cake 264
White Frosting 266
White Fruit Cake 247
White Icing 266
White Oak Hunting Lodge Quail 119
White Salad 71
Wild Duck 120
Wilted Lettuce Salad 71
Wine 19
Wine Jelly or Jello 343

Y

Yeast Rolls 223

Valdosta Junior Service League

P.O. Box 2043
Valdosta, GA 31604-2043

Please send _____ copy(ies)   @ $18.69 each _____
        Postage and handling   @ $ 3.50 each _____
        Georgia residents add sales tax (7%)   @ $ 1.31 each _____
                                                    Total _____

Name _____
Address _____
City _____ State _____ Zip _____
      Make checks payable to *Valdosta Junior Service League*

Valdosta Junior Service League

P.O. Box 2043
Valdosta, GA 31604-2043

Please send _____ copy(ies)   @ $18.69 each _____
        Postage and handling   @ $ 3.50 each _____
        Georgia residents add sales tax (7%)   @ $ 1.31 each _____
                                                    Total _____

Name _____
Address _____
City _____ State _____ Zip _____
      Make checks payable to *Valdosta Junior Service League*

Valdosta Junior Service League

P.O. Box 2043
Valdosta, GA 31604-2043

Please send _____ copy(ies)   @ $18.69 each _____
        Postage and handling   @ $ 3.50 each _____
        Georgia residents add sales tax (7%)   @ $ 1.31 each _____
                                                    Total _____

Name _____
Address _____
City _____ State _____ Zip _____
      Make checks payable to *Valdosta Junior Service League*